EVANGELICALS IN IRELAND

Edited by Robert Dunlop

Evangelicals in Ireland
AN INTRODUCTION

the columba press

First published in 2004 by
the columba press
55A Spruce Avenue, Stillorgan Industrial Park,
Blackrock, Co Dublin

Cover by Bill Bolger
Origination by The Columba Press
Printed in Ireland by Betaprint, Dublin

ISBN 1 85607 443 9

Table of Contents

Foreword

Robert Townley
Dean of Kildare

It is a privilege to be asked by my friend and neighbour Robert Dunlop to write a Foreword to this collection of essays.

This book is not simply an exercise in propaganda. The contributors are self-critical, analytical and disarmingly candid. The diversity and some of the disagreements among Evangelicals are made clear to the reader. This anthology even includes an article by someone altogether unsympathetic to Evangelicalism.

Evangelicals are, however, in my experience much more united than might first be apparent. There is a kinship and family likeness. The supremacy and trustworthiness of scripture in doctrinal authority, the centrality and uniqueness of Jesus Christ as God and only Saviour, the fallenness of humanity, Divine judgement, the necessity of personal repentance and faith, together with the call to practical holiness, bind Evangelicals within a large family of believers. They witness to a sceptical world and often to a sceptical church.

Evangelicalism is within the mainstream of historic Christianity. It has no new gospel, rather it treasures and contends for 'the faith once for all entrusted to the saints' (Jude 3).

May this book help further this faith in Ireland.

St Brigid's Cathedral
Kildare
Easter 2004

In Gratitude

This collection of essays may help to fill a gap in Ireland's Christian story. While much has been written about Evangelicals in their respective churches, they have not been seriously looked at as a body. These pages came together because busy people were willing to put their pen to paper and in some cases stick their necks out to say their say. The views expressed belong to those who wrote them.

I am grateful to all the contributors and also to Seán O Boyle and Brian Lynch, with everyone else at Columba Press, for their support and encouragement throughout the project.

Many people have provided information and given time to get this project off the ground. They include Winston McClean, Fergus Ryan, Godfrey Brown, Finlay Holmes, Warren Nelson, Arthur Chapman, Edward Donnelly, Tony Walsh, Grainne McDonald, John Montgomery, Janet Craven, John Cardoo, Joyce Young, Harold Cunningham, Robert Townley, Helen Shaw, Patrick Comerford, Dudley Cooney, William Croly, John Magowan and Gordon Lewis.

I thank all of them.

Robert Dunlop
Editor

CHAPTER ONE

Looking Over the Threshold

Robert Dunlop

Evangelicals have something of a dubious reputation in many quarters. They have been dismissed as fundamentalists, obscurantists, bigots, schismatics, proselytisers, Bible thumpers and even dubbed 'white mice'. In some respects they need to be rescued from oblivion or at least not treated as some sort of ecclesiastical curiosity fit only to be a cornered artefact in Christendom's museum. This introduction is intended to open up their world and to let their voice be heard.

What Yeats said of the Anglo-Irish Protestants is also true of the evangelical sub-section – they are no petty people. They seek their historical rootage in the New Testament and often see themselves, in Marcus Loane's phrase, as the 'residuary legatees of the great heritage of the New Testament'.

Like every community, Evangelicals are something of a mixed bag. The Irish species bears some distinctive marks and naturally carries both the worth and the weight of its cultural and social heritage. It has plenty of baggage but so has everyone else!

Because of the circumstances in which both the Reformation and the Evangelical Revival occurred, the story of evangelical Christianity on Irish soil has a distinctive hue. This is carefully captured by a contemporary scholar, Mark Knoll:

> 'Irish versions of evangelicalism tended to be more assertive, more eschatological and more missionary-minded than their English counterparts.'[1]

The pages to follow will bear out the substantial accuracy of this observation.

Globally, evangelical Christians are numerically significant, and growing. The World Evangelical Alliance, a global network, is in contact with two million local churches with up to 400 million members in 123 countries.

STRENGTHS AND ASSETS

Accessing verifiable information about a diverse community requires considerable discipline. It is tempting to maximise the aberrations. This is why we need to put some of the better wares in the shop window. A positive view will bring to the surface some of the strengths exhibited by evangelical Christians.

Their love for the Bible
Scripture is taken seriously. An evangelical church will give a prominent place to preaching and teaching. Few other communities have done as much to help with translating and spreading the Scriptures. The Gideons and many of the Bible Societies along with organisations like Scripture Gift Mission, the Postal Sunday School and Aids for Bible Education, make much of ensuring that those who come to faith are people of the Book. Daily Bible reading, Sunday School classes, Bible study groups are an integral part of evangelical life.

Their desire to sing God's praises
Historically, they have produced prolific hymnists. The world church is indebted to the evangelical constituency for the vast majority of its hymns and Scripture songs. Think of Isaac Watts, Charles Wesley, William Cowper, John Newton, William Williams, Charlotte Elliott, Frances Ridley Havergal , Ira D. Sankey, Fanny Crosby, Phillip Doddridge, Augustus Toplady, Horatius Bonar, Christina Rossetti. In Ireland Frances Alexander, Thomas Kelly, Edward Denny, Tate and Brady. In more modern times Graham Kendrick, Timothy Dudley-Smith, Michael Saward, Christopher Idle, Keith Green.

Their spiritual enthusiasm
Sometimes this is their Achilles heel. People see them as 'over

the top' even 'off the wall' but there is a positive side to the presence of zeal in their personal and collective lives. Christians from evangelical churches have been willing to spend and be spent for the sake of the gospel – in missionary work, humanitarian relief and social involvement. It takes more than sentiment to catapult a Cavan nurse from a comfortable Rectory to the inaccessible uplands of Western Papua, a Westmeath doctor from the broad plains of Tyrrellspass to the bleeding heart of Africa, a young engineer from the tightly knit streets of East Belfast to the barren sierra of South Peru.

A commitment to upright living
This strength is not an exclusive preserve but it is a central part of what it means to live out the Christian vocation. People of this orientation would be expected to practice business ethics, personal morality and social integrity. Because of the emphasis on Bible teaching and the 'call to holiness' in the gospel imperative, Evangelicals are sometimes tagged as 'good living', which although not always intended, is actually a compliment.

Their belief in experiential faith
Church membership , charitable deeds, sacramental life, mystical withdrawal, moral reflection do not define the Christian life for evangelical people. They hold out for a personal trust, what George Whitefield called 'a felt Christ' and John Wesley referred to as the 'heart strangely warmed'. However this comes about, it issues in and is causative of the marks of saving grace, including the items in the aforementioned list.

This is part of the story of a people with deep roots and distinctive features who have been part of Irish society for a very long time. While one chapter attempts to unpack the beliefs which are important to Evangelicals, the main emphasis is on the people who make up the community rather than the movement to which they belong. This is about Evangelicals rather than evangelicalism.

Secondly, there is an attempt to assess. While not desiring to

trawl in the muddied waters of failure and inconsistency, blind
spots, prejudices and excesses will not be hidden under the car-
pet. No Christian community can maintain either credibility or
viability without an honest self-audit.

Identifying weaknesses is a healthy exercise, especially if it
comes from within. There is a robust critique taking place in
some sections of the movement which will undoubtedly raise a
whole raft of questions. The list will include some warts or blind
spots which often irritate those on the outside looking in as well
as some who are already on the inside looking in.

1. *It is frequently suggested that Evangelicals are elitist,* therefore
guilty of splitting the church and going down the sectarian road.
It cannot be denied that there are strands of elitism when claims
are made that the 'saved' are clearly countable and that those
who believe certain truths can be sure they are part of God's
elect. However, this charge can also be levelled against the ancient Israelites, other upholders of theological orthodoxy and
even those who like to be classified as 'liberals'.

2. *The tendency to equate Christian and Evangelical.* Instead of
being a sub-stratum of Christianity, a version or species of Christ's
religion, the impression is given that Evangelicals are in the end
the only true Christians. Sometimes this comes out in a clumsy
way – what they have is truth, they have all truth and all they have
is truth. In reality nothing could be further from the truth!

3. *An aptitude to define the gospel too narrowly.* While Evangelicals
cling to theological propositions they often fail by neglecting to
take seriously what are sometimes called gospel imperatives.
They frequently see the gospel solely in terms of personal salvation and this produces the sort of individualism which afflicts
them as a body.

4. *A habit of defining holiness in terms of shibboleths and sacred
cows.* Geographical location has bred cultural captivity and spiritual insularity, opening the way for a contemporay version of
Pharisaism which 'strains at gnats and swallows camels'.

5. *Showing too little concern for the visible church – its catholicity and unity.* The emphasis on being part of the invisible church, entered by conversion or new birth, while a necessary strike at formal traditionalism, can easily ditch or dismiss incarnational visibility.

6. *The paradoxical stance of teaching a grounded secure faith while at the same time exhibiting much fear and insecurity.* Evangelicals all too often seem frightened and threatened. Frequently they are scared of each other, which produces navel gazing and looking over their shoulders.

7. *Permitting their high view of Scripture to descend into obscurantism.* Some fight shy of every form of critical investigation, others make an icon of Scripture and sail close to the wind by flirting with bibliolatry.

8. *Retreating into pietism or separatism.* Going down the first route leads to such habits as proof texting and simplistic responses to complicated questions. The second option, while maintaining distinctiveness can easily cut off the oxygen of encounter with society and being challenged and refined by what comes from outside the circle of faith.

9. *Flirting with an 'other worldly' spirituality,* concerned only with preparation for the life to come and treating this world as a staging post to eternity. Historically, evangelical Christians were in the vanguard of social reform, so the charge is not totally convincing. At the same time, the words of a leading Anglican evangelist should be taken seriously :

'A tragedy of Christianity in the 20th century has been that those who claim to be Evangelicals have turned aside from being hewers of justice and makers of peace and those who have been committed to justice and peace have consequently walked away from evangelical Christianity.'[2]

10. *Polarising the use of reason and the gift of faith.* The words of a notable Archbishop of Sydney provide a necessary corrective

'It has always been the duty of faith to walk hand in hand with reason as far as reason can go. Faith must then go where reason can not go; but not where it is unreasonable to go.

Faith may have to transcend reason; it must never deny reason. The last step which reason itself can take is to confess that there is an infinitude of things beyond its grasp; then it becomes like a sign-post on the path which faith must follow.'[3]

WILD GEESE AND HOMEBIRDS

Ireland has produced distinguished evangelical theologians who have brought enormous benefit to the wider church and the wider world. Most of them are the 'wild geese' who are laying well but laying out! Readers will meet some of them in the pages to follow. The list includes names widely known and respected:

Alister E. McGrath, professor of Historical Theology at Oxford University.

Christopher Wright, formerly Principal of All Nations Christian College and now International Ministeries Director for the Langham Partnership founded by John Stott.

Alec Motyer, a Dubliner who was former Principal of Trinity College, Bristol and a well known Bible expositor and Commentator in Britain.

Elizabeth Johnston, a native of Newtownards, who taught New Testament and Christian Education at Union Biblical Seminary, Puna, India.

The list might be extended to include such people as:

Adam Clarke (1762-1832), a leading Methodist theologian and Bible commentator from Co Derry. His scholarship was impressive encompassing classics, patristics, oriental languages, history, geology and natural science.

Alexander Carson, a distinguished scholar and theologian while minister of a large congregation at Tobermore, Co Derry.

Hugh Jordan, who served as secretary of the Dublin YMCA and went on to be principal of the London College of Divinity.

H. Dermot McDonald, who grew up in Dublin, was a prolific author, writing nineteen books and who became Vice-Principal of London Bible College.

As in many other communities the work and witness of evangelical Christians has been done by the 'foot soldiers' who make up the rank and file members of the community. Even a sample list would include people like:

Patrick McTighe, a Scripture Reader of the Reformed Presbyterian Church active around Cong, Co Mayo in the late 1850s.

Cecilia Mandeville, a cultured member of a notable Clonmel family holding forth on the street at Elvery's Corner in Dublin in the 1960s.

Albert Shaw, against great odds, serving the material and spiritual needs of the poor at the Dublin Christian Mission beside the Four Courts.

Sammy Spence and his 'hallelujah brigade' running the Coalmen's Mission in East Belfast.

The somewhat eccentric Jasper McGowan of Portgelone, Co Antrim preaching with fervour in broad Ulster speech in the fairs and markets of his native territory.

George Bird, a highly respected Corkonian bearing dignified witness through the varied activities of the Cork YMCA.

Aubrey Young, venturing out to rural towns in his Morris Minor to show films and hold rallies under the auspices of Youth for Christ.

Pilgrims of the Faith Mission trudging around country roads all over Ireland encouraging people to come to their Gospel meetings held in tents, halls, schoolhouses and barns.

Belfast City Missionaries traversing the narrow streets of East and West Belfast recruiting the lapsed, consoling the bereaved, assisting the deprived and instructing the young.

William J. Smallhorne, the portly bachelor Rector of St Kevin's, Dublin scurrying round the streets of his parish and then taking off round the country with the Dublin Male Voice Choir to offer Christ in the plainest of language in rural and provincial communities.

'Roaring' Hugh Hanna, the somewhat stormy evangelical preacher from his pulpit in Berry St Presbyterian Church, in the Markets area of Belfast.

A MIXED MENU

Our contributors have offered something of a mixed menu. This collection of essays bears the style, outlook and hallmark of each writer. Thematically varied they are all looking at the same constituency which is by no means homogeneous.

Some have trawled in ancient waters and have managed to pull out a few big fish.

Some have visited the diagnostic bay to examine the state of a community in transition needing to be assured of roadworthiness.

Some have risked chasing a crystal ball and have ventured into prognostic mode.

Some have simply told their story, unembellished with spin or untarnished with make-believe – telling it like it is.

Some have stressed the strengths and highlighted the weaknesses of an elusive body.

Some have simply set out their stall saying this is what is on offer – we have wares that wear well.

Some have made vital connections, visiting many junctions in search of a continuum of faith and faithfulness.

All have demonstrated serious intentionality in portraying a community secure enough to survive and flexible enough to change. Because of their deep roots, strong convictions and expanding presence, Irish Evangelicals are set to stay around for many a day.

Notes:
1. *The Rise of Evangelicalism,* Mark A. Noll, Apollos Press, 2004, p 26.
2. *Makers of our Heritage,* Marcus L. Loane, Hodder and Stoughton, 1967, p 13.
3. *Evangelism and the Local Church,* Michael Green, Hodder and Stoughton, 1990, p 553.

CHAPTER TWO

Re-staging Ireland's Christian Drama

Fergus Ryan

Great dramas are often presented as a series of acts, and the story of Irish Christianity is no different. Evangelicalism, that expression of vital Christian faith which is the subject of this book, dawned in the eighteenth century as what we might call Act IV of Ireland's salvation history. Its principal characters have left their mark on every Irish county – indeed on much of the world, its songs are still being sung wherever people follow Christ, and the 'sets' are still to be seen (if now usually unrecognised) in the buildings of many Irish towns.

The curtain did not begin to fall on Act IV until the 1970s. When it rose again on Act V, the stage that was late twentieth century Ireland was unlike any that had been seen before, and the audience had listened to plays not by the same Playwright; but, unexpectedly, the ancient drama before them continued with a renewed and compelling vitality. This is the unfolding story of Ireland's Act V. To understand it we must review the drama so far.

ACT I: THE CHRISTIAN CELTS

The opening act of our story was that early period during which the evangelistic Celtic church of these islands was a gleaming emerald in the battlements of the city of God. It was Ireland's golden age. The Christianised Gaelic Irish were among the first people north of the Alps to have developed their own written culture. Distanced from fledgling Christendom's Roman centre, the Celts lived out a distinctive but orthodox Christianity that was as beautiful in its art as in its spirit.

In the seventh century, however, a stand off occurred between the Christian Celts and the Roman church that reached its climax at the Synod of Whitby, in Northumbria. The Roman delegation prevailed and England became Catholic. With the coming of Norse invaders, the Celtic church declined further, and with the Norsemen's later conversion to Catholic Christianity the stage was set for the religious and political annexation of Ireland and the suppression of the Gaels by the Catholic Anglo-Normans.

ACT II: THE CATHOLICS

Act II began with the Synod of Cashel in 1101 when, at the command of the only English pope, Adrian IV, the final piece of Roman reform was put in place which brought the Irish church firmly under the control of the English Catholic church. In one of Ireland's great ironies, an English (or Anglo-Norman) king had made Ireland Catholic. But the Gaelic Irish resented the new order, and successive Norman rulers regarded the Gaels as having no rights. For centuries the popes anathematised anyone who would assist the rebellious Irish against the beloved English! Anglo-Norman repression of the Gaels was strengthened in the Statutes of Kilkenny in 1366, which were supported by the Catholic bishops. The races were now worlds apart, with the Catholic Church an instrument of the English crown against the 'King's Irish enemies'. It was a point which would later be made by the Church of Ireland as it sought to lay claim to the true Celtic heritage. Many of Ireland's great cathedrals date from Act II, including Christ Church, Dublin, which was rebuilt by Henry II in 1172 as an expression of the new Norman Catholicism.

ACT III: THE PROTESTANTS

Act III started in the sixteenth century with the Act of Supremacy, whereby Henry VIII declared himself head of the English (and hence Irish) *Catholic* Church. England was not now *Protestant* – in fact Henry had been given the title *Defender of the [Catholic] Faith* by the pope for his opposition to Luther; but being severed from Roman jurisdiction, the English Catholic Church was increasingly open to reforming influences from the continent. The turbulent conflicts between England and the papacy did nothing to improve Ireland's religious situation. Michael Davitt would later observe that Ireland had been crucified between the twin tyrannies of Rome and London. In the plantations of the seventeenth century, the lands of the Gaelic lords were transferred to Anglicans and Presbyterians. During the Interregnum of the 1650s Baptist officers were leading the Irish expeditions of Cromwell's parliamentary forces. The Gaelic Irish might be forgiven for failing to grasp in what sense the Reformation was good news. Indeed C. H. Crookshank, with pardonable hyperbole, reported that Ireland was said to be the only country in which the Reformation produced nothing but evil.[1]

Act III was not, however, without its expressions of 'vital' religion, nor were all outside the Established Church. A revival in the 1670s amongst Presbyterians at Antrim was described by witnesses as 'a bright and hot sunblink of the gospel and one of the largest manifestations of the Spirit that almost since the days of the Apostles hath been seen.'[2] There was limited religious tolerance. Dublin had three congregations of French Huguenots, although Archbishop King complained that Wicklow was 'full of Quakers and dissenters'.[3] Despite some sparks of faith here and there, the Established Church during the time of the Georges was 'a silken prelacy, a slumbering priesthood, a silent laity, a theology precise in form, but pale, pulseless and pedantic'.[4] There was no place for what was derisorily called 'enthusiasm', for awe or wonder; nothing to convert the heart. Presbyterianism was falling captive to the Arian heresy that denied the deity of Christ. It was time for a revival. There were already stirrings at St Catherine's in Thomas Street, Dublin, where Henry Echlin held a weekly celebration. Surely some revelation was at hand.

ACT IV: THE EVANGELICALS

It came in 1746 with the arrival in Dublin of the famous Moravian preacher John Cennick. Cennick was the first flame of a renewal movement that was to last for over two centuries, through two great periods of revival, and which produced an evangelicalism that, in its most familiar features, was to remain strong in the Protestant churches of the south well into the 1960s (and in the north until today). Cennick preached to huge crowds at the former Baptist chapel in the Dublin Liberties, where the windows had to be removed so that he could be carried to the pulpit over the heads of the expectant hearers. When some clergy complained about the negative impact he was having on their churches, Bishop Ryder advised them, 'Preach what Cennick preaches; preach Christ crucified, and the people will have no need to go to Cennick to hear the gospel'.[5]

But while most today have forgotten Cennick, and indeed Moravianism, it was a minister of the Established Church who left the deepest and most enduring impression of 'vital religion' on Ireland's spiritual landscape. John Wesley set foot on Sir John Rogerson's Quay in 1747, the first step of twenty-one tireless visits he was to make to Ireland. Preaching on the corruption of the human heart and the need for repentance, Wesley offered to all a message of salvation by the free grace of God received through faith in Christ's atoning death on the Cross, and – to those who responded – a call to a devout and holy life. To the outrage of many of the clergy he preached in the open air, and used non-ordained men and women to teach his 'classes'. At Dolphin's Barn, Dublin, and at Limerick, the spontaneous praise of God that attended Wesley's visits was so loud that he was scarcely able to begin speaking. Many were quite overcome with remorse, and were shaking with conviction. Others were overcome with rage, and Wesley barely escaped with his life on more than one occasion, most notably at Cork. Wesley gave impetus to what were to become many of evangelicalism's characteristic and lasting features: smaller groups for Bible study, discipleship and fellowship, voluntary societies, itinerant preachers emphasising the need for new birth, flexible forms and structures. Amongst the evangelical societies later to be formed in Ireland were the quaintly-named Dublin Mission for Friendless Females, The Shoe-black, Broomer, and Messenger Society, The Association for the Relief of Distressed Protestants, and The Sick and Indigent Roomkeepers Society (the sign is still visible at the lower entrance to Dublin Castle).

Evangelical clergy who failed adequately to observe the approved forms of the church were considered 'irregulars'. Others, valuing the liturgical forms, expressed their evangelicalism in a more 'regular' manner. After Wesley's death, many of the 'irregulars' joined the newly formed Methodist Church, a development Wesley himself had discouraged. Methodism was brought to America by Limerick's Irish Palatine immigrants.

Biblical preaching was, of course, a defining element of evangelical life in Ireland, and special 'trustee churches', some housing very large numbers, were built for several of the most popular preachers of the Established Church. The most notable in the Dublin area were Bethesda Chapel (now the Wax Museum), Trinity Church (until recently the Gardiner Street Labour Exchange) and St James', Crinken, near Bray, still a thriving evangelical church.

The 'irregular' nature of these meetings led, in a few cases, to the secession from the church of some Irish clergy and their followers to form smaller independent congregations. The new separatist movements were not always stable, and were occasionally of unorthodox or eccentric teaching. In the Church of God, a separatist congregation at Stafford Street led by Rev John Walker, one member insisted on greeting a young newly-married lady with a 'holy kiss' against her wishes. There followed an unseemly fracas between the 'kissers' and the 'anti-kissers'! A more stable and lasting movement, however, grew out of meetings held in the 1820s at the stately home in Wicklow of Lady Theodosia Powerscourt. Her secession from the Irish church caused a scandal, as did that of John Nelson Darby, curate of the nearby Calary church on the southern slope of the

Sugar Loaf. The pulsating Powerscourt meetings which they hosted on the largely unexplored topics of unfulfilled Bible prophecy and the hoped-for recovery of the gifts of the Holy Spirit led to the formation of what came to be known as 'the Brethren'. Without clergy or liturgy, the new assemblies became a powerful force in evangelicalism. It is of interest that in late 2003 the *Irish Times'* 'Irishman's Diary' columnist should explain to a readership largely unaware of what we have called Act IV, the unwitting influence of Darby's teachings concerning Israel and Bible prophecy on the foreign policy of George W Bush, President of the United States! Nor would most Dubliners driving past the grand façade of the Davenport Hotel in Lower Merrion Street be aware of its history as Merrion Hall, until the 1970s the 2800-seater auditorium of what had been the Republic's largest Brethren assembly. The assemblies were usually known as 'halls', not 'churches' and a number continue to exist in larger Irish towns.

The mid-point of Act IV was the Second Evangelical Awakening, usually known as the *1859 Revival*. It began at a farmhouse prayer meeting in Co Antrim and before it had run its course 110,000 new members has been added to Irish Protestant churches. At a Presbyterian church too small to hold the crowds who came to hear of the spreading power of God, many fell on the muddy ground calling on God in repentance.[7] The revival spread from Ulster through the remaining counties of Ireland as far as Kerry, where the county sheriff was converted to Christ. In Dublin Henry Grattan Guinness preached to great crowds at York Street. Thousands flocked to prayer meetings at the Metropolitan Hall and at the gardens of the Rotunda. Thomas Barnardo was baptised as a young adult at the Baptist chapel in Abbey Street. Setting out as a young doctor with the intention of joining Hudson Taylor's extraordinary mission to inland China, he was instead so overcome by the plight of London's homeless children that he founded the Christian charity that still bears his name. Merrion Hall was built in 1863 to accommodate the huge crowds who came to hear Rev J Denham Smith. Evangel-

icalism's familiar agencies and missions expanded after the revival and hundreds of still unsung Irish missionaries lived out
their years in unrecorded service to Christ in the farthest corners
of the world.

Catholic Revival

The Irish Catholic Church had been in a low estate in the early
years of the nineteenth century, not least because of their dis-
favoured position under the Establishment. But in mid-century
a number of developments were to strengthen its position.

First, the unexpectedly successful activities of Anglican
evangelical mission throughout the country were causing concern to the Vatican. Irish-speaking Protestant mission colonies
were established at Dingle and at Achill Island, where Rev
Edward Nangle's original church remains in use today. Dr John
Gregg of Trinity Church Dublin preached in Irish in all thirty-
two counties. Amongst the Methodists Gideon Ouseley was a
fiery evangelist in the native tongue. In response the Vatican dis-
patched to Ireland one of its foremost churchmen, Paul (later
Cardinal) Cullen, who led the Irish Catholic Church to the
prominence it would have for more than a century. Irish
Catholicism, unlike its French counterpart, became increasingly
ultramontane, that is, politically aligned to Rome. Catholicism
and evangelical Protestantism in Ireland came into sharp conflict. Secondly, there was a strong sense that Ireland had been
betrayed during the Great Famine by a government ambivalent
to its fortunes. There was a widespread view, fostered in part by
a threatened hierarchy, that Protestant churches had exploited
the tragedy through 'soup kitchens' established to promote attendance at Bible studies. The theme of 'souperism' would nour-
ish a deep root of anti-Protestantism for more than a hundred
years. Whatever the justification for the charge, more than forty
unremembered clergy of the Established Church died in their
service to the disease-ridden starving population. Evangelical
Quakers in similar service avoided the souperist charge.

The third factor that contributed to the increasing identification of Catholicism with the national cause was the Gaelic Revival, a rediscovery of the heroic era of the Gaelic lords and of the wealth of ancient Irish literature, a heritage suppressed and largely lost in an Established Church that was regarded as 'the Handmaid of the Ascendancy'. Ironically, the rediscovery of Gaelic culture was largely the work of Standish O'Grady, a clergyman of the Church of Ireland. Finally, the Catholic Church deepened its spiritual life through a 'devotional revolution'. While Catholicism was increasing in influence and power as the dominant voice of the Irish people, the Church of Ireland, disestablished by law in 1870, was retreating into the muted voices of its admittedly less-than-Irish culture. There was a gradual decline in its evangelical party, and after 1900 few Evangelicals would be appointed to episcopal office.

After the formation of the new southern State in 1922 Protestantism, along with its own evangelical minorities, experienced gradual and continuous decline. Still, there were notable centres of evangelical life throughout the country. Many Church of Ireland parishes had an evangelical ethos and ministry, and evangelical mission agencies continued to send southern Irish missionaries overseas. The smaller denominations and independent churches tended to be almost entirely evangelical in doctrine and practice. Outreach consisted of open-air gospel preaching, printed leaflets (invariably referred to as 'tracts'), door-to-door evangelism, and special meetings of all kinds. The message of repentance from sin and the free gift of salvation in Christ preached by John Wesley 200 years earlier to an Ireland with a religious soul, was still being preached to a deeply religious society in the mid-twentieth century, but now with little response other than occasional open hostility. A picket on the Dublin Christian Mission by the Legion of Mary and others lasted from 1923 to 1989!

In Dublin, the YMCA served as the centre of an interdenominational evangelicalism that was still unambiguously culturally Protestant, and most notable visiting preachers spoke at 'The 8.30', its crowded Sunday evening after-church service. Despite all these efforts the effect on the general population was minimal. Evangelicalism, at least in the form of its independent congregations, was now something of a cultural backwater, largely invisible and unknown. Despite notable examples of sacrificial and caring charity (e.g. Eva Stuart Watt's ministry to Dublin's prostitutes[8]) Irish evangelicalism might justifiably have been charged with being uninvolved and uninterested in the concerns of general Irish life; its principal aim was the rescue of 'souls'. Not of course that any organised social concern by Evangelicals would have been welcomed, nor when it happened did it avoid the suspicion that it was another form of souperism. Evangelicals were damned if they did, and damned if they didn't. Still, a visiting evangelist from North America exemplified evangelicalism's isolationism and uneasy relationship with human endeavour by remarking to this writer that 'culture is each nation's way of sinning'! By the 1970s Evangelicals in the Republic numbered, by some estimates, barely one-third of one percent of the population. With the closure of the YMCA in the late 1970s and the ending of its 8.30 service, it was clear that the religious and social setting that was Ireland's Act IV was in its closing stages.

ACT V: POSTMODERN IRELAND

Marginalised for centuries by its geographical isolation and by the economic and cultural domination of its closest neighbour, a new era dawned for Ireland with its accession to the European Economic Community in 1973. Few could have anticipated the profound social, philosophical, economic and demographic changes that lay ahead. If evangelicalism was to survive in the deceptively unfamiliar territory that was the new Ireland it would need, like ancient Israel, some 'men of Issachar'[9] who could read the signs of the times, and know how the ancient drama should now be staged.

What were these 'signs' of Ireland's new times that would have to be understood? Some were obvious, others less so. The insecurity of the older generation was being replaced by new youthful self-confidence as Ireland, freed from its old provincialism, began to succeed on the international stage. No one was now listening to a message that might begin by asserting the unworthiness or sinfulness of the individual. With success and a declining sense of need, there began a gradual secularisation of Irish society. This was accelerated by well-publicised moral failings in some religious institutions. It was difficult now to issue a moral call from any altar, and society became increasingly amoral, at least in matters of sexual practice, and tolerant of what had earlier been regarded as sin. In Act IV, *im*moral people might either flaunt or hide their sinfulness; the new *a*moral society found the idea of sin rather comical. Faced with the new secularism, Evangelicals were now, ironically, largely in the same moral camp as sincere Catholics.

Inward investment began to reap undreamt-of benefits when, in the early 1990s, Ireland saw the beginning of an economic climb that would end the decade with it being one of the world's wealthier countries. Few were now looking for a God who would comfort them in times of deprivation. Two other changes set the stage for Ireland's Act V. The first was the simple fact of plurality, resulting from the new immigration from Eastern Europe and Africa and, apart from some localised racial tensions, the decline of older intolerances. It was now acceptable to believe whatever one wished. Irish evangelicalism could now take its place on the increasingly crowded raft of religions. Astonishingly, it would be considered to be a new religious movement!

Just when evangelicalism found its new place in plurality's rising sun, however, pluralism would make it increasingly unacceptable to affirm that Jesus was in any sense the unique Son of God, or his the only way of salvation. All roads, so goes the pluralist mantra, lead up the same mountain – meaning in effect that all religions are equally acceptable only because none of them is, in any absolute sense, true. The new tolerance was, after all, quite patronising.

Evangelicalism now faced a new challenge. In the 'modernist' rationale of Act IV where propositions were regarded as either true or false, its beliefs had simply been viewed by its detractors, both religious and irreligious, as wrong. But a new philosophy had overtaken Ireland without much public debate or analysis. It was postmodernism. Regarded by some as a passing fad, postmodernity looks with suspicion on all attempts to formulate a grand explanation of the cosmos or any 'meaning' to life – just what Christianity claims to offer. Truth is not now so much what is 'out there' behind everything, but what is 'in here'. Each person's truth is valid, even when it conflicts with that of another. No one need be wrong. Postmodern Ireland is therefore a more tolerant place, except of course for those who challenge its grand explanation of the cosmos. Unlike Act IV, postmodern Ireland would not so much regard evangelical Christianity (or traditional Catholicism for that matter) as being in error, but as having the temerity to believe that the Christian message about Jesus was in any absolute sense the truth.

Notwithstanding these developments, the number of evangelical Christians in Ireland has risen steadily since the opening of Act V in the 1970s. The growth comes from a number of sources. First, there was the beginning of what was called the house church movement, independent groups or 'fellowships' that met in private houses or schools for extempore prayer, participative worship and interactive Bible study. These groups reflected society's general drift away from establishment patterns of structure and authority. The strongest were accessible, informal, relational, charismatic and radical. Some developed structures and forms of leadership appropriate for growing Christian communities. Attendance at meetings of one or two of the largest (which now have their own buildings) exceeds 500, and the term 'house church' is no longer appropriate. They are now usually referred to as the *New Churches*.

Secondly, there was the phenomenon of the charismatic movement. Although having similar emphases to earlier Pentecostalism concerning the gifts of the Holy Spirit, the charismatic movement developed within the traditional denominations. The visit of an Anglican charismatic clergyman, Rev David Watson, to the YMCA '8.30' in the late 1970s added impetus to the new developments in Dublin. What was even more unexpected, perhaps, was the outbreak of charismatic experience in the Catholic Church, and large meetings took place at the Friends' Meeting House in Eustace Street, at which some Pentecostal leaders, notably Chris Rowe, taught the scriptures to the new movement. Rowe was the leader of Shalom, a charismatic fellowship attended by most of the members of the pop group U2. The movement spread like a wild fire throughout the country, but was regarded with suspicion by traditional Evangelicals as being 'experiential' rather than Bible-based, and too accommodating of disputed Catholic practices. It was also a matter of some concern to the Catholic authorities, probably for exactly the opposite reasons, and the movement was drawn more closely under their control after a few years. Not all who sought a more evangelical emphasis left the Catholic Church, but many who had had a deep experience of God now found their way into new charismatic groupings along with some of the older Evangelicals who, following Watson's example, had embraced charismatic Christianity. A completely new situation now existed: independent evangelical-charismatic 'fellowships', full-blown churches and Pentecostal denominations in which the larger part of the membership had never been Protestants and did not now regard themselves as being so. Charismatic renewal within the historic Protestant denominations was slower than in other English-speaking countries, with only one or two congregations where charismatic gifts (in the narrow sense) are openly expressed in meetings.

A third stream grew from the revitalisation of older evangelical congregations who were not part of the charismatic movement. Notable examples developed in a number Presbyterian, Methodist and Church of Ireland churches around the country. Some Brethren assemblies restyled themselves as 'evangelical' churches,[10] Baptists experienced an upward trend in numbers and in new congregations. New independent congregations were being formed throughout the country, some planted by overseas 'church planting' mission agencies.

Immigration has given rise to a further major change in Ireland's spiritual landscape. One Nigerian denomination has more than thirty 'parishes' in Ireland,[11] and there are many other African churches, with most larger Irish towns having at least one African congregation. Additionally there are Chinese, Romanian, Korean, and Philippino congregations, mostly Pentecostal or charismatic in expression. Members of mainstream Protestant denominations from overseas have swelled the numbers attending the historic churches, and many of the new immigrants are from evangelical churches in their home countries. The recent census reflects the developments: the percentage of those indicating that they are Roman Catholic has reduced to 88%.

So the Ireland of Act V is witnessing, contrary to some predictions, a resurgence of all expressions of orthodox, biblical, evangelical Christianity. The growth has engendered a new 'engagement' of evangelicalism with Irish public life, and led to the formation of the broadly based Evangelical Alliance Ireland to act as a new 'voice'.

Whether there shall be a sixth Act we cannot yet say, but the Act V drama is getting under way with its ancient and contemporary story. Amongst the growing audiences there may be some like Henry Woodward, rector of Fethard in the 1820s, who seeing what God was doing among the Evangelicals said, 'Why not put up my tiny sail and catch some portion of the heavenly breeze which is blowing so strongly in their favour?'[12] The breeze seems to be picking up lately.

Notes:
1. Crookshank, C. H., *Days of Revival, being the History of Methodism in Ireland* (Clonmel, Tentmaker, 1994) I, p 11.
2. Quoted in Paisley, I.R.K., *The 'Fifty-Nine' Revival* (Belfast, 1981), p 5.
3. Acheson, A., *History of the Church of Ireland 1691-2001* (Dublin, Columba Press, 2002), p 52.
4. The withering comment was made by Archbishop William Alexander. See Acheson, 2002, p 66.
5. Acheson, p 80.

6. Carter, Grayson., *Anglican Evangelicals: Protestant Secessions from the Via Media, c1800-1850* (Oxford, 2001), p 94.

7. The incident was at the First Presbyterian Church in Ahoghill. See Orr, J. Edwin, *The Second Evangelical Awakening in Britain* (London: Marshall, 1949), p 40.

8. Eva Stuart Watt tells her own story of 1940s Dublin in *Ireland Awakening* (Chicago, 1952).

9. 1 Chronicles 12:32.

10. e.g. Dun Laoghaire Evangelical Church, formerly Northumberland Hall.

11. The Redeemed Church of God

12. See Stunt, T. C. F., 'Evangelical cross-currents in the Church of Ireland' in Sheils, W. J., ed, *The Churches, Ireland and the Irish.*

CHAPTER THREE

The forgotten origins of the Irish Evangelicals

Crawford Gribben

Are Irish Evangelicals 'Protestant'? The question seems strangely obvious, and yet an answer is hard to determine. If 'Protestant' refers to an adherence to the central doctrines of the Reformation movement, then the answer must be 'yes': Irish Evangelicals do believe in justification by grace alone, through faith alone, in Christ alone, to the glory of God alone. If 'Protestant' is being used to refer to membership of the Church of Ireland, then the answer must be 'not necessarily': most Evangelicals continue to participate in dissenting churches and those new fellowships that refuse to adopt specific denominational titles. But if 'Protestant' refers to a shared ethnic, cultural or political agenda, then the answer must be 'no': apart from their general support for pro-life causes, Irish Evangelicals, by and large, do not commonly adhere to a substantial political platform, and those northern Evangelicals who are most outspoken about their political convictions do not represent the totality of the movement – especially south of the border. Irish Evangelicals are a complex group that often seems to be divided by as many issues as those that unite it. It is a movement about which it is particularly hard to make general comments – but it is a movement with a general lack of interest in its history.

Despite the politicisation of history in the northern 'Troubles', Irish Evangelicals suffer from an unusual historical myopia. To the extent that they consider history at all, the images they recall are images of resistance to adversity. The Evangelical imagination focuses on the 1641 rebellion and 1690 revolution, the revivals of 1859 and, sometimes, the Belfast missions of the 1920s. What these images have in common is their basis in a black and white worldview. Evangelicals tend to think of their past in terms of 'us' and 'them'. Irish Evangelical identity – to the extent that it is based on the past at all – is based on a series of stressful encounters, a continued rejection of its opposite. These images are rarely drawn from the pre-Reformation period. Even among those Evangelicals most interested in proclaiming their sense of being Protestant, the events and figures of the Irish Reformation are strangely ignored. Orange parades litter the summer social calendar of many northern Evangelicals. Despite the Order's roots in an Irish Protestant consciousness, however, the legacy of the Reformation is notable only by its absence. Banners display images of familiar Biblical scenes, British monarchs, or patriarchs of the individual lodge – but images of the Irish Reformation, pre-1641, are virtually nowhere to be seen.[1]

This forgetfulness contrasts the continued focus on the Reformation among both Scottish and English Evangelicals. While, even there, a decreasing number of Evangelicals seem to be expressing interest in their past, small but influential groups such as the Protestant Truth Society and Scottish Reformation Society continue to promote awareness of Reformation history. In England and Scotland, there would probably not be significant widespread inability to name the most important leaders of the native Reformations: Tyndale and Knox are still seen to be important figures. But no similar organisation exists in Ireland. Despite the rhetoric of the 'Troubles', Irish Evangelicals express little interest in the Irish Reformation.

This evasion of the Reformation might have been a good thing if it had been designed to signal the fact that the evangelical tradition, and the gospel to which it adheres, did not begin in the sixteenth century. As recent interest in the Celtic church has reminded us, the evangelical gospel has roots that reach deep into Irish Christian history.[2] It might also been a good thing if it signalled that Evangelicals were weighing their past in the balance, and finding aspects of it wanting. But there is little sign that evangelical neglect of the Reformation has any kind of strategic or evaluative function. It is, if anything, a sign that the

Evangelical movement – in all its breadth – finds the Reformation too embarrassing to remember.

The results of this inattention have been tragic. Irish
Evangelicals have been imprisoned because they have forgotten
significant aspects of their past; and because they have forgotten
significant aspects of their past, they have forgotten what has
made them what they are. It is profoundly noteworthy, for example, that when Irish Evangelicals – especially in the north –
advertise services promoting the 'Old Time Gospel', their messages, songs and sentiments owe far more to early twentieth-
century American fundamentalism than they do to the longer
continuum of Irish Protestant worship and theology. This 'old
time' worship simply isn't old enough. But fundamentalism,
with its suspicion of academic enquiry and historical scholarship, has so conditioned many of the northern evangelical sub-
cultures that it has provided Evangelicals with a crisis of identity.
The idiosyncrasies of fundamentalism – and its church practices
rooted in the culture of the early twentieth century – have been
allowed to continue only because it is often believed that the
longer past has nothing significant to contribute. Trapped by
their loyalty to this fundamentalist inheritance, many northern
Evangelicals have lost the dignity and significance of a truly
Irish tradition of Protestant life and worship. Whether they like
it or not, Irish Evangelicals need to remember their past for their
religious experience cannot be understood apart from Ireland's
experience of the Reformation.

Forgotten beginnings

Perhaps one of the reasons why Irish Evangelicals are so suspicious of the Reformation is that it challenges the basic duality of
much of their thinking. In mid-sixteenth century Ireland, there
was no hard and fast dichotomy between Protestant and
Catholic churchmanship or thought. The early decades of the
Irish Reformation were a non-dichotomous, pre-denominational
age, an age in which specific theological debates had yet to
emerge from the medieval sea of faith. The Irish Reformation

represents the very real and very slow development of Christian thinking as competing groups within the church moved from the medieval to the modern confessional age.

Perhaps the only thing that many of these groups agreed on was that the medieval feel of Irish Christianity had to change. The improvements they suggested included a range of possibilities. Conservative Catholics appealed for the Irish church to adhere more closely to the dogmatic theology defined by the Council of Trent. Those churchmen with a stronger allegiance to Canterbury appealed for the Irish church to follow the middle path of Reformation that the English church had pursued. As time went on, however, the Irish reformed church attracted more radical spirits, and 'root and branch' Reformation became a sudden possibility. There was no single Reformation movement in sixteenth-century Ireland. All sides were committed to change – the question they debated was which direction that change ought to take. In all the range of possibilities, no one was opting to keep the *status quo*.

Change was popular because of the state of the church. Despite popular ideas that the pre-Reformation Irish church lived in some kind of perpetual Celtic twilight, accounts from the period show Catholic priests lamenting the church's corruption. Irish piety, they feared, owed far more to traditional folk religion than it did to the theological norms defined at Trent. But the problem for the Catholic hierarchy was that this traditional religiosity was more popular than the official canons of their faith. Their concerns focused on the cult of worship at holy wells – a popular form of piety, which continues to the present day. Officially, the holy well cult was frowned upon, but its sheer popularity meant that many priests adopted a more pragmatic pastoral approach at local level. The church pursued an uneasy pragmatism, but its traditionalist consensus was shattered by the sudden impetus for reform in the mid sixteenth century.

Ireland's experience of the Protestant Reformation began in 1536, when Henry VIII proclaimed himself the 'only supreme Head of the whole church of Ireland'. But Henry's Reformation was initially intensely conservative. Edward VI and Elizabeth I presided over the Irish church during a period of active theological reflection, but the 'confessionalisation' of the Protestant church – its defining and propagating a distinctive theological position – really only made significant impact from the early 1590s. From the 1550s to the 1620s, the Irish Reformation was broadly Anglican (though the use of specific denominational labels is anachronistic in this pre-denominational period). The Irish reformed church moved only gradually into a denominational world. Through ethnic migrations and demographic change, distinctive confessional loyalties were fostered throughout the seventeenth century. By the century's end, representatives of virtually every modern denomination – excluding Methodists – existed in Ireland. Irish Evangelicalism, by and large, was born during the church's experience of Reformation.

What was the Irish Reformation?
A cynic might answer that the Irish Reformation was little more than an exercise in English dynastic politics. Certainly, between Henry's proclamation of himself as head of the church in 1536 and the launch of aggressive confessionalisation in the 1590s, English dynastic politics seemed more influential than the imaginative grip of distinctive doctrines. The Irish Reformation made little theological progress during its first two generations. The Thirty Nine Articles (1563), the theological basis of the Church of England, were given no legal standing in Ireland. Apparently content with the Irish church's theological ambiguity, English Reformation leaders set about a programme of redistributing Irish church lands and promoting a policy of anglicisation. Church services were to be conducted either in English or Latin – but the fact that the majority of the island's population understood neither of these languages made little impact on policy makers.

Defining the truth
In the 1590s, this ambiguity began to change. Irish church leaders

set about a programme of defining theological truth. This agenda was to be heavily influenced by a number of intellectuals who shared the Puritan vision of further reform in the church. The new Trinity College in Dublin, for example, was founded in 1592 as a college designed to promote the Reformed faith among the Irish social and political elites. But the atmosphere at Trinity College quickly corresponded to the Puritan interests of the most important of its early Fellows. As a cause and consequence of this trend, the reformed church took on an increasingly polemical role.

This polemical interest is evident in the career of one of the college's most prestigious early graduates. James Ussher (1581-1656) entered the college one year after it had been founded. He graduated BA in 1598, and gained his MA and was ordained in 1601. In 1603 he was made Chancellor of St Patrick's Cathedral; in 1607 he was awarded a BD and was made Professor of theology; in 1613 he gained a DD and was promoted to Vice-Chancellor of the college; and in 1625 he acceded to the Archbishopric of Armagh. Ussher had come from one of Dublin's most prestigious families. His father had been a speaker in the Irish Parliament; an uncle had been Archbishop of Armagh; and another uncle became one of the most significant of Ireland's early modern Catholic intellectuals. Like many other families in the Dublin elite, the Usshers had been divided by the Reformation. But James' loyalties were clear. He was a committed Protestant – and was committed to the Reformation of his island. When he first stepped into the theological breach in 1603, it was as a Protestant participant in a public debate on the identity of the Antichrist – a debate with an imprisoned Jesuit controversialist, Henry Fitzsimons, to whom he was related.

This enthusiasm for the public defence of truth underscores Ussher's central role in devising the confession of faith that would underpin the Irish church during its most Puritan period and go on to exercise immense influence on the confessions of faith of Presbyterian, Congregationalist and Baptist churches worldwide. These Irish Articles (1615) – comprising 104 statements of faith, in contrast to the English church's 39 – constituted a declaration of independence by the Irish church.[3] Their contents committed the Irish church to the kind of emphases that the English Puritans were beginning to share. They consciously built upon the past, including most of the Thirty Nine Articles, the Lambeth Articles (drawn up by English Puritans but never adopted by the English church), and some original material. The Articles dramatised the colonial situation of the Irish church. Their imaginative world was black and white. Their enemies were the followers of Antichrist – and Antichrist was identified as the Pope for the first time in any Protestant confession of faith. The Articles' presentation of the gospel and the Christian life was heavily influenced by Ussher's Puritan predilections. Thus they emphasised Sabbath-keeping, for example, and the importance of covenant theology. They also emphasised the Christian's duty to love his neighbour. And, significantly, they also refused to discuss church government. Of course, there was no doubting that the Irish reformed church was episcopalian: Ussher would, after all, go on to become Archbishop of Armagh. Nevertheless, the Irish Articles' failure to specify any particular form of church government was critical to their success. This muddled ecclesiology proved supremely attractive to those ministers searching for a new home for the Presbyterian convictions that had led to their persecution in Scotland. The Irish Articles therefore provided a theological foundation for an Irish Protestant ecumenism, allowing refugee Scottish Presbyterians to minister alongside other clergymen whose embrace of episcopalianism was more whole-hearted. But, ecclesiology aside, the foundational assumption was clear – the Irish church's period of theological ambiguity was over. Now the Irish Reformation was a clearly defined struggle between the Protestant elect and their Catholic opposition.

It was one thing to define the problem, but quite another to resolve it. The problem from which the Irish reformed church could never escape was the fact that its Protestant elect were so few in number. Nevertheless, existing as a tiny minority in an

island populated by potentially violent enemies, the Irish
Articles showed the church's adherents grounding their faith in
confidence in God. The Articles are expressly Calvinistic – God
is presented as completely sovereign, able to save whomever he
wills, and always effecting that salvation on the basis of an eternally fixed decree. Nevertheless, the Articles are not fatalistic.
This Calvinistic emphasis is balanced by an emphasis on
covenant theology, an emerging theological system that presup-
posed that the ways of God could, to a certain extent, be understood if human beings located their lives within his covenantal
purposes. This covenant theology justified the retention of a
number of practises from the medieval tradition – for example,
the baptism of infants, which was justified on the basis that infants had always been included within the covenant community
in the Old Testament, and no word of their exclusion from the
church was recorded in Scripture. With emphases like these, the
Irish Articles were defining a Puritan reformed church.

This Puritan content ensured that the Irish Articles enjoyed
massive influence throughout the seventeenth century and beyond. In the 1640s, when theologians met in London to discuss
the future shape of a Presbyterian English national church, the
theology of the Irish Articles was foundational to the
Westminster Confession of Faith (1647) they produced. Later
confessions of faith prepared by Congregationalists (the Savoy
Declaration, 1658) and Baptists (the Second London Confession,
1677 and 1689) revised the Westminster Confession without significantly departing from Ussher's central emphases. The Irish
Reformation had laid the foundation for the Puritan programme
of church renewal. The confessional roots of the major evangelical denominations had their roots in the theological consensus
of Ussher's church.

Defending the truth

Despite their interest in identifying the Pope as Antichrist, the
documents produced by the early Irish Protestants do give the
sense that the danger they most feared was not Catholicism but

a variant form of Protestantism. This alternative 'Arminianism' was presented in opposition to the strict Calvinism of the Irish Articles, an alternative that to its critics appeared to blur the opposition between Protestant and Catholic systems of thought. Arminianism had formally emerged in the early decades of the seventeenth century among the disciples of Jacob Arminius. These 'Remonstrants' systematised the opinions of their mentor, but found themselves the subject of an international investigation. The Synod of Dort (1618-19) was an international Protestant council convened in Holland to provide a forum for discussion of the problem. The Synod found against the Remonstrants and, in reply to their claims, issued a statement defining the 'five points of Calvinism': total depravity (human nature is entirely corrupted by sin), unconditional election (if we are to be saved, it can only be because God chose us for salvation before we chose him), limited atonement (although the death of Christ is sufficient for the world, it is only effective for those with faith in him), irresistible grace (those chosen for salvation cannot ultimately choose not to be saved), and the perseverance of the saints (the saved can never lose their salvation).

In the 1620s, English and Irish Puritans were very concerned that the churchmen gaining most influence at court were promoting a variation of this Arminianism. English Arminianism could be theologically more orthodox than its European cousin – but it emphasised the importance of liturgy and the sacraments and denied that the Pope was Antichrist. That latter claim had very different implications in England, with its minority Catholic population, than it did in Ireland, where the danger of Catholicism could never be escaped. Nevertheless, the English administration continued to push for the uniformity of the Irish church on explicitly Arminian terms.

Irish Puritans looked in vain for royal defence. King James believed in the uniformity of the church – English involvement in the Synod of Dort had been possible only because of that conviction. Puritans had concurred while they believed that there might have been the possibility that James' goals were the same as theirs, and that the uniform church might bear the stamp of Puritan ideology. All this had changed by the early 1620s. The king had made a number of ecclesiastical appointments that strongly suggested his interest was no longer in promoting the Calvinism defined in the Irish Articles. The preaching of predestination had been made illegal. The theological convictions forged by the Irish church were quite simply going out of fashion.

Faced with increasing pressure to promote Arminian uniformity in the Irish church, Ussher mounted a desperate rearguard action to preserve the church's independence. Pressure for conformity mounted on the northern Presbyterians. Bishops cracked down on apparent irregularities. Publications complained that the northern dissenters were heretics. Ussher appears to have defended the Presbyterians when he could, but he could not prevent the eventual displacement of the Irish Articles. In the mid 1630s, the courts of the Irish church were pushed into adopting the more ambiguous Thirty-Nine Articles alongside their original confession of faith. Irish Puritanism moved into eclipse.

In response to what they saw of the weight of episcopal pressure, the northern Presbyterians were radicalised. Faced with the same pressures for conformity that had driven them from Scotland, they responded by adhering to Presbyterian government with increased tenacity. Suddenly they were no longer happy merely to be tolerated within the Irish church. Suddenly they wanted a church of their own – and were prepared to rebel to get it. Scotland's Covenanting revolution of 1638 lit the fuse that would explode in Ireland's bloody rebellion.

Spreading the truth
Despite the Protestants' careful formulation of evangelical theology, the Irish Reformation was not a golden age of evangelism. Evangelism was not made impossible because of the church's official commitment to Calvinism – the belief that God 'ordained to salvation' (Acts 13:48) did not do away with the church's responsibility to witness to the gospel. Instead, the church's re-

sponsibility to witness to the gospel became the victim of complex cultural forces.

The reformed church, and the Irish government that supported it, was dominated by the most recent English settlers. These 'new English' had high opinions of the value of their own culture, and disparaged the culture and society of the 'mere Irish' and those earlier English settlers who had gone native. The poet Edmund Spenser, for example, defended the horrific idea that the lives of the native Irish were worth no more than the lives of dogs. Many Protestants never rose above the opinion that Irish was a barbarous language fit only for a barbarous people. As a consequence, reformed leaders missed a unique evangelistic opportunity. Their church made slow provision for preaching in the Irish language, for example. The New Testament in Irish was published in 1602, and the *Book of Common Prayer* appeared in 1608, but the equivocation of the Dublin elite, which debated the value of publishing in Irish, postponed publication of the Old Testament, which had been translated in the 1630s, for fifty years. Instead, the reformed church concentrated its attention upon the Protestant population of Ireland.

At times this concentration seemed to enjoy spectacular success. The 'Six Mile Water Revival', for example, appeared to transform a large part of County Antrim. There, the eccentric preaching of Revd James Glendinning had generated intense concern. Popular accounts of the revival describe how Glendinning had thundered away at the demands of God's law, creating an overwhelming sense of guilt in his listeners, without being able to provide the remedy for their guilt in the gospel. Other local clergy, advising Glendinning to work on his preaching style, instituted a monthly evangelistic sermon in the county town of Antrim. Their emphasis on the gospel of grace found ready acceptance among the 'convicted', and the revival spread like wildfire along the banks of the Six Mile Water, according to popular accounts. Its famous conclusion – at Shotts, in Scotland, in 1630 – has entered the mythology of evangelical revivalism.

Nevertheless, the Irish church's evangelistic ambitions were unclear – and would not be settled for several centuries. That wasn't necessarily a fault of Puritan creation. The situation the Reformers inherited pointed inexorably to the political dangers of an Ireland retaining the same religious sympathies as England's greatest enemies. Irish Protestants were, in effect, presiding over a buffer state between Protestant England and Catholic Spain. It was their misfortune to have to be identified with state policies that demanded the silencing of their opposition. Again and again, Irish Protestants debated the best method of containing the political danger of Irish Catholicism, and again and again their answers veered between persuasion or coercion, conversion or conformity. One conclusion they did share was that Irish Protestant evangelism should be closely connected to the state policy of anglicisation. There was no room for religious alternatives. Dissent was a criminal offence.

The failure of this evangelistic policy became more obvious as the seventeenth century progressed. In the aftermath of the 1641 rebellion, Ireland descended in a decade of civil wars. The involvement of English troops in Ireland's wars was made popular in England because of a groundswell of anti-Irish sentiment generated by populist pamphlet literature describing the horrors of the rebellion in grossly inflated terms. The horrors were real – there could be no doubt about that. But the rebellion could not have involved as many hundreds of thousands of victims as some of the pamphlet literature suggested. And it certainly did not develop into a war of Protestants against Catholics. With a number of Catholic armies under independent command, and a northern Presbyterian army regularly competing against the English Cromwellians in the south, Ireland became a confused and chaotic battlefield where Protestant armies were as often in alliance with competing Catholic armies as they were with one another.

Tensions between the English and Scottish Puritans had been brewing through the later 1640s but, insofar as their forces in Ireland were concerned, the final division was hastened by the

English Parliament's execution of King Charles I in January 1649. The regicide was the symptom of a long series of constitutional experiments that had outraged more moderate Puritans. But Puritan radicals – including many of the English soldiers – had been trained to understand the conflict in explicitly apocalyptic terms. Their campaign did not advance on the basis of evangelism, but on the basis of justice. The Cromwellian troops were encouraged to fight by reminders of the awful brutality of Catholic rebels in 1641. Surviving publications make clear their predisposition to understand the conflict in explicitly apocalyptic terms. They were the elect – and even the Scottish Presbyterians fighting in the north could be among their doomed enemies.

The wars of the 1640s demonstrated the ultimate breakdown of the erstwhile Puritan consensus. Cromwell's 34,000 invading troops had brought with them a cosmopolitan variety of Puritan theologies. Among his troops were Congregationalists, Baptists, and Quakers. Whatever the later impact of these denominations, the troops who first espoused their ideologies have not been remembered for their interest in Bible study, service or worship. It was their involvement in scenes of notorious conflict that brought them their most enduring fame.

But everything changed in 1660. With the Restoration of Charles II to the English throne, the series of ecclesiastical and civil experiments that had characterised the period since the 1640s came to a sudden end. The king was back on the throne; the bishops were back in their palaces. Pressure for conformity to an overtly Anglican settlement was stronger than ever. Theologically, the church was reverting to the theological ambiguity of the pre-1590s, and all the advances represented by Ussher's moderate churchmanship and Puritan theology had disappeared.

The failure of the Irish Reformation
By 1660, with the church back on even keel, there could be little doubt that the Irish Reformation had failed. The Protestant

gospel had failed to convert the nation. Legal sanctions were still necessary to encourage Irish Catholics to attend Protestant worship. Legal sanctions were still necessary to encourage dissenting-minded Protestants to adhere to the establishment.

The Irish Reformation had failed because its leaders had lacked an agreed goal. A sense of unity had been relatively easy to maintain while the church's members and ministers felt themselves in collective danger – but in the Arminian pressure of the 1620s and 1630s, and in the civil wars of the 1640s, Protestants had been offered the chance to mould the national church according to their own ecclesiastical preferences, and they had jumped at the chance.

The Irish Reformation failed because its leaders lacked an agreed strategy. Opinion within the church vacillated between coercion and persuasion, conversion and mere conformity. The Irish church had depended, for its success, on the support of the state. Its consensual ecumenism could not endure when the state withdrew its support for the church's pan-Protestant ethos of minimal conformity.

The Irish Reformation failed because of the church's apocalyptic vision. Native Irish people were not simply neutral targets for persuasive evangelism – they were the sworn adherents of the church's apocalyptic enemy, the Antichrist himself. Unconverted people in Ireland represented something fundamentally different – and more dangerous – from unconverted people in England. A pragmatic sense of fear had eclipsed a sense of holy obligation.

Modern Evangelicals and the Irish Reformation

In succeeding centuries, Ireland's experience of Reformation has exercised massive impact on the lifestyle and belief systems of the island's Evangelicals. Until recently, one marker of an evangelical identity had been a thorough-going adherence to the central doctrines of the Reformation: the conviction that salvation is by grace alone, through faith alone, in Christ alone, to the glory of God alone. Among many Evangelicals, this was regularly combined with a commitment to a basic Calvinism. This basic Calvinism was pronounced among Presbyterians and Congregationalists and relatively common even among Anglicans and Baptists. Methodists, adopting a refined Arminianism that echoed many of this Calvinism's evangelical concerns, were not perceived as denying the gospel, and co-operation between denominations across the Calvinist-Arminian divide was possible because Evangelicals had perpetuated the low-church ecclesiological ambivalence that had marked Ussher's Protestant alliance. Fundamentalism in the early twentieth century provided momentum to this trend. This basic Protestant orthodoxy went hand-in-hand with the conviction that Catholicism represented grave danger for the church – politically and, more importantly, in terms of theology. The rejection of Catholicism was based on the fact that the evangelical emphasis on the Reformation gospel did not seem to correlate to anything that mission-minded Catholics were saying. They were, Protestant leaders argued, preaching an altogether different faith. Evangelicals debated whether the Pope was in fact the Antichrist – and an increasingly influential section argued cogently that he was not. But the Catholic Church was no less dangerous for not being an eschatological enemy.

More recently, this situation has begun to change. Evangelicals have retained their low view of church government, have moved increasingly away from Calvinist theology, and in the late twentieth-century's post-denominational age have channelled their formidable energies into the para-church organisations that have done so much to advance evangelical concerns for mission and, increasingly, social action. Towards the end of the twentieth century, this dismissal of ecclesiological concerns has led to a radical re-thinking of the relationship between Protestant Evangelicals and the Catholic Church. Former generations qualified, then abandoned, the old assertion that the Pope was the Antichrist. More recent thinking has questioned the traditional evangelical repudiation of Catholicism. A series of recent ecumenical evangelistic efforts – such as 'Power to Change'

– has indicated that a growing number of Irish Evangelicals are prepared to work with Catholics – some of whom are now styling themselves as 'evangelical' – in an increasingly secularist Ireland. In this situation of theological flux, Evangelicals seem as reluctant as ever to look at their past. Old dogmas would haunt the new alliances.

This realignment of Protestant and Catholic Evangelicals is increasingly obscuring what 'evangelical' means. Professor David Bebbington's definition has become the scholarly standard: Evangelicals, Bebbington argues, can be defined by their adherence to the centrality of the Bible, the cross, the need for conversion, and the expectation that conversion will be evidenced in an active life of social and evangelistic service.[4] Many of these qualities are reflected in the lives and opinions of those Catholics now styling themselves as 'evangelical'; but the extent to which this new alignment has overcome the old divisions based on the Reformation gospel has led many other Evangelicals to question whether the message it promotes can in fact be described as the gospel. If the situation had arisen in the 1600s, Protestants would have considered that Antichrist was among the elect after all.

How should Evangelicals think about the Irish Reformation?
It would seem then that Evangelicals are more reluctant than ever to assess their present in terms of their past – especially when that past threatens the new alliances they have forged. So what should Evangelicals think about the complex series of social, cultural and theological changes we have described as the 'Irish Reformation'?

Firstly, Evangelicals should not avoid the Reformation. It happened, and the experience continues to influence the way in which Evangelicals think about themselves, their message, and their relationship to fellow Irish men and women. The Reformation continues to haunt Irish Evangelicals to the extent that the non-Evangelical population of Ireland continues to associate the problems of the past with Evangelicals in the present. It would be tempting for Evangelicals to dismiss the Reformation as something terrible for which they were not responsible and therefore something for which they should not be blamed. The dreamy mists of the Celtic church provide an entrancing alternative to the problematic connotations of the term 'Protestant'. But Evangelicals cannot escape their past – Ussher has exercised a great deal more influence than Patrick.

Neither should Evangelicals simply regret the Reformation. They don't need to adopt a hand-wringing lament that the Reformation was a 'tragic mistake'. The attitude is certainly plausible – when the culture of medieval Christianity is compared to the mediocrity of postmodern secularism, it is hard not to conclude that something valuable has been lost, and harder still not to conclude that the process of modernisation actually began at the Reformation. But Evangelicals need to remember that virtually everyone in positions of leadership in the sixteenth century was committed to reforming the church. The pre-Reformation church can look attractive in retrospect, but no-one in the sixteenth century was arguing for the *status quo*. Instead, Evangelicals need to remember that something vital was rediscovered at the Reformation, something so important that it changed the way the gospel was being presented, and radically altered the understanding of how sinners can be put right with God and be assured of eternal life. 'Faith alone, by grace alone, in Christ alone, to the glory of God alone' are not simply the ideas that make us Evangelicals; they are the convictions that make us Christians.

Thirdly, the Reformation should not be uncritically celebrated. Neither should the leaders of the Irish Reformation be elevated above all moral scrutiny. There were mistakes – sometimes tragic mistakes – and sometimes indefensible tragic mistakes. Evangelicals need to learn to prize their history, but never to identify with their past so closely than they lose all moral objectivity when considering it. Evangelical identity is to some extent rooted in the Evangelical past; but ultimately, Evangelical identity is rooted in Jesus Christ alone. Evangelicals are part of God's new society in Ireland – a kingdom people living for a new world, not an historical society preserving the memory of the sainted dead.

Finally, Evangelicals need to learn that, in many important ways, the Irish Reformation needs to be repeated. Something new is happening in Ireland. The Republic is passing through a period of unprecedented secularisation. Adherence to weekly mass attendance is dropping dramatically; charismatic renewal and the sudden impact of immigration are changing the face of the Irish evangelical church. Irish Evangelicals are now served by a range of para-church organisations that are successfully harnessing the energy and creativity of the evangelical imagination. In the Irish Bible Institute, Dublin now has its first major Evangelical Bible College since Puritans lost control of Trinity in the 1630s. All over the island, Evangelicals are gaining in confidence. So why do we need another Reformation?

We need another Reformation because of evangelical irrelevance. Evangelicals now have money, time, expertise, intelligence, organisational skill – and numbers. Per head of population, there are more Evangelicals within a 50-mile radius of Belfast than there are anywhere else in the world. But where is the impact?

We need another Reformation because of evangelical fragmentation. Evangelicals need to remember that orthodoxy of community is as important as orthodoxy of doctrine. Evangelism is, as our Lord explains in John 17, as much the proclamation of the church's relationships as it is the proclamation of the church's message. Sadly, renewal – whether charismatic or theological – has too often led to the fragmentation of the body of Christ. Nothing will hold Evangelicals together as much as a sense of common purpose and the high ambition of working for the kingdom of God in Ireland.

We need another Reformation because of evangelical superstition. Perhaps 'superstition' is too strong. But it is surely true that Evangelicals are selling out to the anti-intellectual character of our post-modern age, and are replacing strongly cognitive

Bible expositions and deeply doctrinal worship songs and psalms with alternatives that successfully appeal to the imagination of the age without impressing it with a deep sense of scriptural truth. Increasingly, these alternatives betray their anti-intellectual character. Claims of 'visions and dreams', spurious or not, too often eclipse the voice of God in Scripture. Evangelicals need to recover orthodoxy of doctrine. That will not be a popular call – but it is central to the renewal of God's new society in Ireland, and to the renewal of individuals who are growing into the image of the one who was full of grace and truth.

Conclusion

So are Irish Evangelicals 'Protestant'? Looking at the evidence, and depending on the definition, it might appear that sometimes they are too Protestant, and sometimes not nearly Protestant enough; sometimes too focused on the badges of ethnic or cultural identity, and sometimes not nearly as interested as they should be in the doctrinal truths that root the evangelical faith. Perhaps that is why Irish Evangelicals so often appear to be caught in an identity crisis, so often appear reluctant to admit where they have come from and the sins they have committed against the other people on their island. But their failure to learn the lessons of the past will sentence them to repeating its mistakes.

That is why Irish Evangelicals need a new Reformation – not a Reformation based on coercion, or state power, but a Reformation springing from the indwelling life of the humble Jesus Christ, a Reformation that speaks always of his transforming power and forgiving grace; of the once-for-all work of the Cross and the Christian's daily obligation to live under it; of the dynamism of the Holy Spirit and the holy life as 'glory in the bud', as Ussher once described it; of the glory of the Father and the dignity of the Christian adopted into his royal family. When that happens, perhaps Irish Evangelicals won't need to be thought of as 'Protestant' any more. It will be enough to be known as the people of the gospel.

Notes:

1. The best study of the Irish Reformation is Alan Ford, *The Protestant Reformation in Ireland, 1590-1641* (1984; Dublin: Four Courts, 1997). For an accessible guide to the wider European Reformation, see Patrick Collinson, *The Reformation* (London: Weidenfeld and Nicholson, 2003).

2. For a helpful qualification of modern interest in Celtic Christianity, see Donald E. Meek, *The Quest for Celtic Christianity* (Edinburgh: The Handsel Press, 2000).

3. The Irish Articles have been reprinted as an appendix to Crawford Gribben, *The Irish Puritans: James Ussher and the Reformation of the Church* (Auburn, MA: EP, 2003).

4. David Bebbington, *Evangelicalism in Modern Britain: A history from the 1730s to the 1980s* (London: Unwin Hyman/Routledge, 1989), pp 2-3.

CHAPTER 4

Things Most Certainly Believed

Warren Nelson

Despite the title of this chapter, there are no beliefs which are peculiar to Evangelicals. The essence of evangelical belief lies in the consistent and committed following of a body of teaching and practice, centred on Christ which is traced back to Scripture and can be seen in the historic Creeds of Christendom. This body of teaching comes well within the bounds of orthodox Christianity and every belief in it has been shared with various other Christians down the centuries. Only the importance or the prominence which Evangelicals attach to these beliefs, and the wholehearted enthusiastic way in which these beliefs are held together as a consistent package, mark out Evangelicals as a body.

In short they believe that God does what he says in his book, the Bible. For them belief moves beyond mere doctrinal assent and acquiescence in church instructions to confident personal trust in God. So when they say 'I believe in God' they are not just giving assent to some propositions about God but really saying 'I am trusting my life, past present and future, to God', or as more poetically expressed in one of their favourite hymns:

When peace, like a river, attendeth my way,
When sorrows, like sea-billows, roll
Whatever my lot, Thou hast taught me to say,
It is well, it is well with my soul.

As a consequence of this sharing of basics with other Christians, Evangelicals have had very few problems with the Creeds and have little desire to change them. A further consequence is that Evangelicals can be found, more or less at home, in all the main churches and have never, as a single body, separated themselves from others.

Perceiving God

There are no surprises in what Evangelicals believe about God. For them he is God Almighty, Creator and Sustainer of the Universe, Lord and Saviour, awfully holy, wonderfully loving, far far beyond us in his nature yet fully involved with us by his choice; very much alive and well. In their theology they do not speculate about trying to find God, God is not lost. Their understanding of God is warm and positive, because they believe that God has always been very positive about his creatures, for whom he often expresses his love in word and deed. They are not embarrassed by hymns about the love of God, whether his love for them or theirs for him, because this is the very centre of their faith. There is sunshine in their souls because 'God so loved the world that he gave his only Son, that whoever believes in him should not perish' (John 3:16). And 'We love because he first loved us' (1 John 4:19). This understanding of a God who loves means that Evangelicals are a people who are happy to be God-conscious in everyday life. The textbooks call this the Providence of God, but on the ground it works out as seeing God's guidance, care and provision in the full tapestry of life, in joys and sorrows, and in events, great and small. Accordingly they can and do bring a most diverse multitude of things to God in prayer, from a car that won't start to the salvation of the world, because they believe he knows and cares, and that prayer does change things. They are as aware of the problem of suffering as others, perhaps indeed more so because for them God is their Father and pain and loss ultimately will be traced back to him, but they do not approach the question as a philosophical conundrum but as an area in which to exercise faith. Having trusted him in the sunshine will they not also trust him when dark clouds arise? Moreover they recognise that many of the accusations laid at God's feet, properly belong to human ignorance, folly or deliberate sin. They strive to high standards of personal holiness because they take seriously the Bible's injunctions to be holy as God is holy.

The 'Who' and 'How' of Creation

Among Evangelicals there are gradations of ideas as to how God created the world and most of the views in the evolution debate will be found among them, from those who hold to a literal six-day and comparatively recent creation to those who see evolution as a creative means which God used. Many are happy with an understanding involving forms of evolution within the created living species but do not accept 'blind chance' evolution. But there is unanimity among Evangelicals that God is the First Uncreated Cause and is sovereign and free in his actions, because he is distinct from his creation. He is not part of the mechanism as New Agers, like their pantheist ancestors, suggest and certainly is not some kind of wish fulfilment crutch for the weak minded as sceptical amateur philosophers claim. God is separate from his creation while at the same time being very involved with it. This means he is in control, and neither limited to the elemental systems of the earth, fire, light, heat, fertility, nor under the influence of the starry constellations. Therefore while Evangelicals may well be as concerned for the environment as the next person, they have not put all their eggs in the basket of this earth. They know that their future is not ultimately tied to it and that it will go the way of an old worn-out suit of clothes, 'rolled up and recycled' to paraphrase Hebrews 1:11-12, a fate of which there is evidence already. Further God is personal, by which they mean he is not a blind force, nor just the outworkings of the so-called laws of nature. This is the reason why God, described in the Bible as 'love' (1 John 4:8), can love and be loved and can communicate with us at profound levels of our being. They are amazed at that rare individual, the true atheist, who appears unable to believe, despite the evidence. From their understanding of God as he has shown himself in Scripture they know him to be indeed this God of love, but of course not just love simply, for he is God of a love which is firmly placed in a setting of justice and righteousness. His is not the self indulgent doting love of some parents, nor the blind love of romance. He knows what we are and what we have done, and what we might

well do – if no one was looking – yet he can love us without com-
promising his righteousness. Love and justice meet in law and
mercy. So with a balanced understanding of the complexities in
the nature of God, Evangelicals are happy and at ease with God,
and even when they speak of 'the fear of God' they mean rever-
ential respect and not craven dread. They know that the true
meaning of the word 'blessed' as found in Scripture is not
'painfully holy' but 'happy'. It is the squaring of the circle between the love and the justice of God that gives meaning and
depth to the death of his Son, as we shall see presently.

The Bible and ultimate Authority
'Bible basher' and 'the bigger the Bible the bigger the hypocrite'
are two of the slurs Evangelicals must wear lightly because they
really love the Bible and apply imagination and intellect to its
study. No one needs to tell them how far they fall short of its
principles, they know that better than anyone. Yet their understanding that God is personal and loving and does communicate
with us, or to use an older phrase, reveals himself to us, is based
on the Bible. Part of this revelation can come across through natural means, from the earth around us and worlds beyond us we
can surmise that he is intelligent, powerful and artistic. But heart
must speak to heart and he gives us a more intimate understanding of himself in the Bible, the Old and New Testaments.
This understanding does not come across in mathematical or
dogmatic statements, though dogma is distilled from it. Rather
it is worked out, very often as a gripping story, through his involvement with his people over centuries. This means that while
it can be richly human and very clear in some places, it does take
the work of good interpretation to get it all into clear focus.
While much credit is to be given to Evangelicals for their love of
the Bible, together with their study and frequent use of it, it also
has to be said that it is sometime misused with a harshness, a
lack of love, and an unthinking wooden literalness that puts
other people off. As well, Evangelicals can be myopic in majoring on the verses that 'prove' their point and gliding over other

verses that would balance the picture more comprehensively. But they do take caution from the jingle:

Wonderful things in the Bible I see,

Most of them put there by you and by me

That said, it is true that they have always been to the forefront in making the Bible known and they consistently try to live and worship in conformity to its teachings. The reading of the Bible appears to some people to be a bore, a duty or a religious function but Evangelicals, taking it as 'a word from home', really enjoy it and some, even after forty years study, will claim that it is still fresh to them and that they look forward to new discoveries all the time.

Within the evangelical family the Bible is held to be completely trustworthy and true, giving light, rule, guidance and support for life and for death. This confidence is expressed by a graduation of different words within their family: inerrant, infallible, true and trustworthy, are among the most commonly used. Some dismiss any analysis or literary criticism of Scripture, and for them every word, just as it stands, preferably in the 1611 King James Version, is the very word of God to be used in any and all ways. This approach is sometimes caricatured as the 'typewriter theory' of inspiration meaning that God put his very words into the pen holding hand of the writers, bypassing their personality. Other Evangelicals are prepared to recognise questions of translation, manuscript variations, cultural backgrounds and authors' style, seeing inspiration more in musical terms, the tune is God's but different writers, like musical instruments, leave the mark of their own personalities on it. Nonetheless all Evangelicals are, as an old writer said: 'People of the Book', loving it, using it and pressing it on others. The computer age has not diminished this – publishers are bringing out ever more study guides, background helps, virtual Biblical events and linguistic aids in electronic format to high standards, and a stirring story of Bible reading, study and appreciation runs unbroken from the ancient scrolls of papyrus to pixels on our computer screens.

Perhaps the issue that most distinguishes the Evangelicals' use of, and reliance on, the Bible from others is the question of final authority. Painting with a heavy brush, we can say that in the realm of religious debate there are three claimants for the chair of final authority: human reasoning, church tradition and the Bible, together with permutations of all three. Aware of the dangers of simplification it can be said that liberals, also known in some quarters as Broadchurchmen, favour reason and the ability of the human mind to weigh and decide all questions. They have grown in theological ascendancy since the Enlightenment, especially in the world of universities, where they may not hold many dogmatic ideas but certainly hold some powerful and influential places. Catholics, by which is not meant exclusively Roman Catholics, favour tradition and the body of precepts built up over the centuries, and Evangelicals favour the Bible. No one, of any party, whether they are aware of it or not, relies on one authority source alone in a vacuum. We need reason to make sense of words and to understand linguistic and cultural matters as well as to weigh the validity of interpretations. Likewise we all use the tradition of the actions, writings and experiences of other Christians to help us understand the present, whether that tradition be held by Cardinals at Rome or by the person who sat beside us last Sunday. This is not where the difference lies. The difference lies in the claim to a Final Court of Appeal, that, now famous, 'bottom line' of every argument, debate and TV pundit. Having studied the issues with our minds, having taken heed of what others have made of the matter before us, having made use of the good and well recognised rules of Biblical interpretation and finding many points to weigh but needing to make a decision, what source of final authority will we go with? Happy if all ideas concur, but they will not always do so, three captains on a football team is no recipe for goals. So when push finally comes to shove what authority do we go by? Evangelicals say the Bible. Richard Hooker, the Reformation era Anglican scholar, known as 'the judicious Hooker' for his sane and balanced wisdom said:

> What Scripture doth plainly deliver, to that the first place
> both of credit and obedience is due; the next whereunto, is
> whatsoever any man can necessarily conclude, by force of
> Reason; after these, the voice of the Church succeedeth.

Their case is strong because taking the totality of the scriptural
revelation of God together with its diagnosis of human nature
and its good news of salvation in Christ they are able to hold a
totally consistent understanding that makes sense of all
Scripture and of the world around them.

Putting Humpty Dumpty together again

It is what Evangelicals believe about human nature that most
frequently brings them into conflict with the values, fashions
and culture of the day. In keeping with the Bible they begin with
a very serious and potentially fatal diagnosis of humanity: 'All
have sinned and fall short of the glory of God' (Romans 3:23),
another genuine instance of that overworked phrase, 'this is the
bottom line'. They understand human nature to be flawed at all
levels, not just in some of our colourful obvious ways, but also in
our pride, in our intellect, our worldview and our understanding. Evangelicals hold that our nature is damaged at the deepest
psychological levels. Just as a carpenter's square which has gone
out of alignment will adversely affect all his work, so the sinful
bias in human nature corrupts all we think and do which, inci-
dentally, is the main argument for not trusting reason alone.
Even our efforts at morality can be suspect, being spoiled by
mixed motives and essential self-interest. We give, but how
much do we hold back? We pray but our own needs get priority;
we help someone but we look for praise. Evangelicals cannot accept the way of the religiously devout and pious who hope that
a few more prayers, some penance and a few good actions will
turn a pig's ear into a silk purse. They reject as too facile the
political hope that better drains, hygiene and education will
bring about an end to law-breaking. Fallen humanity needs
more than soap and cheap copy-books. They give no credence to
the revolutionary's agenda of bringing in utopia by substituting

one group of sinners for another. Nor do they even distinguish between the working lad of rough language weaving his way home from the pub in a cacophony of heavy metal, six-pack in hand, and the cultured devotee of Mozart, renowned for his witty cynicisms, politely inebriated in his own drawing room on best brandy, because they know that our condition is beyond being repaired by a little culture. Like Humpty Dumpty we have suffered a great fall, and all the world's experts cannot put us together again. Most of today's thinking begins with the premise that our 'problems' – for the word 'sins', except in enticing adverts, has almost completely dropped out of polite society – come from our circumstances or from other people who load their wrong doing unto us, who would otherwise be lovely caring, gentle people just like Little Jack Horner able to say 'what a good boy am I'. Evangelicals, who are mostly seen as being conservative, actually take the most radical position of all: that the problems, the evils, the injustices, the sins of society, come from our own nature and wilfulness and they strongly maintain that the only lasting solution will be our individual re-creation. For, as Jesus said, 'what comes out of a man is what defiles a man' (Mark 7:20).

Conversion – The Point of Turning
Some writers and commentators have said, rightly, that an emphasis on conversion is one of the distinctives of Evangelicals. There is truth in this, but not if this only means conversion by itself as a religious experience or the changing from one denomination to another. Conversion is the flag or observable marker of what should be a profound change, a ruffle on the surface denoting deeper goings on. Because human nature is flawed from the centre of our personality out, no sticking-plaster solution will work, there needs to be a root and branch change. And it is indeed a strong evangelical conviction that such a change is both a necessity, for it was Jesus, not some televangelist who said 'You must be born again' (John 3:7), and that this change or conversion should be a conscious happening in our lives. Scripture,

always rich in imagery, uses a number of word-pictures to describe conversion: it is passing from death to life, being able to see, entering the kingdom, being born again, coming out of darkness into light, being set free, being saved, being delivered from the power of darkness and transferred into the kingdom. In fact the Bible does go as far as to say it is a new creation (2 Corinthians 5:17).

The amount and the diversity of these illustrative phrases should impress two things on us: the importance, indeed the necessity of this change, which is why Evangelicals look for conversions; and that no one understanding or experience of it should be considered as the way in which it should happen. There is no unanimity regarding baptism, but they are all agreed that the mere ceremony of baptism will not bring about such a fundamental change. For some their conversion happens dramatically on an ever-memorable occasion, but for others it appears to come about slowly, like a mist clearing. Some come to it easily, well assisted by friends and relatives while others were reluctant and were hard argued into it, and there are those who were apparently converted without the intervention of any human help. Conversion was expected of some because of family or church connection but some conversions were a big surprise to all involved.

The portal, or trigger factors in this profound change are repentance and faith. That is to say – and leaving aside for now deep questions of God's calling and the work of the Holy Spirit in bringing conversion about – we are bidden to turn from self and sin to trust in God. We find that the early Christians frequently urged their hearers to repent and believe the gospel, (see Matthew 3:2, 4:17, 21:32 Mark 1:15, 6:12, Luke 13:3, 5, Acts 2:38, 3:19, 17:30, 26:20) or in Dublin's vernacular to 'Give up your aul sins'. Indeed these are the first words Mark reports Jesus as saying when he began his ministry (Mark 1:15). Powerful, challenging and reassuring as these basic Christian words about repentance and faith are they have been blunted by two very common wrong interpretations. The Latin Vulgate (4th century AD) mistranslated 'repent' as 'do penance' (Matthew 3:2), where the original Greek idea was 'have a change of heart', and so for about a thousand years the call to radical change was muted to one of performing religious duties. The second mistaken idea still clings to the word 'gospel', especially in those churches with strong liturgical traditions. The word itself means 'good news' and as good news it is to be heard, believed and rejoiced over. But the word 'gospel' gets confused with the readings from the gospels which naturally and frequently consist of the teaching injunctions of Jesus to those already disciples. Accordingly the call to 'Believe the Good News' gets translated in popular perception into 'keep the injunctions found in the words of Christ', which is a different message and for another purpose.

If Evangelicals do indeed start with a pessimistic diagnosis of the human condition and are dismissive of easy answers, it is because they have seen a prognosis of great hope. We can be changed, we can be re-made, we can become new people. This comes across dramatically when Paul is writing to the young church in Corinth, he gives a catalogue of sin's nasties, then he says 'and such were some of you, but you were washed, you were sanctified, you were justified' (1 Corinthians 6:9-11). Evangelicals will have their own personal edition of these sin lists, as it were, but they understand what Paul is saying and are able also to say ' I was … but now I am …' More fully elsewhere Paul lists the symptoms of a life lived following our own nature, giving about fifteen perennial ugly traits including immorality, strife, anger and selfishness and then contrasts them with a list of the results of following the leading of God's Spirit: love, joy, peace, kindness and the like, (Galatians 5:16-25). Not unnaturally therefore Evangelicals, having tasted this better, re-made, humanity are recognised, approvingly or not, as people who preach, people who distribute gospel literature, people who talk about their faith; in short, as evangelists. This is because their reasoning is that having discovered the great treasure they want others to have a share in it, like the four lepers of 2 Kings

Chapter 7 who knew they shouldn't keep good news to themselves. Or, as someone put it more simply, 'Evangelism is one beggar telling other beggars where there is bread.'

This evangelical understanding of human nature has produced two different approaches to everyday lifestyle and to involvement with the world around them among Evangelicals themselves. Many, perhaps the majority, looked rather negatively on what in evangelicalspeak is called 'the world'. They took little interest in current affairs and less in the arts. A long list of activities was traditionally frowned upon, some of this from sincere conviction, but often really only because of a created culture of isolation: drinking alcohol, cinema and theatre going, reading Sunday newspapers, engaging in politics or organised Sunday sport. This sidelined the influence of Evangelicals. Others have been more willing to engage the world on its terms, challenge its values and put forward alternatives; the debate continues.

Jesus – the Bringer of Salvation
For the sincere seeker the package of beliefs or emphases held by Evangelicals has in its favour that it holds together logically, it finds resonance throughout the Bible, it does answer questions and it is centred on Jesus. Faced with a loving but holy God and our own lost and sinful condition, people look for a way of escape. Any good psychologist can predict their next actions. They may go into denial – 'I'm not that bad.' Or they may sublimate and throw ourselves into a round of busyness. They may try and bargain their way out – 'Well God, if you will ... then I will ...' But Evangelicals say that there is a sure way of escape, indeed a God-provided way of escape (Hebrews 2:3).

That a man called and titled, Jesus Christ, existed, taught, healed and died on a Roman cross is denied only by the hare-brained, the deeply prejudiced and the anarchically sceptical. Sober secular historians acknowledge the facts. But, of course, Evangelicals like other Christians claim much more than these rudiments, and here again we are on common ground with the majority of professing Christians. Jesus did teach and heal but also with no hint of incongruity or inconsistency he made amazing claims for himself: that he could forgive sins, that he had come from God and was returning there, that he would judge the world and that he was the only way to God. His claims, coupled with his lifestyle and crowned by his resurrection from the dead, convinced the early disciples that he was the Son of God and himself essentially God. Evangelicals do not diverge from this faith in Jesus and, as was said earlier, they readily affirm the primitive Creeds of Christendom. They do, however, to put it briefly, find the centre of gravity for their theology in the death of Christ and in the reasons for it. In other theologies the incarnation, God coming to us as one with us, is central. Evangelicals fully accept this, but press on to look more closely at why he came. They explore all that is implied in Jesus' words: 'the Son of Man came to seek and to save the lost' (Luke 19:10). The understanding of why Christ died comes under the textbook expression 'The Atonement', and short of using other more ambiguous phrases or heaping clauses on top of sub-clauses it is hard to avoid it. A readership that has learned dozens of new words since the coming of the computer should be able to take on board this noble theological term. It is one of the very few words the English language has contributed to theology and means exactly what it looks as if it should mean: at-one-ment – the state of two parties being reconciled.

The atonement comes out of the love of God, set alongside the justice of God. How can God, who is the upholder of the moral law, forgive those who have broken it repeatedly? He cannot say, 'It doesn't matter' for that would be universal cosmic and eternal anarchy. He cannot say, 'No harm done' for terrible harm has been done, our lawlessness lies behind every waste of human potential and an ocean of tears. He does not say, 'Fix it up yourselves', because he knows we cannot, even if we wanted to. And he loves far too much to say, 'Right, if that's the way you want it you can have it.' Much of the Old Testament tells of preparing God's people for the concept of Someone, at great cost, filling a mediating role. In its pages ideas like sacrifice, re-deemer, blame taker and representative occur. So it is no sur-prise that when Jesus came to this world the same ideas came quietly into the equation, all pointing to the events outside Jerusalem on the first Good Friday. After the death and resurrec-tion of Jesus, and with the Old Testament as background the first Christians brought it all together and the cross became their core message. This was hardly the best way to win friends and influence people and not what a PR agency would think up: that you should put yourselves forward as the followers of someone who died as a criminal. Indeed one very early graffiti depicts a Christian worshipping a donkey, i.e. a fool, on a cross. That the first Christians did nevertheless place the crucifixion to the fore in their preaching speaks of its central urgent importance.

Sometimes when a rope is made with a number of strands there is one coloured tracer cord running through it. This may help us to understand the Atonement, for, like a rope, it is in-deed multi-stranded and no one theory or illustration can ex-plain all its richness. The New Testament brings the strands in the Atonement before us: it was a ransom paid, an example given, a bond or debt cancelled, a sacrifice made. And the coloured tracer deeply entwined? Yes, Evangelicals hold that at its deepest level the Atonement was a substitution, that Jesus was the lamb slain for others, the just for the unjust, or as Evangelicals, with Paul, would personalise it: he loved me and gave himself for me (Galatians 2:20). An anonymous second century Christian put it:

> How overwhelming the love of God! Instead of hating and rejecting us, remembering things against us, He bore with us and took our sins upon Himself and gave His own Son as a ransom for us. The Holy for the wicked, the Sinless for sin-ners. Oh happy swap, the wickedness of many covered in the One, the holiness of One justifying the lawless. *Epistle to Diognetus 9* (paraphrased)

From this they get their confidence in God, their assurance of sin forgiven and of a new relationship with God and, not least, their joy. There is little in all this, in terms of its various parts and pieces, that marks out the thinking of Evangelicals from the understanding others have of the Atonement. They are unique only in the centrality it occupies in their theology and worship, in the completeness with which they believe in all the strands, and in the robust assurance they derive from it as being complete and a 'done deal'. Their older textbooks speak of 'the finished work' of Christ, reflecting his own cry from the cross, 'It is finished.' This means that by his offering of himself, once and once only in time and place, he achieved all that was needed in order for us to be forgiven and found acceptable, therefore Evangelicals strongly reject the idea that anything we do: suffering pain, giving money, doing penance, supposedly offering Christ again, can add anything to a transaction that is complete and is the only God appointed basis for our forgiveness. This is not to say that there is no virtue in good deeds, but it is saying that with regard to seeking eternal life we can but accept salvation as a gift given freely of God's grace. This also means that they are not constantly looking back over their shoulder in concern about their own standing with God, but rather, knowing their own spiritual security they are set free to work for others.

All these benefits come in a package, as it were, which is given the name 'Salvation'. Common synonyms for salvation are: deliverance, rescue, recovery, escape; and all these have Biblical weight. We are delivered from evil and lostness, rescued from the downward pull of self, given God's own Spirit to bring about recovery, and we finally escape the fate we should deserve. Not surprisingly, therefore, Evangelicals often speak about, sing about and preach about salvation. This can come across as shrill and arrogant when unthinkingly urged on some buttonholed victim by someone who is not only 'saved' but can give date, location and time for the event. A fuller, more scriptural and loving picture is given by those who explain that the salvation package has past, present and future dimensions. So while Evangelicals do claim to have been saved from the penalty of sin when they repented and turned trustingly to Christ and

Merrion Hall (now the Davenport Hotel) built around the time of the 1859 Revival to accommodate crowds who sat under the ministry of Rev J. Denham Smith, previously a Congregational minister in Dún Laoghaire. It became a centre of interdenominational mission and later a Christian Brethren Assembly.

Photo: Fergus Ryan

Rose La Touche (1849-1875) was a member of the notable Huguenot family who settled in Ireland in the seventeenth century. This portrait was drawn by her lover and admirer, John Ruskin.

Power le Poer Trench, a leading evangelical churchman in the 19th century, the last Church of Ireland Archbishop of Tuam

The Church of St Thomas, Dugort, Achill, Co Mayo, built beside the Missionary Colony founded by Rev Edward Nangle during the Great Famine
Drawing: Fergus Ryan

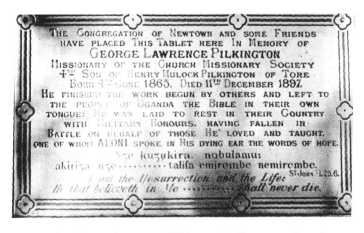

THE CONGREGATION OF NEWTOWN AND SOME FRIENDS
HAVE PLACED THIS TABLET HERE IN MEMORY OF
GEORGE LAWRENCE PILKINGTON
MISSIONARY OF THE CHURCH MISSIONARY SOCIETY
4TH SON OF HENRY MULOCK PILKINGTON OF TORE
BORN 4TH JUNE 1865, DIED 11TH DECEMBER 1897.
HE FINISHED THE WORK BEGUN BY OTHERS AND LEFT TO
THE PEOPLE OF UGANDA THE BIBLE IN THEIR OWN
TONGUE: HE WAS LAID TO REST IN THEIR COUNTRY
WITH MILITARY HONOURS, HAVING FALLEN IN
BATTLE ON BEHALF OF THOSE HE LOVED AND TAUGHT,
ONE OF WHOM ALONI SPOKE IN HIS DYING EAR THE WORDS OF HOPE.

Nze kuzukira, nobulamu:
akiriza njo............talifa emirembe nemirembe. ST JOHN 11.25.6.

I am the Resurrection and the Life:
He that believeth in Me ....shall never die.

Memorial to George Lawrence Pilkington in Newtown Church near
Tyrrellspass, Co Westmeath. See page 220.

ST. KEVIN'S CHURCH, BLOOMFIELD AVENUE SOUTH CIRCULAR RD. DUBLIN

Buses 17, 19, 20 & 22

PAROCHIAL MISSION

October 31st—November 9th, 1947

Missioners:
CANON T. C. HAMMOND, M.A.
REVD. E. M. NEILL, M.A.

———— *Services* ————

SUNDAYS: 11.30 a.m. & 7 p.m.   WEEKDAYS: 8 p.m.
CHILDREN: Sundays, 3 p.m.; Weekdays, 5 p.m.
WOMEN'S SERVICE: November 2nd, at 4 p.m.
MEN'S SERVICE; November 9th, at 4 p.m.

CANON T. C. HAMMOND, M.A. was Curate and later Rector of St. Kevin's. Became Superintendent of the Irish Church Missions and is now Principal of Moore Theological College, Sydney, Australia.

REVD. E. M. NEILL, M.A. who will take the Childrens' Services, is Rector of Crinken and Irish Staff Worker of the Children's Special Service Mission.

" Behold, I stand at the door and knock; if any man hear my voice and open the door, I will come in."—REVELATION iii. 20

PRAY! COME! INVITE OTHERS! EVERYBODY WELCOME!

Parish or Congregational Missions were held frequently throughout the
20th century and often attracted substantial audiences from different
churches.

Trinity College, founded in 1592 for the spread of Protestantism and the training of Anglican clergy, contributed much to Irish Evangelicalism during the Puritan era, the Cromwellian period and the years of the Second Reformation in the nineteenth century. Samuel Winter, an Independent, became Provost in 1652. The aptly named 'Trinity Evangelicals' were influential in promoting evangelistic endeavour in both the Established Church and Nonconformist congregations during the Victorian Revival.

Drawing: Fergus Ryan

Christ Church Cathedral, Dublin. Baptist and Independent ministers
preached from its pulpit in the Cromwellian years.
Drawing: Fergus Ryan

Multi-denominational camps for children and young people have been
part of evangelical life in Ireland for generations. These campers and
their leaders are pictured at Killashee School near Naas, Co Kildare, in
the 1980s.

A church youth camp outside Rostrevor, Co Down, in the 1960s

Veteran Dublin
YMCA evangelist
Johnny Cochrane

Gathering at the Irish Church Missions building in Townsend Street, Dublin, c. 1933

Rev T. C. Hammond, well known evangelist, theologian and apologist, c. 1930

A Bible Churchmen's Missionary Society (now Crosslinks) rally in the Lurgan area in the 1920s

Pastor Robert Boggs who ministered in Tobermore, Co Derry for almost forty years.

were forgiven, and they consider this as settled and in the past. They also affirm that they are being saved from the power of sin as the Spirit of God changes them, sometimes slowly, sometimes painfully into conformity with Christ. And they do believe that one day they will be finally saved from the presence of sin and presented without blemish before God's glory (Jude 24). It is like a man rescued from the sea and being brought to shore, he has been saved, he is being saved and he will be finally saved unto dry land. These three tenses of Salvation, past settled, present ongoing and future assured can be found coming together in Paul's words at Romans 5:1, 2:

> we are justified by faith, we have peace with God
> we have obtained access to the grace in which we stand
> we rejoice in our hope of the glory of God.

The explanation of this was given flesh and blood by Jesus in the story of the returning Prodigal (Luke 15: 20-24). And for post-modern twenty-first century people it is best understood in terms of that most human of ideas, the idea that lies behind film after film, soap opera after soap opera: relationships. We were alienated, our backs turned to God, our heart set on our own way. But we were turned around, we became sons and daughters of God (John 1:12, 13), members of his family. The textbook, and biblical, word for this operation is 'justification'. We are justified – accepted as not guilty by means of, but not on account of, our faith in Christ's atoning death for us, and given, again on Christ's account, the standing of being righteous in God's sight. We find this all the way back to Abra(ha)m who trusted in God and God 'reckoned it to him as righteousness' (Genesis 15:6). In the Psalms we read of the happy position of 'he whose transgression is forgiven and whose sin covered' (Psalm 32:1). In Isaiah we read of the servant who will make many 'to be accounted righteous' (Isaiah 53:11). But, of course, it is when we come to the New Testament that we find this truth in full flower. In the stories of Jesus it is the sinner at the back of the Temple who goes home justified (Luke 18: 9-14), it is the swindling rich Tax Collector, Zacchaeus, coming down from his tree a changed

man (Luke 19:1-10) and the Prodigal alive to his Father again
(Luke 15:24). After the death of Christ the matter was even more
fully understood as the implications of the cross as the ultimate
sacrifice sank in, and it become a central plank in the church's
message. Paul urges it strongly on the Galatian church when
they appeared to be falling back on self-justification, (Galatians,
chapters 3, 4 and 5), and then gives a full exposition and reasoned presentation of it to the church at Rome, especially
Romans, chapters 3-8. There is a distinction in theory – but none
should exist in practice – between our justification and our subsequent growth in righteousness, technically known as our
sanctification. Justification is about our legal standing before
God, it has no graduations for it is complete, it is God's doing
alone and is based on the relationship 'Christ for us'. Sanctification is about our quality control as Christians. It is a process,
that creaks and groans at times, it requires our co-operation and
is based on the Holy Spirit forming Christ-likeness in us.

At times the truth of justification and the potential of a new
relationship with God by faith was forgotten and even denied,
but has always re-surfaced to give new courage and impetus to
God's people. It was an issue, we could almost say *the* issue, at
the Reformation. Every time people sing the much loved hymn
'Rock of Ages' they are, aware or not, reaffirming its truth:

could my zeal no respite know,

could my tears for ever flow,

all for sin could not atone,

thou must save, and thou alone.

It is argued that believing that we are now right with God, just
by faith alone, leads to indifference about good works, and indeed it will always be possible to point to an example of someone thinking it gives licence to sin. This is no new charge, for it
was apparently urged against Paul who strongly refutes it
(Romans 6 :1, 2). To enter into this new relationship of forgiveness and reconciliation with God is to begin a whole new approach to Christian living – we now find that we want to serve
God from the heart out and not from the ears in. When I have

been given a clean sheet of paper I want to do clean work. Besides it is, in fact, the only way to actually have good works, because if we think otherwise and are supposing that there is some way that our good actions will stand to us in earning eternal life, then those actions are not single-minded purely good actions, they are being performed with at least some thought to earning merit. Only when we realise that eternal life is gifted to us can we begin to be good for goodness' very own sake. It is as if a mother plans to bring her children to town for a treat, if she says: 'If you don't wash your face I won't take you with me', she is entering into a bargaining situation, and the children go and wash with bad attitude. However if she says: 'I am taking you to town, now go and wash', they go with the assurance of their mother's good favour and wash readily. This second approach best reflects the connection between justification by faith and good works. And while it is to be sadly acknowledged that Evangelicals can sin grievously, yet surely the empirical evidence is that they, in general, have a good reputation for living to high standards. There is a fine distinction that must be understood. The Evangelical says he is justified (right with God) by faith alone, it is a gift (Romans 6:23) and he is saved by grace, not by works (Ephesians 2:8, 9); if this is misunderstood his opponent will say, 'how can you be justified without good works? Doesn't that mean you can then do what you like?' The Evangelical will reply, 'No, the faith in God by which I am justified is found to be not alone, but brings with it good works as surely as your shadow follows you, nevertheless it is by the faith only that I am justified.' The good works which follow are the evidence of faith, it is like cart and horse, horse being faith, cart being works, the horse comes first and brings the cart after it.

Freedom in the Spirit
Older Evangelicals, while quite orthodox on the subject of who the Spirit is and what he does in and for believers, did not however preach or teach often on the subject. And once again we find no basic difference between Evangelicals and the generality

of Christians on the classical definitions of the Holy Spirit as the third person of the Trinity. Yes, they held that he brought conviction and opened hearts and interpreted Scripture, helped us pray and could 'come upon' preachers to help them speak for God. But in practice it was taken that we had to do these things very much for ourselves. The rise of the Pentecostal movement from the beginning of the twentieth century and the charismatic movement from mid-century on has made Evangelicals do some re-thinking and has spiritually enriched them. They have now taken more seriously the Spirit's work in enabling all Christians to have a ministry through his gifts for service (Romans 12, 1 Corinthians 12, Ephesians 4, 1 Peter 4). And they have opened doors for him to bring more freedom and joy to worship. In their older textbooks of dogmatics it was certainly written that he brought life to the church, but now this is passing from theory to practice.

Enjoying the new life
Where this is happening in evangelical circles it is bringing together again two influences that should never have been separated: the study of the Bible and the work of the Spirit; the Bible for soundness, the knowledge of God and correction, and the Spirit to make that knowledge alive, warm and attractive. Just as there is a lot of difference between rashers in the freezer and rashers sizzling on the pan. It is by the Spirit working with our spirit that we have the confidence and assurance that we belong, that we are sons and daughters in God's family and that we can have the happy boldness to call God 'Daddy', for such, culturally adjusted, is what Paul means when he says that it is by the witness of the Spirit we can say 'Abba, Father' (Romans 8:15).

Once again the teaching and example of the first Christians is being studied as people want to see in their churches evidence that the gifts of the Spirit are being used to foster growth, and want to experience the fruit of the Spirit in their own lives producing the beautiful qualities: love, joy, peace, patience, kindness, goodness, faithfulness, gentleness, self-control (Galatians

5:22, 23). It would be fair to say that Evangelicals hold a middle position on questions of the life of the Spirit in the church. Over against those who consider the structures, ceremonies and due order of the church as of first importance and who expect the Spirit to be in attendance at the place and time of the church's choosing, they appeal for liberty 'for the Spirit blows where he wills' (John 3:8) and they encourage the expectation of life and growth. Their understanding and experience of the Spirit has dynamism. But on the other hand they are distinctly cautious about some of the claims of healing and power made by charismatics and others, and certainly will not accept every claim some people make of speaking by or for the Spirit. So some accuse them of being undisciplined or at least a bit free and easy with rules, while others accuse them of being too stiff and cerebral. They are like buses which operate freely, within certain constraints, in a world of unrestrained cars and rigid trains.

The church and Christian living

It will surprise some to know that Evangelicals have a 'high' view of the church, and they agree that it is One, Holy, Catholic and Apostolic. They are zealous for sound caring churches and endeavour to have healthy congregations which reflect the lovely illustrations given in the New Testament of what the church is. For in Scripture it, sometimes 'she', is described variously as Branches of the Vine, the Flock, a Temple of God, a Body, a Bride and most comprehensively as the Household of God. But they do not give these attributes or titles to any one single organisational visible church. When they speak in high terms of 'the church' they are referring to the company of believers worldwide, indwelt by the Holy Spirit and with Christ as Head. This company of people then is considered to be 'invisible', not however like some quirky TV character who cannot be seen, but because the actual membership cannot be determined by counting adherents to any or all denominations. Rather, although members of the church live here on earth, as some are already 'with Christ', they actually constitute a spiritual reality whose exact and full extent is known only to God. And it is this spiritual body that is One, united by faith in Christ as Lord, Holy by calling and privilege, Catholic by being truly everywhere and Apostolic in following the teaching of the first Apostles. This 'invisible' body must, of course, in order to fulfil its purposes in the world, have visible buildings to use, written constitutions to follow, recognisable leadership and membership and will have, as we know, varying traditions and ways of doing things. But none of these things is the church. Therefore in the sphere of their 'visible' manifestations we find diversity among Evangelicals. Likewise there is diversity of attitude to the large established churches. Some Evangelicals believe that their spiritual home is in the mainstream denominations where they can serve, have influence and bear witness to biblical truth. Others are happier to belong to denominations where they are the majority if not the totality, some pursue the will-o-the-wisp of belonging to 'perfect' churches, giving some Evangelicals the reputation of being divisive. Where they have numerical strength they are found to indulge more often in division and exclusivity, where they are few they forgo those harmful luxuries. The same is also true of the extent to which they co-operate with other denominations – where they are numerically strong they often take an independent line, where few in number they more readily can be found working alongside others.

The sacraments – no ex opere operato

As for the sacraments, or ordinances of the church, Evangelicals hold to baptism and the Lord's Supper as being normally and generally necessary for good church order and life, and the means by which God's favour towards us becomes more fully known. But they are of the firm belief that God is not tied to them and that no sacramental function can be considered as absolutely essential for salvation, neither sacrament is effective without faith. Both of these sacraments have an outward visible aspect and an inwardness which comes by faith. Baptism, with its outward sign of water, is indicative of washing and new life and is a mark of membership. The New Testament does press the importance of baptism, but is a little vague as to how it should be carried out, so some by their practice of sprinkling show that for them the amount of water is not vital, whereas others press for total immersion. Perhaps by analogy with Scripture's way of speaking about the Spirit being 'poured out' we get closest to New Testament usage where some form of pouring is practiced. More contentious in the evangelical family is the question of who should be baptised. Baptists and a large number of others contend that only those of sufficient years to have insight into what is involved and who express and show active faith should be baptised. This is a strong and simple position which goes far to safeguard the responsibility to repent and believe before being accepted into membership. However, with equal sincerity, other Evangelicals regard the children of believing parents as welcome into membership and therefore eligible subjects for baptism and support this position by appeals to the place of children within God's Covenant in Old and New Testament and they see the examples of household baptism in the New Testament as supporting their case.

The Lord's Supper, called The Breaking of Bread by some Evangelicals, the Holy Communion by some and The Eucharist by a few, is highly valued. It is participated in with reverent solemnity and observed, with degrees of frequency from weekly to quarterly, in keeping with Jesus' own instruction to 'Do this in remembrance of me'. In the mainstream Protestant churches it is carried out by appointed recognised ministers very much along the same lines as by other clergy, with perhaps more simplicity. In the smaller and more independent churches there is greater liberty as to who supervises the administration and which words and actions are used. A range or scale of ideas about what is actually happening is held, not necessarily consistently or constantly by any individual or congregation on every occasion. Since the understanding of the ceremony can be very personal and subjective, it is unlikely that many could spell out exactly their thoughts. But in as much as there is a scale or range it goes from 'mere' thankful remembrance for the death of Christ through ideas of being spiritually fed to appreciating the sacrament as a means of blessing or grace for those who believe. But on all sides any idea of a physical presence of Christ in or with the bread and wine is rejected, the bread is bread and does not change in substance or essence, nor does the wine. Christ's presence is in the believer's heart.

Church Life

For Evangelicals the life of their local church and their own spiritual life are very much entwined. They do not consider their religion to be a once-a-week exercise to be got over with quickly so that they can 'get on with their lives'. Prayer and Bible study, personally and with others is considered a vital lifeline, so they make time most days for both, and will probably attend a mid-week meeting at the church for what is loosely called 'fellow-ship'. This means being with others of like mind to encourage them, and to be encouraged in their faith. This close attachment to their congregation helps to maintain Christian standards of conduct for, as explained above, Evangelicals are concerned to live according to the high calling and privileges they have been given.

A visitor from one of the larger denominations coming along to a morning service of worship in a church building housing a modern 'free church' evangelical congregation would find all these differences in theological emphasis we have looked at re-flected around him in the 'feel' of the place. The architecture of the building would show an attempt to give chief place to the preaching and teaching of the Bible. Therefore the preaching point would be centrally located as opposed to that prominence being given to an altar, as in Catholicism. In as far as the build-ing allowed, seating would be 'user friendly' and egalitarian with no especially 'holy' or sacred place. If he found himself in a Baptist church he might be intrigued by the pool used for bap-tism by total immersion. He would be aware of an informality which he might even mistake for irreverence. With no priestly order and because Evangelicals internalise their spirituality more, there would be no special robes, attendants, ritual or holy objects. There would be more, if not indeed complete, lay involvement in all aspects of the worship. And there would be more books and much congregational singing; the visitor would be given a hymn book, or two, and be expected to sing along, and perhaps choose a hymn. He might be given a Bible, and in an understated way be expected to follow the readings and the sermon from it. The notices or announcements would indicate a high level of prayer activity, missionary involvement – local as well as overseas – and lay participation in the business matters of the church. Unless he had struck an exception to the norm, people would be friendly and there would be an underlying current of joy. Finally the Pastor / Preacher / Minister / Leader would be ahead of him in getting to the door and whilst perhaps exchanging a pleasantry about the weather would be searching his face for a sign of some interest in what he had heard.

Behind their livestyle, their ways of worship, otherworldliness and their sometimes seemingly awkward approach to other people Evangelicals, individually and corporately, do have a genuine concern for the souls of others. From the eager 'Are you saved'- type to the person who gives years of their life quietly working with relief projects hoping that even just one person might ask 'Why do you do this ?', there is a strong motivation to bear witness to the salvation available freely in Christ and to loving service. Effort, prayer and money go into the unceasing task of taking the good news into all the world by every means possible. And Evangelicals do rejoice with the angels when another sinner repents.

Multiple Ministries
In keeping with the teaching of the New Testament Evangelicals fervently believe in a called and recognised ministry or leadership in the church, established for the good order, growth and defence of the church. However they find that the New Testament is not over concerned with exactly what form that ministry

should take. In the New Testament we have 'elders', 'deacons', 'deaconesses', 'overseers', 'teachers', 'evangelists' as well as even less clearly defined roles such as 'leaders' and 'those over you', and nowhere in Scripture is any one of our many present forms of church government given specific description or endorsement. Consequently we find a very varied usage among Evangelicals, especially where they have formed 'free' or independent churches. However, there is wide consensus on the basic ideas behind ministry. With very few exceptions it is agreed that some form of leadership/ministry is necessary. It is also agreed that the key element of ministry is in serving the church or flock, feeding, teaching, leading, and generally caring for people. So we find 'minister' (in older congregations), a word which emphasises service, or 'pastor' with ideas of shepherd, among the preferred names for leaders. Leadership should itself be under some form of oversight, as there is no place in the church for people to set up and run their own personal little empires, but there is no unanimity as to how such oversight should be exercised. Some see this oversight in the work of bishops, some in various councils or committees of elders, others see it in the confederation of a number of local congregations and some in the gathered membership of the local congregation. The worldwide debate about the role of women in Christian ministry also arises among Evangelicals. Some are conservative and quite definite in restricting the work women can do, while others value, and have valued since long before the current debate, the contribution of women to all aspects of ministry. Most Evangelicals would want to recognise biblical patterns of male leadership exercised with due regard for love, care and protection. Finally there is agreement that leadership is not a hierarchical 'caste' separate from the laity, and Evangelicals contend that no leadership can play a mediatorial or priestly role between the people and God. 'Put no man between your soul and God' was an old saying. In this regard Evangelicals only use the idea of priesthood in the inclusive sense of the 'priesthood of all the laity' offering grateful praise to God, which is the priestly work of all the people of God (1 Peter 2:9, Revelation 1:6). By this they are affirming that the death of Christ, once for all time (Hebrews 9:25-28), has put an end to any need for a priestly class to offer atoning sacrifice for sin. And so the only 'offering' that now needs to be made is the offering up of praise and thanks to God (Hebrews 13:15), something which all the redeemed people of God can do, and it is a Christian task that is the duty and privilege of all. It may be helpful here to mention also that following New Testament use (Acts 9:32, Romans 1:7, 1 Corinthians 1:2 and similarly over fifty times), Evangelicals consider all believers to be the 'saints' (with a small 's') since being a saint is the result of God's calling, forgiveness and indwelling Holy Spirit, not of degrees of personal sanctity. They certainly are not happy with teaching that exalts some individuals to any special category or status, though most Evangelicals do, for convenience, go along with such common usage as 'Saint Patrick'.

The end of all things

Where mainstream churches have shifted their interest to other concerns such as ecumenism, Third World debt, anti-racism or whatever is flavour-of-the-month, Evangelicals have kept alive the expectations of heaven or hell and the Second Coming of Christ. The grave is not the end and human destiny is more than hoping we will be remembered for a generation or two. And again it must be said that they teach nothing in these areas that would not have been the widely held views of Christians for hundreds of years. They live with a conscious expectation that Jesus will return to this earth, they point out that his Second Coming is mentioned over three hundred times in the New Testament, whereas the Lord's Supper/Communion is only mentioned a handful of times and baptism not much more often. There are graduations of this expectation – one business man is said to have had on his desk a little plaque with the words 'Perhaps Today', how it influenced his planning decisions we are not told. But the generality of Evangelicals do hold firmly to belief in a sudden, visible and personal return of the same Jesus

that they know from the New Testament. Beyond this certainty
they are not always in agreement as to the timetable of his return; some have elaborate schemes they have worked out from
Scripture, each step supported by a verse or two from somewhere in the Bible, though it is less clear whether their overall
timetable as such is found in, or could be supported by, the
Bible. Others are content that he will come, one day, and that his
coming will be the end of this present world and the beginning
of a new heaven and earth which will be without sin or its ef-
fects. This great hope of his coming rests, as we have mentioned,
on hundreds of verses of Scripture and does not depend on any
quirky mis-interpretation of a few obscure verses tentatively
patched together. Moreover for Evangelicals it is entirely consistent with their experience of God. A great and powerful creator
can bring about a new world – a just God will not allow the evil
of powerful men to go unchecked and a loving and true Saviour
who has said that he has gone to prepare a place for us can be
taken at his word. And the Spirit has given us inward longings
for a final redemption that will not be disappointed.

Our Victorian forebears lived in a time when many died
young and most lived at just about existence level. Not surprisingly they were very heaven conscious and fond of melodramatic
deathbed scenes, as we can see from their writers such as
Dickens, and this was prominent in their hymns. Evangelicals
today, like the rest of the population, have higher expectations
for this world and so it can be said that thoughts of heaven have
receded a little. But the sure hope of dwelling in the house of the
Lord forever is the goal of their faith, the confidence of their
daily walk and what they want others to enjoy assurance about.
In keeping with the Bible they cannot be specific as to what
heaven will be like but would think in terms of the fulfilment of
true human potential and being with Jesus and all the redeemed
people of God in peaceful active happy righteousness beyond
all expectation. They do not however expect to sit around all
day, in white, playing harps. They are also less specific than previous generations about the nature of hell. There is in fact a very

lively debate ongoing among them on the subject. Some support the traditional understanding of everlasting fire, others think in terms of the burning woe of everlasting regret, some expect a destruction with finality. But all would be in agreement that hell exists, that it is not 'of your own making on this earth'. It will be a sore loss of opportunity and a separation from love because it will be a separation from God, and it is to be avoided especially since we have the great alternative of turning to Christ for deliverance.

Evangelicals do not believe in a profit and loss, balancing the books type of Judgement Day in which people hope that their good deeds will outweigh their sins, especially if God would just tip the scales a little in their favour. As we have seen above, for them the issue of their eternal destiny has already been settled, they have been forgiven and made members of the family, indeed, following John in his gospel, they believe that their eternal life has already begun: 'he who hears my words and believes him who sent me has eternal life and does not come into judgement but has passed from death to life' (John 5:24). And with Paul they rejoice that 'there is now no condemnation for those who are in Christ Jesus' (Romans 8:1). However, they certainly do believe that they will have to give account of their stewardship while on earth, and that there will be graduations of reward and loss, yet their eternal life itself will not be at stake.

Finally – back to the beginning

Two things must be said in order to finish with a true picture. This chapter has attempted to comprehensively cover the main beliefs of Evangelicals and the more important shades of thought within those beliefs. But attempting so to do could give the impression of a people stuffed with dogma and Bible verses arguing among themselves over sub-clauses within sub-clauses. This would be a very definite distortion of the truth, so we must stand back now a little and look at the full picture.

Firstly, Evangelicals whether in or out of the main denominations are very united on the essentials of salvation and are able to enjoy warm fellowship with fellow Evangelicals. The distances between any of them on secondary questions such as baptism or the end programme for this world are measured in centimetres where differences between them and some other forms of professing Christianity are measured in metres. Any of them can recount moving stories of meeting Evangelicals from other areas or even from across the world without even language in common, and yet being aware of complete agreement of heart. There is also strong co-operation, irrespective of denomination or secondary issues, among them for evangelism and in agencies for mission, publishing or famine relief.

Secondly, while this chapter has attempted to survey systematically all the beliefs that Evangelical hold dearly, the average Evangelical does not spell out his faith in dogmas, he, or statistically more likely: she, lives by a warm rounded trust in God that brings peace, hope, joy and purpose to their life, and which is so much a part of everyday life as to influence a hundred and one decisions, whether those decisions be what to watch on television tonight, what to spend money on, whom to marry or whether to leave their job and work overseas for a relief agency. They do not consider their time, talents or their money to be at their disposal to use on self. In a world growing ever more frenetic they enjoy the peace of God. In a world that measures 'success' only in monetary terms they have a priceless contentment and where some people consider a 'relationship' to be meaningful if it lasts more than six months they value lifelong love in marriage. No Evangelical would want to go back to what they were in the days when they lived without Christ.

CHAPTER FIVE

A Theology of the Heart

PART ONE: MY FAITH JOURNEY
Ken Clarke

Sorry … thank you … please … are three of the first words many
parents teach their children to say. For me, they gave shape to
the most significant prayer in my life. It was a defining moment.
Each person has defining moments. In my life this was the most
important one of all. I was a 12-year-old boy at a Scripture Union
Inter Schools camp lying on a top bunk bed in Guysmere,
Castlerock. It was late at night. The others in the room were
going to sleep. I was reflecting on things I had heard in the talks
during the camp. I knew I had to make a response. In a simple
and undramatic way I prayed an utterly sincere prayer. From
the very depth of my being and with all the sincerity a 12-year-
old could muster, I prayed 'sorry … thank-you and please.' I
knew that Christ had been speaking to me. His promptings were
unmistakable. His love captured me. His friendship captivated
me. His death moved me. His mercy overwhelmed me. His
grace staggered me. His word spoke to me. I could almost hear
him say to me personally, 'Behold, I stand at the door and
knock! If any man hear my voice and open the door I will come
in' (Revelation 3:20).

I knew I had confessed my sins many times at church. I knew
Christ loved me and died for me. I had no doubt he had been
raised from the dead. However, I also knew that I had never
specifically and intentionally responded to his invitation to
open the door. Now it was RSVP time! Gently and apprehen-
sively I decided in my mind that I had heard his voice and that
this was the time to open the door. I prayed. 'Lord Jesus Christ, I
am sorry for my sin. Thank you for dying on the cross for me.
Please come into my heart and life and make me a new person.'

A New Beginning

The next day I told someone I trusted. I began reading the Bible
and praying each day. I factored into my life what was called in
those days 'A Quiet Time'. It has been part of my life ever since.
It was considered essential for Christian growth and maturity.
Since before birth I had been a church attender but after that
summer church took on a whole new meaning. I listened and
participated with much more interest. I became more involved
in my local parish. I joined the Scripture Union Group in
Sullivan Upper in Holywood where I was a pupil and I also
joined an interdenominational Bible Class movement called
Crusaders. My Christian nurture in my teenage years was firmly
in the evangelical tradition.

At Trinity College Dublin my involvement in the University
Christian Union followed on naturally from my school Scripture
Union. My conversion to Christ was in line with the teaching of
my Dad and Mum and the influence of my Sunday School teachers. My parents had taught me to love and pray to Jesus. Such
training was reflected in my immediate reaction to a frightening
experience.

When the Ghost train broke down I believed that Jesus could
help me. I was sure of that truth. I will never forget my childhood experience of the Ghost train breaking down in the darkness of the journey in Barry's Amusements in Portrush. From
waves of fear and from the very depth of my heart I cried out for
divine help with unreserved earnestness and compelling ur-
gency. One of the first lessons I had learned about Jesus was that
he helps us and that he is with us wherever we are. Such convictions did not flow from extensive reading of the Bible because I
was too young to read. They flowed from the teaching of my
parents. The first hymn I ever remember singing was one they
had taught me. Unknown to me I had been learning theology
from hymns and in this situation of stress and distress it rapidly
became applied theology!

'Jesus loves me this I know.

For the Bible tells me so.

Little ones to him belong.

They are weak but he is strong.

Yes Jesus loves me …

A child's mind can understand this and some of the greatest minds in the world are humbled by this same simple truth. He loves us and he helps us because he loves us.

A Sheaf of Essentials

The lessons I learned as a child and the primary elements of a conversion have stayed with me for the whole of my life. I am intrigued that it is these same truths which are the very essence of evangelical faith. Some of them are…

The generous grace and love of God.

The centrality of Christ, his cross and resurrection.

The trustworthiness of God's word.

The reality of sin.

The importance of personal repentance and faith.

The dynamic of personal conversion which leads to community transformation.

The empowering work of the Holy Spirit that we might be Christ's witnesses.

The aspiration of holiness and righteousness.

The Jesus I still know fifty years later is the same Jesus I knew then Of course I no longer visualize him in long pristine white robes, immaculate flowing hair and surrounded by perfectly behaved children, as he was in my first book of Bible stories. However I now have a lifelong experience of his unique kind of love … love of a different kind. The Jesus who walked on earth and the Jesus I know is someone whose love is a selfless, muscular love. His love is not a wishy washy, wimpish kind of love. His love is surprising in its expression, disturbing in its extent and profoundly overwhelming in my personal experience and the experience of millions of others across the nations and generations.

Jesus The Trailblazer

The Jesus I know is a trailblazer, courageous in his actions, astonishing in his attitudes, a breaker of moulds but always in line with his Father's will. He profoundly disturbs religious people. He constantly engages with needy people. He, a Jew, spoke with a Samaritan woman. When I was younger I had no idea of the revolutionary nature of this unusual encounter. In this meeting with the Samaritan woman he was crossing national, cultural, social and religious boundaries. He was walking where the strict religious Jews would not walk. He was building friendship where others would not. St John wrote that Jesus was 'full of grace and truth'. Amazing, overflowing and never ending grace, which is loving and showing favour to those who do not deserve to be loved, marked his whole life. That is real grace! If we need anything in Ireland we need to discover the Jesus of the gospels who reached out to all in his society and who forgave even his enemies. From the Cross he prayed, 'Father forgive them for they know not what they do.' This is Jesus who loved 'the other side', the despised, the outcast, the misunderstood, the last, the least and the lost. This is the Jesus I am still getting to know and he disturbs me.

He challenges my prejudices. He calls me to be radical. He confronts my hypocrisy. He sees my secret struggles. He is hurt by my sin. Yet I still see the moisture of grace in his eyes and I still know the depth of his mercy in my heart. I have said sorry many times for my rebellion and folly. I recognise the reality of his forgiveness in my life. I hear him whisper in my ear, 'Your sins are forgiven. Go and sin no more.' They are but I do. The Jesus I have come to know forgives and forgives and forgives again. Like the apostle Paul I cannot get over the fact that he loves me and gave himself for me. It is an incredible thought but such a releasing truth. I know that the truth, his truth, sets people free.

Rest and Restlessness

To some this may seem strange but the Jesus I know has enabled me to know a sense of rest and an ongoing restlessness. I have known peace but I can never settle. He constantly calls me to new adventures in my mind and life. He stretches me and repeatedly in my inner being I hear his words, 'Follow Me.' Following means change. Obedience is sometimes painful. He takes me where I am not sure I want to go. He leads me in the known and the unknown. Yet the alternative is to miss out on what it means to be a disciple. In bereavement, disappointment and in those personal and family pains, which you are not sure you want anyone else to know about, I have known Jesus Christ. He is the Jesus of the cross and of suffering. He is the Jesus of resurrection and hope. The two are inseparable. The longer I know him the more convinced I am that his call to follow him is a call to suffering and glory. Heaven will be all glory. But that is yet to be. Romans chapter 8 is the classic teaching on this tapestry of trial and triumph.

The Jesus I know is the Jesus who knows me. I'm back where I started. I am still overwhelmed by his love as I travel on a different train, not a ghost train but the train of mid-life. For this I have Jesus! The words of the following hymn have meant much to me in recent years:

For the joys and for the sorrows, the best and worst of times.
For this moment, for tomorrow, for what lies behind.
Fears that crowd around me, for the failure of my plans.
For the dreams of all I hope to be, the truth of what I am.
For this I have Jesus.

For the tears that flow in secret, in the broken times.
For the moments of elation or the troubled mind.
For all the disappointments, the sting of old regrets,
All my prayers and longings that seem unanswered yet.
For this I have Jesus.

This hymn means so much, not primarily because I have Jesus but, primarily because Jesus Christ has me. His hold is secure. His grip is strong. His people cannot be separated from him! The Cross and resurrection are the foundation of Christian hope. His Word is the promise of Christian hope. His people are an expression of Christian hope. This eternal journey of life begins in the heart of God and is received as we echo those words with life changing honesty … *sorry* … *thank you* … *please!* Without hesitation and with profound gratitude I thank God for evangelical essentials.

PART TWO: MY STORY, MY SONG
Moya Brennan

In the 30 years of my time with Clannad I have stood in the wings of the *Late Late Show* on numerous occasions, but I have never felt so sick with nerves as I did that night. With a tight knot in my stomach and perspiration on my palms, I listened to Pat Kenny's introduction and prayed that I might be able to say the right things: 'Now, ladies and gentlemen, my next guest is no stranger to the *Late Late Show*. She is the girl from Donegal, the one we all know and love as the voice of Clannad. But tonight she's here to talk to us about her autobiography and let me tell you, there are some shocking revelations. Do we actually know the real Máire Brennan? Let's meet her.'

I took my seat to the audience's welcoming applause, taking a moment's comfort as I made out the silhouette of my husband, Tim, sitting on the front row. As expected, Pat Kenny honed in on the darker aspects of my story. I knew that there would be revelations which might be shocking to some people, including an abortion I had had when I was younger, but I wanted to get across my message about God's forgiveness and to share how my broken life has been healed through turning to him.

For the next few days I felt like I wanted to hide. I found myself on the front pages of Ireland's newspapers.

Numerous times I was stopped while out shopping when a woman would thank me for my honesty and tell me how encouraged she was by my story. Stories (from readers) continued to flood in, making me more and more grateful for the things God has done in my life and the opportunity I have, through my story, to help others. All too easily we wrongly fear the judgement of these people who, perhaps more than most, might reveal compassion and forgiveness. Some people say, 'There but for the grace of God go I' but I suppose I came very close to going there.

Some memories that stay with me:

Out on a Lonely Road

I had been trying to ignore the sickly feeling in my stomach, but now there was no doubt about it. I had to face the fact that I could be pregnant. Panic-stricken, I had no idea what to do. What I feared and focused on most was the potential I had to hurt so many people. What kind of example was I? The eldest of the family, and here I was, only one year out of school and pregnant through a night of silliness at a festival.

I awoke, back on the ward with a pounding head and lurching stomach. I was terribly sick and longed for the numbness of sleep. It was dark and quiet on the ward, except for the restless stirring of other haunted dreams. Eventually, I quietly cried myself to sleep.

I'd never smoked as a teenager. I knew some of the girls at school did it, and later in my father's bar the air used to be thick with nicotine fumes, but we'd grown up in a cigarette-free household and admired our parents' stance against it. Then again, life on tour was different. We were musicians and that's what musicians did. It was in Germany that we were also introduced to cannabis. It seemed quite widely available, though I was shocked when I was first offered it. The first time I tried it, I hated it. But it was 'cool,' so I persevered. That's the worst thing about young people with drugs, drink and sex. It becomes the 'thing to do'. It was all part of 'having a good time'. More and more we found ourselves surrounded by people who indulged and supplied us, and a joint every now and again helped us wind down after a show.

The *Theme from Harry's Game* was touted around some of the

major record companies and RCA (who later became part of the BMG group) rose to the challenge. The *Harry's Game* film was broadcast over the next three nights and by Wednesday the sales of the single had rocketed.

Bono tells a story that he nearly went off the road when he heard it on his car radio. He had to pull up and listen to it properly. It was so unusual and, of course, Bono recognised that the singing was in Gaelic. We were very flattered when U2 later used it to open and close their show and also in their concert video filmed at Red Rock.

Even with Clannad's success, my confidence had been gradually, and fatally, eroded.

Though I probably didn't realise it at the time, my self-esteem had plummeted and inside I was dreadfully lonely. It was easy to drink and smoke a joint. It helped me forget all that and meant I didn't have to think too deeply about anything. I should have been excited and on top of the world with the way my career was going, or thinking about starting a family of my own, but no, my future didn't get beyond the next couple of hours in a day.

People had gone crazy and our music was being played everywhere. When the night of the British Academy of Film and Television Arts awards came around we were all in very high spirits.

I cringe now to think what I must have looked like among all the other guests – the 'beautiful people' – actors and actresses, models and general celebrities, all in their designer gear and glitzy hairdos. Still, when Ronnie Scott made the announcement that Clannad had won the award for the best soundtrack, I couldn't have cared less what I looked like. The moment (going on stage to accept the award) was simply breathtaking.

Champagne flowed and we chatted and laughed our way through the rest of the evening – to the point where we were getting angry looks and eventually a telling-off from the table next to us because they couldn't hear Charlton Heston do his speech. Later we joined the lineup with Heston, Jane Seymour, Roger

Daltry and other stars from the stage and screen to be presented to Princess Anne. The next morning the film company sent over bottles of champagne which we sipped over breakfast in the hotel room as we giggled at our pictures in the newspaper.

Drugs were always available through the crowd I now mixed with. Looking back, it's hard to understand why it did not become more of an addiction. For some reason it didn't get a grip on me the way it does with so many others. Perhaps it had something to do with Mammy and Daddy back home on their knees praying, as they always had, for the protection of their children.

A Change of Direction

I met my (now) husband, Tim on a photoshoot and saw him whenever I was in London. After a while I told him that the next time I was over in London I wanted to go to his church. I think he was quite horrified. He tried to make an excuse for us not to go, but I was intrigued and determined. This was a part of his life that was alien to me and I wanted to understand more of it. I think he thought it might scare me or emphasise the difference between us, and he tried to warn me what it might be like.

But in a way he was right. Even his warnings had not prepared me for what I discovered the Sunday morning we walked into his church. I was amazed at how casual it seemed. Everyone was really friendly, laughing, chatting, hugging each other, and the vicar had a hard time getting everyone's attention to start the service. When the music started I didn't know what was going to happen. There was a proper band playing and in minutes people were singing, dancing and throwing their arms in the air. While the music was upbeat they danced and clapped, then the worship leader brought the music down. There followed about 20 minutes of gentle songs that seemed to stir people's emotions even more.

I looked around. Some were crying, others just stood with their eyes closed and their hands held up towards the ceiling. Over to my right I watched one of these women start to shake, then before my eyes she collapsed backwards and lay on the floor. It made me jump and I was amazed that the people around just left her lying there. There was also a strange muttering coming from some people, like a different language. I didn't understand it. It was very strange to me, quite mad in fact, but I was interested in what was going on and what was being said, especially when the vicar gave his message. He spoke with power and passion about the love of God, how Jesus died to take on our burdens, to wipe away our sins, to be our personal Saviour. It was a new language for me, but I found myself quite gripped by what he was saying.

I came out of the church with many questions. I had never heard people talk about Jesus in such a close and loving way, and as Christmas approached I was beginning to look at the nativity story that I knew so well in a new light. I suppose I was seeking a deeper meaning to my life and, through the faith of my childhood and my meeting Tim, I was beginning to find it.

During Christmas that year my family witnessed a smile on my face and lightness in my spirit that they had not seen for years. There were still many clouds overshadowing me, but as I lived each day I found myself looking ahead with anticipation and hope, perhaps for the first time in my adult life.

I had a lot to learn. I had no doubt about the existence of God, but what I had to grasp hold of was the fact that he heard my prayers and cared enough to pull me through. I knew that handing myself over to his mercy was my only hope. When you get that desperate, the rules and trappings of any kind of religion disappear. There was no dramatic experience or great spiritual awakening, but I was beginning to understand that the God who had watched over me since my birth was carrying me now.

The love (Tim and I) shared was special and the more we explored our faith together, the more we wanted our relationship to develop on solid ground.

At our first Easter together, Tim had offered to buy me an Easter egg. I'd asked if he would get me a Bible instead. He had been thrilled and inside wrote some words I have always cherished: 'To dear Máire – Never forget how much God loves you.

May he always give you strength and encouragement and may you always be able to show his love in your life.'

My Bible had become a treasured companion, along with my grandmother's prayer book. I had taken it on tour with me, quietly and shyly seeking my way on my bunk in the bus while the others played cards or watched videos. All through the tour I made sure that I went to church regularly. The others never took much notice. Sunday morning was usually the time to catch up on sleep and they rarely missed me. One of my visits took me to a large cathedral in Christchurch, New Zealand. The worship was wonderful and it was a great service, but it is neither the music nor the teaching that lingers in my memory. Something happened that day; I came out of the cathedral feeling more alive than ever.

'Tim, don't laugh at me,' I said, 'but I think God has spoken to me.' I went on to tell him what was going on in my head. It was hard to explain. There had been no audible voice and it wasn't even anything the preacher said, but somehow I felt God was telling me that I would be used to help break through some of the barriers of prejudice in the Northern Ireland situation.

One of the most amazing things about life is that you never know what's around the next corner. In many ways my life was complete, happy and fulfilled. I had a wonderful family (having married Tim), I had my career with Clannad and I was enjoying church life at St Mark's. One day my dear friend, Ann Trainor, who leads one of the worship teams at the church, invited me to sing a Gaelic Psalm for the morning service. Gradually I found myself becoming a regular member of the worship team. When Ann discovered that Tim played the cello when he was younger, she eventually coaxed him into the team as well.

Coming from Ireland, and seeing the misery caused by such factions, I am ashamed that such obvious bigotry still exists among those who profess to love and serve the Lord. Is there any wonder that the outside world looks at the church with a certain disdain? The impression so often is of a body of people who wallow in self-reflection and are bound by guilt and rules.

Yet, the reality of Christianity is that Jesus Christ, the man from Nazareth, blew away the bondage which leans only on rules and regulations and replaced them with love – a love that does not condemn and judge, but breaks down barriers and unites people.

Thankfully this is the heart experience of some people I have met around the world. Toward the end of 1999 I found myself performing at a Presbyterian church in the Loyalist stronghold of East Belfast. I had to double-check that the pastor knew what he had set up. There I was, with my band, our traditional Irish instruments and Gaelic songs in a place that traditionally has had no tolerance for the things of Irish culture. And yet that night the church was alive and electric with joy as I performed in concert. It is in areas such as this where the seeds of unity are beginning to flourish. As the politicians struggle to bring peace to Ireland, the people of God – from all backgrounds, denominations, classes and walks of life – are seeing their prayers answered, and I cannot help but remember the conviction I had all those years ago in Christchurch. Once again, he is working out his perfect time in my life and I am honoured and privileged beyond words to be able to play a small part in uniting God's people in my music.

Condensed from *The Other Side of the Rainbow* (London: Hodder and Stoughton, 2000).

CHAPTER SIX

As Seen by An Other

Malachi O'Doherty

The first reports that I heard about Evangelicals were from my mother and some boys in my class at school, who left early and took jobs in the civil service and post office. They talked a lot about the saved because they were fascinated by them. There were two elements of this fascination. One arose from the discovery of the religious Protestant; our prejudice before that was that Protestants were not really religious at all. We could see that not many went to church. The other element of this fascination was horror that Evangelicals were breaking one of the fundamental rules which had been instilled into us, which was that we should not talk about religion to people of another faith. We understood that Northern Ireland was a divided society and that religion was contentious and that the best way to get on with your neighbour was not to advertise your differences. Evangelicals advertise their difference all the time.

Mixed Memories with Strong Emotions
My mother was a night sister in a hospital in Belfast and she would come home from work in the morning carrying with her the exasperations of the long night. So at the breakfast table she would tell us stories about the other nurses and orderlies on the ward. Someone may have crossed her and annoyed her and she would say, 'And her all goody-goody, having seen the light.' I asked her what this light was that the Protestant orderly had seen and at first she simply mocked the notion that they had seen any light at all, but one day she addressed my question more seriously. She said: 'I am not sure that they have actually seen a light. Perhaps they are speaking metaphorically, yet sometimes by the way they talk it seems they mean to say that they have seen something'.

This amazed me. I was a religious child. I believed the stories I read about the lives of the saints, that they had had visions and great disturbances in their souls. I took it for granted that religious transcendence could only really be part of the Catholic experience. Yet where were the Catholics who were reporting this transcendence? None were that I knew of.

It dawned on me that my mother's contempt for the saved was part of a more general suspicion of religious enthusiasm which included the Catholic.

It would be years before I had any closer acquaintance with Evangelicals. I would see them in Belfast, handing out tracts on the street, preaching at passers-by through loud hailers and I took these people for eccentrics.

As the political temperature rose in Belfast, Evangelicals appeared more in the media, advancing their political arguments in theological terms. Their suspicion of the rest of Ireland was informed by a suspicion of the Roman Church. It was during this political debate that I began to see what Evangelicals thought of the world to which I belonged. They thought clearly that Catholics were slavish people, dominated by the priests who took their orders from Rome. Many said frankly that they made no distinction between the Catholic Church and the IRA. They regarded the church simply as a force for evil in the world, the devil's counter to salvation.

Now I can look back with more detachment and see that there were then two religious blocks, each making the clear statement that it was right and right alone. The Catholic Church that I grew up in before the Second Vatican Council held the conviction that it was the one true church. Belonging to that one true church, it was easy to imagine that other people were not really religious at all. The Evangelicals believed that they alone were the saved of God. They held the one true clear understanding of the Bible; they committed themselves to Jesus Christ, accepted his salvation and met the single condition which could entitle them to entry into heaven. They believed we were damned; we believed they were damned.

Then years later still I worked as a religious affairs journalist for the BBC and began to meet many Evangelicals. One thing that became clear early on was that the religious tradition which I had read as very narrow included considerable diversity of attitude. For people whose primary assumption about me was I was damned to hell, some were extraordinarily civil. Their human contact with me overruled the information about my destiny which their theology provided. Some of them rationalised this. They said that, though I clearly wasn't saved like them, it wasn't for them to presume to know the mind of God. God was free, if he chose, to accept into heaven someone who didn't believe in him.

I could tell the story of how an Evangelical pastor and I shared cigars and a bottle of whiskey and some bawdy humour in my flat, but I will spare him the embarrassment.

Some had no interest in me at all other than a desire to save me. They would say things like, I love you because the spirit of God is in you. I had no wish to be loved on such terms. I wanted people to like me for the person I was, for my humour and my intelligence. Love that bypassed these seemed to me not to be love at all.

Still, they believed that it was important to save me and always made their pitch. The Reverend Ian Paisley has reminded me every time I have met him that I need God's grace, and that I am lost without it. I was in his home once with a camera crew and as they set up the camera and lights, Dr Paisley and I went into another room to discuss the interview. Before he would talk about the political issues we would air on camera, he took the opportunity to remind me that many Catholics before me – he made the assumption that I was a Catholic – had come to his church and received God's grace. He told me I would be very welcome there myself. Every time we have met he has extended the same hope in one form or another that I might be saved. I think he would regard it as discourtesy and negligence to do otherwise.

He holds his religious beliefs with deep conviction. The immanent God is as real to him as the weather.

As real to him also is the historic battle between Christ and Satan, embodied in the saved people and the Roman Catholic Church, which is anti-Christ. From my perspective, Catholicism and Evangelicalism are no longer alike in their assertions that they are exclusively true. The contest between them is one from which Catholicism has retired. It does not proselytise and it no longer asserts that it is the one true church. When it has made claims in recent years to being more true than other churches, and even presumed to dismiss other churches as mere ecclesiastical communities, most Catholics have been embarrassed if they cared, contemptuous if they didn't.

Though some in the hierarchy of the Catholic Church would like to reverse Vatican II, most Irish Catholics would not. I doubt if there is that same disparity within Evangelicals between popular feeling and theological instruction.

Irritations and a Hint of Admiration
Let me tell you what annoys me in Evangelicals.

I hate the way they describe themselves as Christians. Not that I want to apply the word to myself, but I hear them in their usage excluding all other churches. I hear them claiming not to be a church or denomination when clearly they represent a specific strand or type of Christian belief. Okay, perhaps it is fairer to call them a tendency than a church since there are Evangelicals in many churches. But their insistence that they are the true Christians, still in the intimate circle of Jesus, is a claim on a par with the one the Catholic Church made.

Evangelicals appear sometimes to be deftly seeking unfair advantage for themselves with their claim to be nondenominational. For instance, the BBC, which could never broadcast a programme presented by a Catholic priest for the purpose of winning converts to Catholicism, nonetheless broadcasts programmes in which Evangelical Christians seek to win converts to their type of Christianity. Those Evangelicals, I think, would say that they do not represent a type of Christianity at all but only simple, essential, true Christianity. That is trickery with words. That is dismissing other Christians as entirely invalid, and refusing to acknowledge that you are part of a range of churches and interpretations of the gospels. It is not the BBC's understanding of Christianity. And it is what a Catholic priest would have said in 1960.

But the born-again Christian is vindicated by experience. That cannot be ignored. People do feel shaken to the foundations and transformed in a moment by the touch of God. And rather than tell them that they don't, or that they are imagining it, perhaps we have to understand more about the human heart and the cataclysms that may occur within it. Evangelicals themselves perhaps have to understand too that the range of human emotional experience may be wider than they know and that seismic upheaval in the human frame is normal, and that numinous wonder is normal and is human and that rapture is normal.

Evangelicalism, I believe, is founded on bad psychology, the inability to grasp that the range of human emotion includes the sublime and the willingness to be told that your own sense of wonder is not your own at all, but something from outside you.

Within the evangelical tradition I have perceived a great naïvete about human nature. There are clearly a lot of confidence tricksters in that section of religious belief, great charismatic preachers who can attract huge amounts of money to themselves. There are lesser crooks who maybe have not been so successful but have nonetheless won the support of evangelical groups which think that it is enough for a man to say he is saved for him to be judged good. There are also mountebanks and clowns, great entertainers who perform healing rituals, exorcisms and speak in tongues who even though they may believe in what they do and are excited by what they do, preach nonsense and convey the impression that the excitement is its own reward.

Opting for instant salvation is opting out of human nature and the need to understand other human beings in their psychology, but Evangelicals who give up on psychology leave themselves wide open to abuse.

I have seen a preacher enthral an audience with his stories about driving out devils and healing the sick. It seemed to me that the audience was vulnerable to him because it did not have the critical tools with which to test him. The world he described was biblical, therefore it was true to life as they understood it.

I spoke to the preacher Heinrich Bonnke and asked him about reports that he had brought a baby back to life in the womb. He couldn't tell me where it had happened or what the name of the mother was, or even for sure that he believed himself that it had happened. He had, therefore, agreed to meet a journalist without the least expectation that he would be asked about such things. I got the impression that he rarely if ever met anyone who doubted him.

I was asked recently to participate in a debate at Summer Madness, an evangelical festival for young people in Belfast. The motion was: this house believes that Christians have the right to evangelise any time, any place, anywhere. I was opposing that. I said, if you post a notice on the door of this building asserting that right, people will take you for being arrogant and imperialistic.

In the discussion after the main debate, a young woman of about twenty rose to speak. She told me that she had been doing missionary work in London and that she had called at the house of a Jamaican woman. The woman welcomed her and introduced her to her children. She said it was lovely to meet another Christian; she was a Christian herself and went to the local church. The young woman telling the story then made a point which I expect everyone in the hall anticipated. She said, 'I had to explain to this woman that she wasn't a Christian at all'.

I said to her, 'Where under God does a child like you get the cheek to address another person like that?' And I wondered what sort of church it is that sends children out into the world convinced that they already know all they need to know.

Of course, if they are right then they are right and it is pointless for someone like me to try to correct them. If they are right I am lost. If I am right, they are misguided and in a sense they are lost too because I believe that what counts is what you learn by reflecting on life's experience. I believe that the young missionary wasted a great opportunity, when an older woman offered her friendship and hospitality and perhaps, if she was really lucky, a little of her wisdom.

I also believe that this insensitivity to what matters to others is potentially very dangerous, and has been destructive of good relations in Northern Ireland. I cannot trust to the respect of an Evangelical person who thinks I am damned. I can make allowance for the common disparity between what people say they believe and what their behaviour shows they actually believe, so I can be friends with Evangelicals. But I am not sure that they are good Evangelicals in their own terms, those that are friends of mine.

The proselytiser who has no interest in me for what I believe or for what I have experienced but wants only to change me, can never be a friend. And those whose theology tells them that people I have loved are burning in hell must accept the damage this assumption does to my ability to hear them. More, I must wonder about the petrol bomber, whose religious background tells him that his victim is damned to burn anyway, whether he is capable of a realistic sense of what he does.

Some Evangelicals express a decent shame for the way in which their religion bleeds through their community and expresses itself as raw sectarianism. I have quoted this before and I refuse to accept that it was an insignificant incident: at the Catholic Church in Harryville, during the picket by Orangemen, I asked a man why he was protesting at that church. A little boy beside him heard the question and shrieked out, 'It's not a church, it's a Fenian hole.'

I am not suggesting that that boy's insult would have been approved by decent Evangelicals but I did notice that when many Evangelicals came forward to defend the right of those Catholics to worship, they stayed outside the church. They did that because, like the little boy, they did not regard it as a legitimate place in which to worship God. They stayed out so as not to find themselves worshipping a heathen God alongside heathen people.

I wonder what terms those people would have used to correct the boy who said that that was not a church and that defiling it with protest was not morally equivalent to disrupting real Christians like themselves.

What impresses me about Evangelicalism is the core idea that God is to be accessed from within. This seems to me a far better idea than the alternative, that God is to be found through messages preserved within monolithic institutions. The Evangelical idea, at its heart, acknowledges human freedom to explore. The institutional churches are saying to us in effect, don't bother your little head about God, we've taken care of that.

This accords with my own instinctive response to the question of God. As a teenage Catholic I was inquisitive and rebellious. I was one of those schoolboys who was good at disrupting religious instruction classes with awkward questions. It seemed a wholly inadequate treatment of these questions for a teacher simply to say, as they did in those days, that the church had given much thought to these things, was inspired by the Holy Ghost, and I should just pray harder for the strength to accept the church's guidance.

Compared to this, the teaching that a person might find spiritual affirmation from within and might trust that affirmation, seemed revolutionary and encouraging. When I sought to test that idea myself, I did it within a Hindu environment and submitted myself to the discipline of an ashram and a guru to learn how the mystics there had explored the soul. I was of course – though it took time to realise this – merely submitting myself to another institution. In recoiling from that I arrived at the firmest possible conviction that one must face the crucial questions of meaning and mortality alone.

The evangelical spirit, at its purest I think, is motivated by the same insight but naturally enough, like religious people everywhere, baulks at living with uncertainty and accepts the hollow promises of others. I wonder if a George Fox or John

Wesley would recognise in our mission halls today, among the Irish saved, the same spirit that quaked within them or strangely warmed them. I'm sure they would among a few but that the widespread assumption of salvation won so cheaply would not impress them.

Today Evangelicalism more commonly teaches people conformity and restraint. It tells them that they have no interest in other people other than to direct them to the Bible.

Freedom has become obedience; and spiritual imagination is giving away to literalist and utilitarian readings of the Bible. The injunctions to the Evangelical to listen to God from within and to read his word in the Bible, I'm afraid, contradict each other and it pays little respect to the human heart and the promptings within it to urge those who have difficulty with those promptings simply to open a book and look for an answer there.

That determination to allow the individual the freedom to find a sense of God within now seems to have deteriorated into a spirit which allows social and cultural uniformity and restricted imagination.

Evangelical sermons and radio *Thought for the Day* pieces often betray a kind of emotional insulation from the world and from human suffering.

I'm thinking of a recent piece in which a pastor started off reflecting on the Holocaust, took us to Churchill and his contemplation of the afterlife and from there to the speaker's confidence that his own soul was saved. A moment's reflection on millions dead served only as a springboard to self-congratulation.

It wasn't always like this. There was a time when Evangelical religion empathised with human suffering and the struggles of the poor, when it was essentially revolutionary, when the dignity of freedom extended naturally to the right to know God for yourself.

The energy of the evangelical religions is astonishing though, and it may be that the compensation for accepting simplifications about life and mortality and destiny is that the mind is freed to devote itself with greater concentration to work. As a nonevangelical, it is inevitable that I will regard proselytising work a waste. I recently had an audience with the Catholicos of the Armenian church and he expressed great anger that missionaries from here, who had helped in the evangelical relief work after the Armenian earthquake, had presumed to try and convert Armenians.

In Northern Ireland, however, some of the most enlightened work towards reconciliation is being led by Evangelicals within ECONI, the Evangelical Contribution on Northern Ireland. Members of ECONI have dialogued with all paramilitary groups and worked hard to get Protestants in Northern Ireland to question the interaction of the religious faith and their political unionism. I have been invited to write several articles for ECONI's magazine, *Lion and Lamb*, because the editors and the organisation have a genuine concern to hear contrary views.

Where many Northern Protestants justify their political positions with reference to the Bible, I have seen discussions among them about ways of using the Bible to explain or justify radical and more generous political positions. On the one hand you will see a pastor reading from The Book of Joshua to enthuse Orangemen with a sense of their right to walk the Garvaghy Road, while another uses scripture creatively to explain that God does not require his people in Ulster to be British forever. The Lord said to Abraham, leave your father's house. Are you ready to leave your father's house?

I started off by explaining that my early suspicion of Evangelicalism was rooted in narrow fundamentalist Catholicism and in the sense of sectarian etiquette. Now I am essentially secular in my thinking. I make no claim to knowing the truth about God or the universe but I do sense that some religious traditions are better than others. The Evangelical tradition strikes me as one that demeans humanity. It says that the generous and cheerful life can be a waste. I do not believe that. It supposes the person may acquire great understanding and achieve heroic compassion and still have failed God, and yet that another, who learns nothing about human nature, may rise up over all need to do so, simply through establishing the sense of personal relationship with the invisible Jesus. I do not believe, and cannot believe, that salvation, if there is such a thing, can be available through a route which is not also the route to maturity and wisdom. For me it is just a question of how far the road goes. This life is a journey through knowing who we are and what we're worth, towards coming to terms with our own mortality. We can stray off that road into alcoholism, obsession and even into the arms of Jesus.

But we are the losers if we do.

CHAPTER SEVEN

Into All the World
Irish Evangelicals in Global Mission

Drew Gibson, Deborah Ford and Lynn Stanfield

In their attitude to global mission, as in most other things, Irish Evangelicals differ little from their counterparts throughout the world.

Like Manchester United and football, Evangelicals and mission are intimately linked. The first element in both couplets is a group of people and the second is an activity associated with that group. For many Evangelicals the parallel with Manchester United is very close because, just as football is the defining activity of Manchester United, mission is the defining activity of Evangelicalism, the activity that sets Evangelicals apart from other Christians. They tend to see other Christians as either uninterested in mission or engaged in a pallid kind of mission that is a mere shadow of the real thing. They accuse other Christians of being involved in 'good works' (often a term with negative connotations) but without any significant engagement in evangelism. Good works are fine, in their place, but they are no substitute for evangelism because evangelism is the heart and soul of mission. Thus, they often consider themselves to be the only ones doing 'real' mission.

The root of this self-understanding is not difficult to identify. The definition of the term 'evangelical' includes a commitment to evangelism as a core element of one's faith; in fact this commitment is so close to the heart of Evangelicalism that many people treat the terms 'evangelical' and 'evangelistic' as synonyms. In ordinary conversation and even in reasonably serious publications the two terms are sometimes used interchangeably. This builds the impression among Evangelicals that they, and only they, are doing evangelism and hence they, and only they, are doing mission.

As we shall see, this understanding of mission and evangelism has meant that evangelical mission endeavours have regularly been accompanied by an inability to work alongside other
Christians and even an inability to work alongside other
Evangelicals. This has led to some significant heartache but, in
the providence of God, it has sometimes worked out for good
and for the spread of the kingdom of God.

We shall look at the involvement of Irish Evangelicals in
global mission from three perspectives and finish with some
general comments.

First we shall look at the involvement of the main Protestant
denominations in global mission, then we shall look at a number
of independent evangelical agencies and thirdly, we shall comment on the work of a few individuals who have made significant contributions to global mission. In the first two sections we
shall concentrate on the early years of the agencies and from
these stories identify broader principles that underlie evangelical
mission activities in general. The first section is the longest of the
three as the mission interests of the denominations is the context
in which the independent societies and individuals must be understood and the early years of this denominational interest set
the tone for the attitudes and actions of succeeding generations.

'THAT LITTLE IRISH CHURCH' – THE DENOMINATIONAL CONTRIBUTION

Any assessment of the contribution of Irish Evangelicals to
world mission depends upon a prior consideration of their
home context. An obvious, but nevertheless noteworthy fact
must first be considered: none of the major Protestant denominations was indigenous to Ireland.[1]

The gentrified Church of Ireland was very much orientated
towards England and the Whigs politically, economically and
spiritually; its main members were landlords and tenant farmers, and it was preoccupied with preserving Establishment,
Ascendancy and, later, the Union. In the 1650s when our story
begins there was a serious shortage of active preaching ministers and the parochial system had largely broken down.

Originally an evangelical movement within the Anglican fold, the proponents of Methodism who arrived in Ireland in the 1740s inevitably attracted few native Irish. Methodism as a distinct denomination in Ireland did not emerge until 1878. Consequently, Irish Methodists were very much dependent on and subordinate to the mainland, and this undoubtedly affected their involvement in world mission.

If the Anglicans and Methodists were orientated towards England, the Presbyterians and Reformed Presbyterians were very much bound to Scotland. Irish Presbyterianism developed as chaplains from the Scottish army campaign of 1642 reached out to the settler community and took a number of parishes under their care. The sober Ulster-Scots appear to have regarded the native Irish as essentially pagan: historian Patrick Adair likened the fledgling Presbyterian community to Israel, the people of God, in a foreign land 'surrounded by hostile idolatrous Canaanites and threatened from within by delinquents among their own people'.[2]

The social and economic difficulties encountered in Ireland offered little motivation for the various shades of local Protestants to sever these emotional umbilical cords tying them to the mainland. This is understandable because seventeenth to nineteenth century Ireland was characterised by poverty, crop-failure, large-scale unemployment, landlord tyranny, and widespread community disorder. Between 1780 and 1845 1.1 million Irish flooded into North America; a tidal wave whipped even higher by the disastrous famine of the late 1840s.

Dissenters faced additional distresses. As early as 1661 Irish Justices had declared assemblies of 'Papists' and 'Presbyterians' 'unlawful' so that many gatherings were forced underground, meeting house-to-house or in barns. By 1684 we learn that 'the majority of ministers intend emigrating because of persecutions and general poverty abounding in these parts, and on account of their straits and no access to their ministry ...'[3] The infamous 1704 Test Act, designed to prevent further growth of 'Popery', barred all who did not take the sacraments in the Established

Church from civil office. The Church of Ireland continued to take their tithes and held jurisdiction over their marriages, educational prospects, inheritances and burials: a thorn in the flesh that lasted until 1780.

Revolutionary fervour was another obstacle to evangelical outreach. With the onset of the French Revolution, Dissenters were regarded with increased suspicion; and even among the Dissenters themselves support for foreign missions was viewed as dangerous 'radicalism'. Presbyterians and Covenanters were involved on both sides in the Ulster Rebellion of 1798, which further exposed the grave dangers of the Roman threat to 'the brethren' in their own land. Add internal wrangling over royal bounties and Arian heretics, and prospects for missionary endeavour outside Ireland scarcely seemed auspicious.

A Pioneering People
Yet in spite of their difficulties, (even, indeed, because of them), Irish denominations lay claim to many missionary 'firsts'.

Between 1706 and 1721 over twenty-six Church of Ireland clergy served with the United Society for the Propagation of the Gospel (USPG), including William Smith, first missionary to the Bahamas, and Charles Inglis, the first colonial Bishop (of Nova Scotia). Numbers decreased in the latter half of the eighteenth century, but the years 1824-1870 saw over 106 Irish clergy sent to Canada, Australia and South Africa. The Church Missionary Society (CMS) was to send over 87 missionaries from Ireland to India, South Africa, and Sierra Leone.[4]

The Irish presence in the early formation of the Anglican church in Australia and Canada was particularly strong. Hard on the heels of the Inglis clan (the doughty bishop was supported by a son, nephew and son-in-law) came the fiery Benjamin Cronin, Bishop of Huron (1867) described, (somewhat enigmatically) as 'a great fighter and fisher of men'.[5] In turn this dynamo of the Canadian church recruited three young Dubliners, Edward Sullivan, James Carmichael and John Philip du Moulin, a prelatical trio known collectively as 'the three Musketeers'.

The Church of Ireland also contributed much to the
Protestant churches of France and Italy, (spearheaded by the
Dublin Waldensian Aid Society). Dublin rivalled Oxford and
Cambridge in its establishment of University Missions – the
Fukien Mission (1886) and the Chota Nagpur Mission (1890).
Irish Anglicans also pioneered in Burma, Korea, and Japan.

The mission support-base was much wider in the Church of
Ireland than on mainland Britain. The Anglican Society for the
Propagation of the Gospel was formed in 1701, its Irish counterpart in 1714. The Irish branch was to include prominent laymen
as well as prelates on its committee, including Dr Marmaduke
Coghill (a wealthy businessman) and Robert Boyle, (son of the
1st Earl of Cork). Unlike its English counterpart (founded 1799)
the Hibernian CMS (1814) could list earls, viscounts, mayors,
judges, generals and honourables amongst its committee, including the prominent Disney, Guinness and La Touche families, and the redoubtable Thomas Parnell: a broad nucleus of interest which gave the Church of Ireland a lasting 'missionary
character'.[6]

Such was the strength of interest in mission in Ireland that
the CMS as a whole sent its candidates to Trinity College,
Dublin for training until its own institution in Islington was
founded, considering the theological formation offered by
Dublin to be more 'progressive' than either London or
Cambridge.[7] By 1900 the HCMS was contributing over £20,000
to the London headquarters and had sent out some 133 missionaries.[8] Almost half of Trinity graduates were serving in England
or overseas, and the commitment to mission within the Church
of Ireland was envied throughout the Anglican Communion. In
1898 the General Secretary of CMS wrote to the Honorary
Secretaries of the General Synod, commending Irish zeal as 'an
example and stimulus to the other churches'.[9]

Methodists from Ireland were particularly predominant in
that denomination's earliest outreach. Thomas Coke announced
his plan for a society 'for the establishment of Mission among
the Heathen in the British dominions of Asia' in 1783. Amongst

his early pioneers we find the Irishmen William Hammett (first Methodist missionary to St Kitts, 1787), John Stephenson, (Bermuda, 1799), James McMullen, (Gibraltar, 1804) and John McKenny (Cape Colony, 1814).[10] In 1813 Coke sailed on his inaugural mission to Asia. Three of the seven men who accompanied him were Irish, and it is little wonder that he regarded Ireland as his premier recruiting-ground. Irishman James Lynch took over the leadership when Coke tragically died at sea, organising the work in Ceylon into Tamil and Singhalese districts and establishing the first permanent Methodist mission in India.[11]

Nor was the pioneering spirit of Irish Methodism confined to those who went to the far ends of the earth. The British Conference of 1786 is regarded as the official inauguration of Methodist Foreign Missions; yet even before the mainland had approved the scheme, the first Irish subscriptions had already flooded the coffers. Irish generosity quickly became renowned: The Canadian Christian Guardian opined that Irish Methodists, 'though far from wealthy', contributed the largest amounts to overseas mission in proportion to their numbers.[12]

Inevitably, however, it is the Irish influence upon the North American Colonies that predominates. Alongside the Anglicans, Methodist ministers and laymen alike made outstanding contributions. Laurence Coughlan served as pioneer missionary to Newfoundland (1765) while Barbara Heck, Philip Embury and Robert Strawbridge, early emigrants from the Palatine community near Limerick, introduced Methodism to New York and Maryland. One William Ryland became leader of the Foundry Church in Washington and Chaplain to the Houses of Congress, while Charles Elliot from Donegal became the first President of Iowa Methodist University. Two of the greatest missionaries of the Methodist Episcopal Church (MEC), James Thoburn and William Butler, had Irish origins.[13] A message from the Methodist Episcopal Church to the Irish Conference in 1857 declared that: 'The very foundations of our Methodist church were laid by Irishmen – and a large proportion of her ministry and membership are natives of Ireland.'[14]

In Canada, by 1866, there were 170 Irish Methodist ministers, compared with 167 ministers in Ireland! By the beginning of the twentieth century Methodism was the largest Protestant denomination and it is not coincidental that its heartland in S. Ontario was also the heartland of Irish immigration. The fulsome 1873 message from the MEC was not far wrong when it read: 'You cannot place your foot on any colony of the British Empire that does not include a convert of that little Irish church.'[15]

Presbyterians were also quick to turn their attention to the colonies in the wake of persecution and emigration. William Trail, Clerk of Laggan Presbytery, went West recognising there was little prospect of true church order being established back at home. Together with Francis Makemie he formed the first Presbytery on American soil in 1706. The latter quickly incurred the wrath of Deputy Governor Cornbury in New York, who forbade the sermons of this 'strolling preacher' and his 'pernicious doctrines'. Experiences of religious persecution in Ireland, however, inured him to repeated jail sentences in New York and Virginia, and resulted in the inception of the Act of Toleration.

From the 1680s onwards, Presbyterians in Ireland received requests for godly ministers for Barbados and Maryland, gave grants to newly-established colleges, (the literally-named 'Log Academy', Nashaminy, a wooden precursor of Princeton, was founded by William Tennent of Armagh), and set up funds for distressed emigrant ministers, widows and children.

'Foreign Mission' as understood by the 1834 plan submitted by the Presbytery of Dublin to the Synod of Ulster was primarily a matter of giving pastoral support to expatriate Irish Presbyterians, rather than Irish Presbyterians bringing the gospel to the indigenous inhabitants of foreign parts.

This prevailing emphasis can be seen in the rapid expansion of work in the colonies, as opposed to the slow trickle of pioneer evangelists to India. By 1841 Thomas Buchanan was sent to South Africa; 1846 saw the foundation of the Colonial Mission, which was to serve in Australia, Canada, South Africa, America and New Zealand. Typical is D. Macrae Stewart's assessment that 'Presbyterianism in America owes more to the Irish Church than to any other in the world; and to the stalwart North of Ireland the Church in Victoria is indebted for much of its vigour and many of its distinct characteristics.'[16]

The Reformed Presbyterians[17] followed a similar pattern, firstly establishing a mission to the colonies, secondly a mission to their own members within Ireland: mission to 'the heathen' *per se* was the last to develop. Emigrants to New York, Pennsylvania, and South Carolina formed themselves into two-or-three-family Covenanting Societies and appealed for ministers to join them, and one John Cuthbertson, ordained in Scotland in 1750, sailed for Pennsylvania a year later. Occasionally, the call developed the other way round, as in the case of the enterprising Rev William Martin of Kellswater, who sailed for the USA after advertising in *The Belfast Newsletter* for like-minded families to join him. By 1820, the focus became more overtly missionary, with a Synod resolution to expand beyond America 'to New Brunswick and other areas where some of our people are scattered'.

Vision

The early missiological vision of Irish Evangelicals appears both radical and far-reaching. Adam Clarke, born in South Derry in 1760, was one of the nine men appointed to the inaugural Methodist Missionary Committee of 1790; he shared general responsibility with Coke for the direction of mission overseas as well as particular responsibility for the West Indies. William Arthur, a fellow-Irishman, served as WMMS Secretary for two lengthy periods, following a tour of India: he emphasised that the Methodist denomination was essentially a missionary movement; the multitude of believers are not 'mere adherents' but 'living burning speaking agents in the great movement for the universal diffusion of God's message'.[18]

Likewise James Morgan, Director of the Presbyterian Foreign Mission, 1840-73, realised the necessity of stirring the Presbyterian Church into action as a missionary institution in itself, rather than a passive supporter of the independent societies. He even proposed getting rid of 'tours and auxiliaries', arguing that 'the congregations are the auxiliaries and the sessions the committees'. The Presbyterian principle that foreign mission is integral to the church owes a lot to Morgan's deeply-held convictions.[19]

James McKee, Presbyterian missionary to India in the mid-1800s, stressed the importance of holistic mission, education and indigenisation: 'To confine ourselves just to oral preaching appears narrow-minded and unwise in the extreme. Neither German nor Scotch nor Irish missionaries should be the immediate agents in the evangelisation of India.'[20] By this he meant that in any given mission situation, converted local people were the most appropriate evangelists and that expatriates could be better employed in supporting their endeavours. From this it appears that a commitment to indigenisation was part of the Presbyterian agenda from the beginning.

The rather more militant 'great Crusade against Popery and Infidelity' championed by Cookstown Presbyterian Rev Henry Cooke nevertheless helped to develop a natural empathy with minority Protestant Churches in the Catholic heartlands of Central Europe that continues within the Presbyterian Church in Ireland to this day.

Particularly interesting is the developing awareness of the importance of overseas work for the maintenance of spiritual vision at home. Thus *The Irish Christian Advocate* of 1884 argued that: 'The foreign mission enterprise is essential to the prosperity of the work of God at home. It does not sap our strength but acts as a spiritual tonic, preparing the churches for the more vigorous prosecution of the work at home. We are ever in danger ... of becoming protracted in our views and our sympathies, and even in matters spiritual we need to be lifted out of our insularity.'[21]

'An Unhappy Procrastinating Spirit'

Yet, while to believers in Britain 'that little Irish church' appeared to be a Thessalonian model of faith and generosity, in her own eyes the dangers of protraction, insularity and 'an unhappy procrastinating spirit' (as an early Presbyterian missionary noted)[22] were constantly present. It was perhaps understandable in view of the tense religious climate that most denominations placed the far-off 'heathen' well down on the evangelistic list of priorities. The Reformed Churches were, however, unusually slow to engage in this form of mission. It was not until 1820 that the Reformed Presbyterians agreed to expand their missionary ventures beyond the colonies, and not until 1827 that the first candidate for New Brunswick was ordained: despite frequent minutes on the blessings of a church which actively propagated the gospel and divine displeasure on the church which neglected it, records note that 'no immediate action was taken to establish a mission'.[23] A legacy of £100 for the establishment of a mission to the heathen in 1843 produced more than 156 letters of enquiry as to a suitable mission-field, but no actual missionaries; a request from the American Reformed Presbyterians for volunteers for Aleppo was rejected for lack of suitable personnel, and it was not until 1871 that Syria was finally selected as 'the foreign mission field'.[24]

The Presbyterian record was equally uninspiring. Prior to the visit of Alexander Waugh, representative of the London Missionary Society (LMS) in 1812, Irish Presbyterians evinced very little interest in mission; the unfortunate Waugh's request to speak at the Synod of Ulster 'was not cordially received' and many considered the very idea of mission to the heathen both 'utopian and absurd'.[25] Only in 1829 was the first volunteer, Rev Hope Masterton Waddell, sent to Jamaica, and under the auspices of the Scottish Missionary Society at that. Hailing him as 'the first foreign missionary from Ulster' *The Orthodox Presbyterian* bemoaned: 'How long shall he be the only missionary among the Presbyterians of Ulster?'[26] Thomas Leslie, Minister of Kilraughts, inspired fresh hope by following in Waddell's footsteps in 1835; sadly, it took his premature death to stir nascent Presbyterian pride. A 'Mission to the Heathen World' was recommended in 1837, as exercising 'a more salutary influence upon the church', and two candidates, Glasgow and Fisher, were identified for India in 1838. Institutional resistance was then followed by congregational resistance: Fisher was relieved, on the grounds that his infant congregation in Galway would not survive the blow of his removal, Glasgow's Castledawson congregation also objected, while Fisher's replacement Kerr confided that 'the great bulk' of his Portadown flock regarded his new call as 'tyranny and robbery' on the part of the Directors .

Surviving correspondence from the two eventual pioneers suggests constant deep frustration. As early as 1841 Kerr was disillusioned by the fact that 'so little was being done', while Glasgow admonished 'What could two of you do, if left alone in Ulster?'[28] The 1848 announcement of 'a drastic curtailment in support' moved Glasgow with such 'deep agitating emotion' that 'I cannot hear such tidings and not weep.'[29] The need for reinforcements was a constant thorn in the side; hearing reports of the Revival in Ulster in 1859 Glasgow confessed that the lack of missionary candidates left him quite 'bewildered'.[30] For their part, the General Assembly admitted: "All we have done for them during this year is pay our missionaries their salaries ... we have simply kept them alive at their posts.'[31]

Personal frustration, however, was not just the prerogative of the Presbyterians. All denominations complained that the Revival had minimal immediate impact on overseas mission, John Venn expressing disappointment that Irish recruits were not 'immediately delivered' to CMS.[32] Very few Methodist missionaries went out from Ireland following the death of Coke in 1814; not until the closing decades of the nineteenth century do they re-emerge.[33] Nor was generosity of spirit always in evidence: Hugh McKeag, secretary of the Hibernian Methodist Auxiliary, 1902-3, complained that 'income has not kept pace with the increase in the Church's numbers and their wealth'.[34]

It seems, in fact, that the Revival was more immediately concerned with the ungodliness at home than the idolatry of the heathen. There was no immediate impact on foreign missions, although the fresh motivation to prayer and religious commitment and the new activism of the laity undoubtedly impacted the growth of missions in the closing decades of the century. Eugene Stock of the Church Missionary Society, for example, realised that the slow delivery of recruits bemoaned by Venn was in fact 'only delayed'.[35] It may also be the case that the Revival's impact was greater on independent, non-denominational faith missions, as these would be more likely to appeal to the uneducated lay men who now found themselves 'revived'. The fact that these societies did not start to arise until well into the second half of the nineteenth century might be another part of the explanation of the delay.

Two inhibitors to overseas mission may be summarised at this point. Each denomination was suspicious of the other and even the early non-denominational societies were not free from denominational suspicion: churchmen who disliked 'ambiguous undenominational activity' refused to support the general mission societies founded by Anglicans around 1810 for the support of LMS, CMS etc,[36] while in 1812 Presbyterians rejected a request to support the Mission to the Jews for fear of excessive Anglican influence. Many Presbyterians became suspicious of the LMS because of its association with the (Anglican) Evangelical Society of Ulster.[37] This trend is one that has gradually waned over the years and Evangelicals are much happier today to make common cause with other Evangelicals and in some cases prefer to work alongside Evangelicals of other denominations rather than non-Evangelicals within their own denomination.

A second problem is illustrated by the Methodists' struggle with a more 'in-house' challenge: their subordinate status within the Wesleyan Methodist Missionary Society (WMMS). The Hibernian Society was placed on a par with other overseas districts, and up to the nineteenth century Irish Methodists had no direct involvement in the formation of mission policy. Not until Robin Booth was sent from Cork to China in 1899 under the influence of the Christian Endeavour Movement did Irish

Methodists really feel that they had a missionary whom they could call 'their own'.[38]

The tension between Ireland as a sender of missionaries and as a mission field was very real. This was seen in the above tension within Methodism as the daughter church in Ireland was still regarded by the English parent as something of an adolescent. While the other denominations did not have this particular problem, all shared another aspect of the same tension. A significant number of people believed that the evangelistic needs of Ireland should take precedence over the needs of the unevangelised regions outside the island. Addley suggests that Presbyterian concern for 'the special duty of preaching the gospel in our native land' (1833 Missionary Synod) resulted in the relegation of foreign mission. The 'paramount importance of work at home' is demonstrated by the comment of Mrs Leslie, widow of James Leslie, first Presbyterian missionary to Jamaica, who even in the wake of her husband's premature death 'was not convinced of the appropriateness of sending out more missionaries, since Ireland is itself an important field at present'.[39]

Even the Methodists, who were the first amongst the major denominations to see the importance of mission to the heathen *per se*, appeared genuinely torn by the missionary need of their own land. In 1806 Coke claimed that Ireland was Methodism's most important mission field, because 'three million of its people were plunged in the deepest ignorance and superstition'.[40] McArthur saw a more strategic missionary importance in maintaining a strong evangelical witness in Ireland to meet the Romanist threat. Bearing in mind the high rates of emigration from Ireland it was better to export sound evangelical Christians to other parts of the world than Romanists![41]

However, while there is some evidence that concern with the home situation was a barrier to the promotion of foreign mission, the major preoccupation was preservation of existing Protestant communities rather than outreach to Roman Catholics *per se*. Holmes suggests that the Irish were seen as essentially 'pagan';[42] Adair's description of the Presbyterian community

bears repeating. 'Like the Israelites settling in Canaan, surrounded by hostile, idolatrous Canaanites and threatened within
by delinquents from their own people'[43] was a constantly resur-
facing motif. Popular Protestant anti-Catholicism further
harmed the cause, while the Revival (a sign of God's blessing
and vindication of the Protestant community) only served to
further differentiate the two groupings. There was also some
realisation that evangelistic preaching was too cerebral and intellectual to appeal to illiterate Irish peasants; 'preaching will
not do, for the vast majority do not understand it' was one missionary's verdict.[44] David Miller suggests that such evangelistic
outreach was by its very nature a lost cause: 'In targeting the
poor of Catholic Ireland the Presbyterians were seeking to win
from the Catholic community the very stratum they had already
lost within their own society.'[45]

A Pugnacious People

It must also be recognised that the qualities of the Irish that
made them great pioneers, fighters and Musketeers in the
colonies and stalwart apostles to the heathen could also make
them intractable trouble-makers, or even, at times, dissidents.
The peaceable Quakers of New England found the Ulster Scots
to be 'an uncouth and pugnacious people'[46] – hardly surprising
when personified by Davey Crockett, the son of immigrants
from Co Down! Archdeacon Owen's support of African rights
earned him the tag 'Archdemon Owen' among the less than
amused colonial settlers of Eastern Africa. Even under Coke
some Irish Methodist personnel had been disciplined or returned home early; following the demise of this charismatic
leader and the emergence of a more formal society Taggart sus-
pects 'an unofficial agreement that Irish involvement overseas
be discouraged for a period'.[47] The missiologist's mind boggles!

Sometimes, Irish intractability on issues of government and
practice slipped into disunity, or even schism. Holmes notes that
Ulster Presbyterians frequently came into conflict with more re-
laxed New England Presbyterians over issues such as subscrip-

tion to the Westminster Confession of Faith and the authority of
the church courts.[48] Many Irish Methodist personnel in North
America protested against what they perceived as authoritarianism and unbiblical directions in the church, and some, like
Robert Strawbridge, James O'Kelly, William Hammett and
Alexander McCaine, were involved in the formation of schism-
atic Methodist denominations.[49] Edward Johnston from Co
Tyrone, a returned volunteer missionary to Canada, remarked,
with disillusioned perspicuity: 'the business of a missionary is to
keep up a religious war, and in many instances to be employed
in making division in other Methodist societies.'[50]

Individuals who made their mark
Any survey of the early involvement of Irish denominations in
mission will reveal that it was not, in fact, the institutions, but
the individuals who were most important. Churches as a whole
struggled to commit to mission, and were dependent on individuals, families and other small groups for their involvement.
Particular figures spring to mind: the Anglican George Berkeley
of Cloyne, frustrated in his attempt to establish a missionary college in Bermuda; the Honourable Lady Charlotte O'Brian, who
formed the CMS Ladies' Association from her castle in Co Clare;
the charismatic personality of Thomas Coke; Limerick Methodist
Barbara Heck who importuned fellow-settler Embury to start a
class for Irish immigrant neighbours in New York when she saw
their 'religious indifference'; Alexander Waugh of the LMS
whose appeal to the reluctant Synod in Cookstown left not a dry
eye in the house; Presbyterian James Morgan whose impromptu,
impassioned call to mission in 1838 'pervaded the whole
Assembly with the most extraordinary silence', and evinced a
never-before seen 'feeling of fervent zeal amongst sober
Presbyterians'.[51]

     The last word, however, should be left to lesser-known indi-
viduals: Anglican gentlewoman Charlotte Pym of Monkstown,
whose drawing-room meeting led to the formation of what is
now the Leprosy Mission; Methodist Thomas Dawson, who em-

igrated to Prince Edward Island in 1801 and, struck by the spiritual deprivation of the colony, exchanged long-term family dreams for the life of a travelling preacher; a certain Sgt McBride of Banbridge, converted in the West Indies, who persuaded the military authorities in Karachi to set up a church, 'so that if ever a missionary is sent, he will find a church ready and waiting.' Last but not least come the rather more colourful pioneers such as Henry Fulton, native of Lisburn and Rector of Monsea in Killaloe, who was convicted of sedition in the Rebellion of 1798 and transported for life to New South Wales; Edward Eager, forger, visited in prison by Methodists, spiritually awakened, and transported to Australia where he became pioneer evangelist in the same region (did they ever meet and swap notes?); and Elisabeth, sister-in-law of William Digby of Geashill in Kildare Diocese, who developed a missionary vision upon eloping with her soldier-lover Henry Pilot to Florida. Having taught the faith to black servants there, she returned home to found the Irish Auxiliary of the Church's Mission to the Jews in 1809.[52]

The patterns and characteristics that we have outlined in the Reformed, Methodist and Anglican traditions are repeated in the other denominations albeit on a much smaller scale. For example the Baptist Irish Society was founded in 1814 for the purpose of evangelising in Ireland. The society became the Irish Baptist Home Mission in 1888 and Baptist Missions – Ireland in 1977. Overseas mission began in 1924 with a single family who originally went to Argentina but, when they found that others were already working in the place to which they had been assigned, moved to southern Peru. Baptist Missions still works in southern Peru and also in France and Spain. Two comments can be made which are true not only of the Baptists but of all denominations.

First, all denominations give roughly equal priority to mission in Ireland and to mission overseas. Both in terms of personnel and finance the denominations are firmly committed to evangelisation and to various forms of social action throughout the world; they are also firmly committed to both in Ireland.

Second, all denominations have more of their members working with independent mission agencies than they have with their own denominational societies. One need only look at the number of independent agencies with offices or representatives in Ireland to understand this.

Having looked at the period up to 1900, what can we say about denominational involvement in the twentieth century and into the twenty first century? While we have focused on the major historic denominations, during the twentieth century a number of other denominations have taken root in Ireland. Some of these have been imported while others, such as the Elim Pentecostal Church, the Evangelical Presbyterian Church and the Christian Fellowship Churches have indigenous roots. Each denomination has its own story to tell but it is fair to claim that all denominations have faced the same tensions, dilemmas and problems as those we have already seen. The names, locations and details differ but the pattern is the same in each case. In particular there have been two most tenacious problems.

First, no denomination has really got to grips with extricating evangelism in Ireland from the socio-political chains that have bound it for so long. Protestantism of all shades is regularly associated with Britishness or, at least, non-Irishness. This is most tragically true of Northern fundamentalists such as the Free Presbyterian Church of Ulster whose high public profile gives them an influence beyond their numerical strength and prejudices many against Evangelicalism and even against Christianity as a whole.

Social class also remains an issue to be addressed. The Anglican ascendancy may have gone and the domination of the middle class by Presbyterians may also be a thing of the past but the unarticulated assumption of many both within Evangelicalism and outside it is that to become a Christian is to embrace a raft of broadly middle class values and aspirations. Those who see these values and aspirations as either unattainable or undesirable are not likely to be well disposed to the Christian gospel.

The belief that to be Irish is to be Catholic is significantly weaker than it used to be but is still strong enough to be a significant barrier to evangelical evangelism. When this is set beside the traditional attitude of Evangelicals to Catholics the problem becomes even greater. The traditional evangelical belief that Catholics are, by definition, not Christian means that Evangelicals have thought of Catholics as they would think of Hindus, Moslems or Atheists, that is as objects of evangelism.[53]

The second missiological issue with which the denominations wrestle today returns us to the international arena. Irish denominations have not been unaffected by the changes in mission in the last half century and one of these changes is particularly relevant here. The daughter churches, planted by missionaries from Europe and North America have now grown to maturity and have virtually all achieved autonomy. They now stand as equal partners with the European and North American denominations. Indeed many African churches are much larger than the churches whose missionaries first brought the gospel to their homelands. This has made an evangelical understanding of mission much more complex. In the nineteenth century the situation was quite simple: 'we' had the good news, 'they' did not, so we took the good news to them. Now 'they' have as much of the good news as 'us', so what is our role to be? Some Evangelicals simply ignore this trend and continue to believe that the pattern of sending evangelists around the world is as simple as ever; others understand global mission to be Evangelicals in Ireland supporting the work of Christians in other parts of the world to do mission in their own places. This latter position is the view that dominates within denominational mission agencies although some nuance this by saying that 'we' should be prepared to take initiatives if local churches in their places are unable or unwilling to do so.

In some of the disputes that disturb the Christian church as a whole, Evangelicals in Europe are making common cause with Christians from the developing world against the liberalising tendencies that are so much in evidence at present. The debate over the acceptability of homosexual 'partnerships' as a Christian option has seen evangelical Anglicans in Europe and North America in conversation with Anglicans in the developing world and if a schism occurs the lines of fracture will not be purely geographical.

Conclusions

Given the often inhospitable home situation, it is clear that all denominations in Ireland have produced missionaries who have made an outstanding contribution to global mission. Occasionally, however, that contribution was rather more controversial than charitable. While the Irish were models to those around them, no Irish denomination appears satisfied that it has done what it could have done. Indeed, the most significant Irish missionaries may be the individuals and emigrants of whom few, if anyone, have ever heard. To the present day concern in each Irish denomination for global mission remains an interest of the enthusiast rather than an orientation of the denomination as a whole. When the enthusiasts have been in a majority or have enjoyed positions of influence, global mission has risen higher up the agenda but it has always had to compete with other interests and enthusiasms for finance and personnel.

THE CONTRIBUTION OF IRISH EVANGELICALS
IN INDEPENDENT MISSIONARY SOCIETIES

Independent missionary societies, that is those organisations that are run independently from the denominational mission agencies, have had a significant impact on world mission, enabling people across a wide variety of denominations to work in many different capacities around the world. These independent societies have usually been started when an individual has become involved in mission work, has shared the need with others, brought people alongside them and an organisation has been founded.

From the mid nineteenth century there was a new drive in world mission, the desire arose to reach as many people as possible. Along with the increase in trade and Western colonialism, new avenues were opening for missionaries. With developments in communications and transport the 'wider world' was becoming more accessible. There was a new motivation to present the gospel to every people and a new focus on unreached people groups, going beyond what was already being done, moving into new territories.

Some of those who went on to found new independent missionary societies had approached the existing classical missions initially, desiring to work with them but, as we have already seen, the older boards often did not have enough funds, personnel or interest in breaking into new fields and thus the individuals, still feeling very much that this was where God was calling them, would go off on their own. Often, after a few years as lone workers, they founded a new mission to further the work. This new focus on the unreached can be clearly seen in the names the new groups took, China Inland Mission, Sudan Interior Mission, African Inland Mission, Unevangelised Fields Mission, etc. This focus on the unreached meant that these new societies were not encroaching on areas already being worked by classical missions and therefore they were not in 'competition' with one another – indeed in some cases the denominational missions requested the independent missions to come and work in new areas that they felt unable to tackle.

Hudson Taylor's China Inland Mission, founded in 1865, was not the first independent missionary society (there were two other smaller ones started shortly before that) but it was the first 'Faith Mission' – so called because of the faith principle of financial support. The independent missions founded at the end of the nineteenth century and into the first decades of the twentieth largely followed the faith missions principle. This meant that they felt able to proceed to mission work on this principle rather than having to spend a longer time establishing financial structures at home first.

Aside from the faith missions principle there were other principles laid down by the China Inland Mission that many subsequent independent missions also adopted. These ideas were spread through people like Grattan and Fanny Guinness from Dublin who founded the East London Training Institute in 1873 as a missionary training college. These training institutes were another distinctive feature of the new independent missions – the denominational missions work had been mainly carried out by educated, and often ordained men, now men and women who would not be accepted as candidates for the older missions found new opportunities for service. These training institutes were often the nucleus for the founding of new societies.

More than 45 mission agencies have sending bases here in Ireland, sending people, resources and money around the world. Some, such as the Acre Gospel Mission, Mission Africa and Youth for Christ have their UK headquarters in Northern Ireland. Others have an office with a full time or part time staff or a formal representative who shares the needs of the organisation in local churches. Space will not permit any further comment on societies based outside Ireland; we shall simply recognise that for many of these societies Ireland is a significant source of both prayer and financial support and of recruits.

We shall look at four missionary societies, each one started by an individual who learned of a need and acted on it. These four are typical of many others; they are just some of the stories that could be told, of individuals who have made their own contribution to mission, and whose example has led others to follow in their footsteps.

Mission Africa

At the East London Training Institute in 1887 a young student from Belfast heard a letter being read from a group in Nigeria asking for a missionary to come and live among them. This letter had been sent originally to the Scottish Mission working at Calabar in Nigeria, but they had lost many missionaries through illness and death and were not able to spare anyone. The letter was passed on to Grattan Guinness to be presented to his students and was read out one day at breakfast where it was heard by Samuel Bill. He had been born in Belfast in 1863 and had gone to the East London Training College in 1886. On hearing this letter he felt that God wanted him to go to work in Africa and, despite meeting and becoming engaged to Grace, he headed out later that same year. On arrival, on his own, with no organised support behind him, he frequently became sick but, as soon as he was able, began attempting to reach the people with the gospel. He quickly made friends with the Ibuno people who lived as fishermen and traders and followed traditional religious beliefs. They had requested a missionary because they thought if they had a white man living among them their enemies would be afraid to attack and they also wanted their children to learn to read to help them in trade.

The first convert was a man called David Ekpong, and he soon became a good friend and a fellow worker alongside Samuel Bill, becoming the first Ibuno pastor. Bill also made friends with the local chief, by getting together to build a school/church building and the chief also became a Christian. After a year he was joined by his friend from home and former fellow student, Archie Baile. By this time there were over a hundred attending the weekly church service and a core of believers.

Samuel Bill had gone out as a totally independent missionary. His colleagues were able to help a little the first year, but he had planned to support himself by trade. He quickly saw that this would not work, it would put him in competition with the people he had come to reach, would not provide enough to support him and would leave him no time for Christian work. At the same time a small group of friends back home in Ireland decided to undertake to support him and formed the Qua Iboe Missionary Association. When he and Baile came home in 1890-91 they were able to speak and share the work with the association. They brought David Ekpong with them to help to share the vision. At this time Samuel and Grace married.

By 1896, the old church building at Ibuno was no longer big enough and a new church was built. As early as 1889 Bill and Baile had begun making trips up river to other language groups and as time went on and the mission gained new recruits some were sent up to these other groups. Missionaries joined them from Ireland from Presbyterian, Baptist, Quaker and other backgrounds. The church grew and is now the United Evangelical Church of Nigeria with over 5,000 churches nationwide. It became independent of the Qua Iboe Mission in the 1960s and now the two work in partnership.

Mission Africa (as the organisation was renamed in 2002) still works in West Africa today currently with eight missionaries from Ireland among seventeen in total in Nigeria, Burkina Faso and Chad, and the headquarters is based in Belfast. Missionaries serve in theological education, church planting, medical work and literature distribution.

It is noteworthy that the combination of evangelistic activity and addressing social needs that has been part of the ethos of Mission Africa is typical of most evangelical societies working in the developing world. Other societies with Irish origins such as the Acre Gospel Mission and Amy Carmichael's Donahvur Fellowship, which have had a primarily evangelistic motivation have recognised from their earliest days that evangelism could not be done in isolation from other aspects of the lives of the local people. The same is also true of some evangelistic societies that work in Ireland. These include the long established, denominationally based urban missions of the Methodist and Presbyterian Churches and societies that focus on particular groups such as the Seaman's Christian Friend Association and the Sandes Soldiers' and Airmen's Centres.

The Leprosy Mission
The Leprosy Mission, which works in 29 countries around the world bringing hope and medical help to millions with leprosy, was also founded by a young man from Ireland. Wellesley Bailey was born in Abbeyleix in Co Laois in 1846, at the height of the potato famine. He had planned to make his fortune in Australia and New Zealand, but in 1866 just before he left with his fiancée, Alice Grahame, she persuaded him to go to a church

meeting with her. He did so and felt God speaking to him and that evening committed his life to Christ. In 1868 he returned to Dublin and decided to join his brother who was working in India. In November 1869 he travelled to Ambabla in India as a teacher with the American Presbyterian Mission. Here he met people suffering with leprosy for the first time – 'I felt, if ever there was a Christ-like work in the world it was to go amongst these poor sufferers and bring them the consolation, the hope of the gospel.' Wellesley began to visit regularly those suffering from this disease.

Wellesley and Alice were married in 1871, and were both committed to the work of helping those suffering with leprosy. Having returned to Dublin in 1873 Wellesley talked about the needs of people with leprosy in India at the home of his and Alice's friend, Charlotte Pym and such was his passion for this work that a public meeting was arranged at the Friend's Meeting House in Monkstown. Following that meeting, in 1874 the Leprosy Mission was born, with a group of people agreeing to raise £30 a year. In the first year they raised £600. The work grew and eight years later in 1886 Wellesley gave up his other work and became the full time secretary of the Mission, a role in which he continued to serve until his retirement at age 71.

Initially the aim of the work was to provide support and care for those suffering from leprosy but from the 1940s medical treatment to cure leprosy began to be introduced. Treatment has since further advanced so that often leprosy can be cured after between 6 to 12 months on a course of drugs. The stigma of suffering from leprosy remains and The Leprosy Mission now also has a strong focus on 'care after cure', helping with rehabilitation and work retraining.

Both Mission Africa and The Leprosy Mission were born out of the vision and commitment of two young men, one from Belfast and one from Dublin, who learned of a need and not only sought to meet that need, but who inspired and challenged others to also get involved. They initially started on their own, with a few friends, and over time their efforts grew into organisations that still bring the gospel and God's love to many people over 100 years later.

The Leprosy Mission was a mission born out of compassion for the physical and emotional welfare of suffering people and Irish Evangelicals have a consistent record of involvement in such mission. Many doctors and other health workers, teachers, agriculturalists, engineers and tradesmen have gone from Ireland to work in some desperately hostile situations. Some have committed their lives to this aspect of global mission while others have offered their services for short term work and it is to this relatively recent development in global mission that we now turn.

The world has changed much since the formation of Mission Africa and The Leprosy Mission. Some of the biggest advances have been in terms of technology, communication and travel. The world is a much more accessible place. This has changed the shape of mission today. It no longer takes several weeks to travel to another country, to stay for months or years. Now an individual can go and make a useful contribution to mission in a few months or even weeks. This new short-term aspect has not diluted mission from Ireland, rather it has opened it to a wider range of individuals. Both the denominational and the independent mission agencies have become increasingly involved in this growing aspect of mission and the short histories of the following two independent missionary societies reflect this changing trend.

LIFT

LIFT (Labour In Faith and Trust) was founded in 1999. It grew out of a visit in 1997 by two men from Belfast, John Purse and Gary Moore, to Guinea Bissau to fit a suspended ceiling in a church. Working alongside another six men on this project, they were inspired and challenged to serve God again in this way in the future. They invited a couple of other men to form a management team, gathered a council of reference and in March 1999 LIFT was launched. Since April 2003 John Purse, who was previously working for a local plumber merchants in Belfast as stores supervisor, has been working as the full-time secretary for LIFT and in the same year a building was purchased as headquarters for the organisation.

LIFT sends teams of practically skilled workers from Ireland to work on construction projects for one or two weeks. From 1999 to 2003 there have been 17 projects with 115 people involved. They have worked in Africa, Europe and Asia with the team members ranging from skilled professionals to 'handy enthusiasts'. In the early days LIFT members identified jobs that needed to be done in missionary situations with which they were familiar and offered their services to the agency involved. As the organisation's reputation became established, missionary agencies began to send requests for a LIFT team to come and help with a particular project and teams are put together with the skills required to do the work.

LIFT not only fulfils an important role in providing assistance to meet practical needs, they also seek to encourage the missionaries whom they are visiting and to share fellowship with local Christians. The teams provide opportunities for individuals to become involved in mission on a short-term basis, who otherwise might not have that experience. This not only benefits the project they are working on, but also the individuals in the teams, deepening their relationship with God and giving them a bigger picture of mission, which they then share with others on their return.

Abaana

Abaana is another new independent missionary agencies based in Ireland, having been set up in January 1998. The name 'Abaana' comes from a Ugandan word meaning 'children' and the needs of children in Uganda are the main focus of the organisation. The story of its origins follows the pattern with which we are now familiar, that is of an individual becoming aware of a need and seeking to meet that need. In the case of Abaana, that individual was Scott Baxter, who visited Uganda in 1997 when he was 18 years old. This experience had a deep impact on him; he saw children living in poor conditions and wanted to do something to help. On his return home he took up his studies in Mathematics and Computer Science, graduating with first class honours, but also began fundraising to help support children in Uganda. Abaana was registered as a charity in 1998 and now sponsors over 55 children and has raised over £40,000 for various projects. Scott Baxter now works full-time on a voluntary basis for Abaana, giving presentations to churches and youth groups. Abaana sees itself as having a different focus from many of the longer established missionary societies, whose supporters are often the older members of churches. Abaana seeks to get young people excited about mission so they run sponsored events in which young people can become involved in raising money. They say their goal is 'to motivate, challenge and empower, especially young people, to make a difference', and in this they are not so different from the older independents in their early days and from organisations such as Logos Ministries, which began under the name Youth Evangelical Missionary Fellowship. It will be interesting to see whether the support base of youth based organisations such as these ages with the passing years.

It is encouraging to see organisations such as Abaana and LIFT, amongst others, who are helping people to become involved in mission in very practical ways, and in doing what they can to reach out around the world with God's compassion. These new organisations have a part to play alongside the many existing mission agencies that are facilitating individuals to go from Ireland and be God's witnesses in different countries in ways that were completely impractical just a generation ago.

Three concluding comments may be made at the end of this section. First, the distinction between Ireland as a sending base for mission and Ireland as the recipient of mission, either from within or from outside that we noticed when considering denominational mission, is also present in the independent agencies. Agencies such as Youth For Christ, Scripture Union (including the Children's Special Service Mission) and the Faith

Mission both recruit in Ireland and have large programmes of evangelism throughout the island. Curiously, the Faith Mission has both its largest annual conference and its greatest concentration of missionaries in Ireland. Even more curiously UFM Worldwide (Unevangelised Fields Mission) includes Ireland as a 'Field'.

Second, there are a number of means by which evangelical mission societies have been working together over the years. Perhaps the most significant of these is the Bangor Worldwide Missionary Convention, held annually in the seaside resort of Bangor, Co Down. This is probably the largest event of its kind in the UK and draws together dozens of mission societies, both denominational and independent, for nine or ten days of worship, teaching by internationally respected mission leaders and fellowship. Founded in 1937 by Herbert Mateer, the convention provides a forum for the sharing of information, recruiting and mutual encouragement. The blurring of the distinction between local and global mission is evident here also, perhaps most obviously in the exhibition halls where stands representing Dublin Christian Mission or Belfast City Mission sit beside stands from Africa Inland Mission and Frontiers.

INDIVIDUALS IN GLOBAL MISSION

Irish Evangelicalism has always contributed gifted individuals to the cause of Christ throughout the world. This has been true across the spectrum of Christian activity from academic scholarship to hymn writing, so it should come as no surprise that a number of Irish Evangelicals have become household names in global mission. We have already seen how the mission activities of the various denominations can be understood as activities of committed individuals rather than activities of whole denominations and we have discussed the work of a number of individuals who founded what are now international mission societies or who made significant contributions in a denominational context. The people discussed below are not unique: rather they exemplify the way in which individuals have made their contributions to global mission without identifying themselves with Irish evangelical societies or denominational bodies. These examples stand for many thousands of other individuals whose contributions will never be widely known.

The second comment is that too often Irish Evangelicals have engaged more in conflict with other Christians than with the non-Christian world. The desire for a pure church has led many to separate themselves from fellow believers with whom they differ on relatively minor issues. In turn this has led to genuine evangelistic activity being supplanted by denominationally-based proselytising. It is arguable that much of the growth of Brethrenism can be attributed to Christians being attracted from other denominations rather than to the conversion of non-Christians. Having said this, we must still acknowledge that, from J. N. Darby's day to the present, Brethrenism has provided missionary personnel and financial support beyond what one would expect from what is still a small group of Christians.

Henry Grattan Guinness (1835-1910)

Henry Grattan Guinness was born in 1835 into one of the best known families in Ireland, whose name is now known (and whose beverage is drunk!) worldwide. As a young man of twenty he began to preach evangelistically around Ireland and later moved to England, Wales and Scotland and thence to the Continent and, for six months in 1859, to North America. Some have claimed that he was the greatest evangelist of the mid-nineteenth century and certainly contemporary records show that his campaigns regularly met with significant response.

However, it was in March, 1873 that Guinness' most significant contribution to global mission began. In that month he founded, along with Dr Barnardo[54] and others, the East London Institute (later the Harley Bible & Missionary Training College), which marked the beginning of what has now become known as the 'Bible College Movement'. Up to this point the only significant training for cross-cultural mission had been done in the preparation of clergy within the main historic denominations. It had been assumed that the clergy would evangelise and that other workers could be treated as ancillary to them. Guinness had learned from Hudson Taylor that lay people had much to offer and that people of lower academic levels could be as valuable as anyone else. Therefore his new institution offered training to anyone who desired it, on condition that they were committed to global mission. The Institute grew rapidly and led to a stream of similar schemes on both sides of the Atlantic.

Guinness died while the most important missionary conference of the twentieth century was in progress in Edinburgh in 1910. Such was his stature in mission circles that the conference meeting which was in session when the news broke was suspended as a mark of respect.

If we were to draw a net of relationships in evangelical mission worldwide the name of Grattan Guinness would be linked to a huge number of other individuals and groups. Likewise the inclusion of Samuel Bill in this chapter illustrates that Irish Evangelicals cannot be separated from the bigger network and cannot be understood without reference to this bigger context.

J. Edwin Orr (1912-1987)

Until relatively recently one name stood out above all others in the history and theology of Revival, J. Edwin Orr. His work on the subject was for many years the only substantial treatment of a subject that many Evangelicals had engaged with in practical and emotional ways but had never submitted to any thoughtful reflective study. Orr applied both his huge intellect and his extensive experience of personal involvement in evangelistic enterprises throughout the world to the subject and produced a number of important works, both academic and popular.

From humble origins in Belfast, Orr began his evangelistic preaching in his late teens and moved to London to begin an itinerant ministry in 1933. From there he toured Europe and before the outbreak of war in 1939 he had preached in dozens of countries, on every continent. During the war he served as a military chaplain and for twenty years following his demobilisation he based himself in southern California from where he travelled and wrote extensively. In 1966 he became a professor at Fuller Theological Seminary's School of World Mission. It is perhaps appropriate that Orr died while involved in an evangelistic campaign in 1987. He died at the age of seventy five, doing that for which he was supremely gifted and to which he had committed his life.

J. Edwin Orr represents a trend within Irish Evangelicalism that has given rise to some sad reflections. It would seem that many of the most gifted people have made great contributions on the world stage without having any significant creative impact at home. This is not to cast aspersions on any particular individual but it does seem a pity that some creative thinkers and activists have brought so much innovation to other parts of the world while much missiological thinking and practice in Ireland remains firmly wedded to the past.

On the other hand, Orr also represents a trend which surfaces in some much younger groups such as Crown Jesus Ministries, an evangelistic agency formed around the year 2000 by a Monaghan man, Cecil Stewart. All of these began their mission interest as a passion for local evangelism.[55] This interest then expanded outside their homeland to include mission in the rest of the British Isles and throughout the world.

Stewart represents a development of Irish evangelical involvement in mission that is firmly tied to the technological developments of the last three decades. In previous generations, once an individual's ministry had grown beyond the geographical boundaries of Ireland he or she had to make a choice: commit to home while maintaining a global interest, or commit to the globe and retain little active interest in the homeland.

For every Samuel Bill or J. Edwin Orr who has given up secular work there have been many anonymous donors whose often sacrificial giving has been essential to the success of their mission enterprises. The commitment of Evangelicals to mission cannot be measured simply by the proportion of their number who spend shorter or longer terms directly involved in mission activity but by the proportion who engage in mission support activities. Empirical data is not available but it is beyond doubt that the vast majority of Irish Evangelicals give money with some degree of regularity and sacrifice to support global and local mission. It is also beyond doubt that many pray regularly and specifically for missionaries and mission organisations known to them. Missionaries and mission organisations are well aware of the crucial need for this twin support and have always been careful to nurture both aspects.

T. B. F. Thompson of Garvagh set up a Charitable Trust as a means of supporting a wide range of worthwhile causes, not only Christian but secular. This charitable work is clearly the action of a Christian philanthropist in which he endeavours to link his faith to the secular world and to use the fruits of his business success to do good. It is unlikely that he understands this as mission but even if he does, it is still clearly mission done in the context of work rather than work done as mission. In doing this he again is engaged in what is quantitatively rather than qualitatively different from activities common to most, less affluent, Evangelicals.

Evangelicals have always recognised that the everyday secular life of the Christian is an important theatre for mission although opinions have differed concerning how mission is to be done in this sphere. One of the best known examples of this has been Sir Frederick Catherwood, an Ulsterman by birth, who saw clearly that his life as an industrialist and his witness as a Christian were closely related. Perhaps more controversially, Evangelicals who have become involved in politics have often approached their work with a sense of mission. Some have been very robust in linking their Christian and political goals together, while others have preferred to allow their faith to guide their political actions in a more subtle fashion. Ironically it is people such as Ian Paisley and William McCrea who have most clearly identified their political work with Christian mission. They have understood the cause of Christ and the cause of Ulster to be intimately linked and to be engaged in promoting the latter is to be engaged in upholding the former. However, even they would be reluctant to refer to their political endeavours as mission, believing that mission is synonymous with evangelism and that politics is by no means an evangelistic activity.

Very recently a few Evangelicals have begun to think and speak of their work *per se* as mission. They see secular employment as more than an opportunity to have an evangelistic impact or to be a moderating influence in a sinful world. Within this group, there is a growing tendency to see the fabric of one's secular employment from a missiological perspective and to claim that there is a distinctively Christian and missionary way to be (say) a civil servant, plumber or farmer. This approach to work and mission is still in its very early stages of development but does show some hopeful signs for the future.

New challenges – fresh directions
In conclusion, we would like to offer three reflective observations.

Many Irish Evangelicals believe themselves to be more committed to global mission than any other group of Christians. They compare themselves favourably with other Evangelicals worldwide and with other Christians in Ireland, claiming to send more missionaries overseas, to give more money to global mission and to pray more for the cause of Christ throughout the world. However, we are unaware of little more than anecdotal evidence that these claims are true and some evidence that they are at least open to dispute.

In favour of the claims it has been shown above that in the nineteenth century and much of the twentieth century, Irish Evangelicals were disproportionately well represented in denominational missions and in certain strands of the independent mission societies. It is also clear that independent mission societies recognise that maintaining an office or full time representation in Ireland is an investment worth making. In addition, some of these societies have a relatively high number of active prayer groups in Northern Ireland, compared with the rest of the

United Kingdom and have a significant number of recruits and financial support flowing from the Province. However, when various social factors are taken into account the situation may not be as clear cut. For example, as noted earlier, Ireland has long had a tradition of emigration and there is no reason to set the movement of Evangelicals in mission outside this broader social trend. Also, if Irish Evangelicals are compared with their counterparts in the USA or South Korea it is far from certain that their degree of commitment to global mission is anything other than unspectacular. Another telling comparison is between Irish evangelical commitment to global mission and Irish Catholic commitment. The role played by Irish priests, nuns and others throughout the world in the last hundred and fifty years may well compare favourably with the role played by Irish Evangelicals.

But all of these comparisons are little more than guesses and the field is open for more robust research to be undertaken.

Our second comment is that the Irish Evangelical understanding of mission is often 'That which we in Ireland do in the rest of the world.' In other words their contribution to global mission can be seen as their contribution to mission in total. It is relatively easy for Evangelicals to become deeply involved in mission 'out there' on the 'mission field'. There are many valid opportunities to do this as part of the 'home support'. This demands some time spent in private prayer, some money in the collection envelope, perhaps some evenings at the mission society prayer meeting. It also brings some heart-warming feedback as accounts of evangelistic success or development projects completed allow Evangelicals to pat themselves on the back and enjoy a job well done.

This involvement may be very real, very valuable and something to which we are called by God but it can never be the core of our understanding of mission. To make this the core of our understanding of mission is a type of 'displacement', doing at a distance that which we ought to be doing with intimacy, as part of the fabric of our lives. Our fear is that Evangelicals can be guilty of being cobblers who leave their children shoeless. This criticism needs to be clearly understood. We are not saying that the support of evangelism across the world is being used as a substitute for doing evangelism at home. This is clearly not the case; if anything, Ireland is one of the most heavily evangelised parts of the world. Rather the criticism is twofold.

The first concern is that much of the evangelism that is carried on in Ireland is woefully unsuccessful. The return for the effort put in is often very small, yet too little questioning of evangelistic strategies and methods is done.

Second, the arm of mission that reaches out to deal with social, economic and political issues has been badly neglected by Evangelicals in Ireland.

These are two of the most important areas in which Irish Evangelicals have much to learn at home from the experiences of their own missionaries overseas and from the Christian communities founded and supported by Irish missionaries. The experience of the church in the developing world has been one of developing patterns of evangelism and social engagement that have been appropriate to the local context. This lesson has been slow in the learning at home as outdated methods of evangelism are treated with almost idolatrous respect and some still cling to the almost universally discredited notion that evangelism and social engagement are to be seen as separable or even antithetical.

However, we must not paint a completely negative picture. There have been some very hopeful signs in the last decade or so. Groups such as ECONI, CARE and Habitat for Humanity have been active in Ireland, combining a recognition that the spiritual and social needs of individuals and communities are closely intertwined. Within the Protestant denominations social concern has become more acceptable to Evangelicals and many strongly evangelical congregations are developing social programmes. However, there is still not the seamless integration of a holistic understanding of mission in Ireland that is evident in other parts of the world.

Our final comment is to reinforce what has been hinted at above, that Evangelicals in Ireland need to develop a greater degree of humility with respect to mission. They have been quite willing to learn from American Evangelicals but much less willing to learn from non-evangelical Christians and from Christians in the developing world. Many still find it difficult to get to grips with the fact that others (apart from American Evangelicals) sometimes do mission better than themselves. In particular the paternalism that has often attended Christian mission still lingers so that the idea of being able to benefit from interaction with churches that our forefathers brought to birth has yet to take firm root. It is our conviction that the future of the church in Ireland is dependent on the degree to which it is willing to learn from other places, where God is doing great things, and to become recipients in mission as well as donors. It may be that the many Africans and others who are coming, sometimes as refugees or migrant workers, to live in Ireland may be the means by which God speaks to the church on this island. Perhaps Evangelicals, more than any other group, should rejoice, and give thanks for people from other parts of the world who in the twenty-first century may be bringing good news from God to Ireland, just as Irish Evangelicals brought good news to their forefathers in the nineteenth and twentieth centuries.

Bibliography

Acheson, Alan, *A History of the Church of Ireland 1691-2001*, The Columba Press, Dublin, 2002

Addley, William Palmer, *A Study of the Birth and Development of the Overseas Mission of the Presbyterian Church in Ireland up to 1910*, Queen's University, Belfast, unpublished PhD thesis, 1995

Addley, William Palmer, 'Irish Presbyterian Attitudes to Mission before 1840' in Thompson, Jack, 1990, 11-24

Boyd, Robert, *Couriers of the Dawn: The Story of the Missionary Pioneers of the Presbyterian Church in Ireland*, Foreign Mission Office of the Presbyterian Church in Ireland, Belfast, 1938

Brown, Godfrey, 'The Colonial Mission' in Thompson, Jack, 1990, 163-73

Gallagher, Robert, *Pioneer Preachers of Irish Methodism*, Nelson and Knox, Belfast, 1965

Holmes, Finlay, *The Presbyterian Church in Ireland: A Popular History*, The Columba Press, Dublin, 2000

Loughbridge, Adam, *The Covenanters in Ireland*, Outlook Press, Rathfriland, 1984

Taggart, Norman W., *The Irish in World Methodism 1760-1900*, Epworth Press, London, 1986

Thompson, Jack (ed), *Into all the World – A History of the Overseas Work of the Presbyterian Church in Ireland 1840-1990*, Overseas Board of the Presbyterian Church in Ireland, Belfast, 1990

Notes:

1. This statement refers to post-Reformation churches – we do not wish to minimise the considerable evangelical impact of Celtic Christianity, which falls outside our present remit.

2. Patrick Adair, first historian of the Presbyterian Church in Ireland, cited in Holmes, 2000, 28.

3. Statement from Laggan Presbytery to other Presbyteries, 1684, cited in Holmes, 2000, 45.

4. For statistics relating to the USPG, see Acheson, 1996, 90-91, 185; for statistics relating to CMS, Acheson, 1996, 185-6.

5. Philip Carrington, cited in Acheson, 1996, 187

6. On the SPG, see Acheson, 1996, 29; on CMS, Acheson, 1996, 125. The quotation is from J. H. Singer, 1829, cited in Acheson, 1996, 135.

7. Stuart Piggin, cited in Acheson, 1996, 149.

8. Acheson, 1996, 221.

9. cited in Acheson, 1996, 222.

10. Taggart, 1986, 8.

11. On James Lynch, see Taggart, 1986, 104-107.

12. cited in Taggart, 1986, 13.

13 For Heck and Embury, see Taggart 1986, 52-54; Ryland, Taggart 1986, 8; Elliot, Taggart 1986, 9; Thoburn, Taggart 1986, 170ff; Butler, Taggart, 1986, 168-180.

14. cited in Taggart, 1986, 45.

15. cited in Taggart, 1986, 45.

16. cited in Brown, 1990, 166.

17. The Reformed Presbyterians had their origins in the Second Scottish Reformation of 1638-49. Regarding the settlement under William of Orange as a complete surrender of spiritual independence, they dissented from the constitution and separated from the 'sold-out' Presbyterians. Small groups of disaffected Scottish émigrés formed 'covenanting societies' in Co Antrim, Co Derry, East Donegal and North Down. Their fortunes were very much tied to the Scottish Reformed Presbytery, under whose supervision they remained until 1761.

18. cited in Taggart, 1986, 96.

19. See Addley, 1995, on Morgan.

20. cited in Boyd, 1938, 236-237.

21. cited in Taggart, 1986, 192.

22. Glasgow, cited in Boyd, 1938, 147.

23. Loughridge, 1984, 79.

24. Loughridge, 1984, 78-84.

25. Boyd, 1938, 16.

26. cited in Boyd, 1938, 18.

27. cited in Boyd, 1938, 43.

28. cited in Boyd, 1938, 112.

29. cited in Boyd, 1938, 188.

30. cited in Boyd , 1938, 199.

31. cited in Boyd, 1938, 146.

32. cited in Acheson, 1996, 195.

33. Taggart, 1986, 14-15.

34. cited in Taggart, 1986, 13.

35. cited in Acheson, 1996, 196.

36. Acheson, 1996, 133

37. For further information on this, see Addley, 1990, 17ff

38. See Taggart, 1986, 30ff for the history of this 'unequal partnership'.

39. cited in Addley, 1990, 15-16.

40. cited in Taggart, 1986, 143.

41. op.cit.

42. Holmes, 2000, 97.

43. cited in Holmes, 2000, 28.

44. cited in Holmes, 2000, 202.

45. cited in Holmes, 2000, 102.

46. S. E. Ahlstrom, cited in Holmes, 2000, 67.

47. Taggart, 1986, 16.

48. Holmes, 2000, 67.

49. Taggart, 1986, 10 ff.

50. cited in Taggart, 1986, 83.

51. Berkeley, Acheson 1996, 82; O' Brian, Acheson, 1996, 126; Heck and Embury, Taggart, 1986, 52-54; Waugh; Boyd, 1938, 16. The effect of Morgan's speech was reported by *The Belfast Newsletter*, 2nd July 1838; Boyd, 1938, 32-33.

52. For Pym, Fulton and Pilot, see Acheson, 1996, 127; 91-92; 89; for Dawson, McBride and Eager see Taggart, 1986, 70; 51; 55-59.

53. The belief that Catholics cannot be Christians is much less common among Evangelicals today than it was a generation ago.

54. Much more could be said about Dr Barnardo, the founder of the famous children's homes and other Evangelicals such as Miss Margaret Lyttle who founded the Girls' Brigade in 1896 in Sandymount, Dublin.

55. As yet Crown Jesus Ministries have engaged in little work outside Northern Ireland.

CHAPTER EIGHT

Living with Difference:
Evangelical Diversity

Patrick Mitchel

There are probably more types of evangelical Christians than there are brands of cereals in Superquinn. To an outsider it can be difficult to 'get a handle' on the, at times, almost bewildering diversity within the evangelical world. Derek Tidball writes that 'contemporary Evangelicalism, now over two hundred years old, has grown to be an immense tree with all sorts of shoots and branches, which often seem to have little in common, yet which clearly draw off the same roots.'[1]

If Warren Nelson's chapter has described these roots that form the core beliefs and attitudes which connect Christians within an identifiable movement called Evangelicalism, in this chapter I will move upwards into the often tangled foliage above. Here I hope to identify and describe some of the more important branches within the canopy – which has grown denser and more complex over time.

This image captures how difficult it is to define neatly what it is to 'be evangelical'. Modern Evangelicalism – and the Republic of Ireland is no exception[2] – incorporates a multiplicity of different churches and organisations within a loose network of relationships, united not by any common creed or single unifying structure, but shaped by a common commitment to certain core theological convictions and their practical implications. The theologian Alister McGrath describes Evangelicalism as 'essentially colligatory in that it finds its identity in relation to a series of central interacting themes and concerns.'[3] In other words, Evangelicals find common ground through a sense of shared beliefs, a belonging to a shared heritage and broadly similar objectives rather than in organisational structures.

Historically Evangelicalism has been a Protestant phenomenon, tracing its roots to the Reformation and subsequent revivalist movements. As Protestantism has diversified and fragmented, so evangelicals are now found in varying strength, within all the following denominations and groupings: Anglicans, Baptists, new churches, Pentecostals, Mennonites, Methodists, Brethren, Lutherans, Presbyterians and Charismatics. One of the fascinating and I believe significant aspects of recent evangelical history in Ireland, is how Evangelicalism is no longer confined within a small Protestant minority. Christians, committed to an evangelical understanding of the gospel, and from a Roman Catholic identity and culture, have been forming themselves into new churches and fellowships and also finding spiritual homes within Protestant churches with an evangelical ethos and focus. Such churches are now found in practically every town all over Ireland. Many of these Christians would certainly not describe themselves as 'Protestant' – with all the alien cultural and political implications associated with that word. They do – as the emergence of Evangelical Alliance Ireland (EAI) demonstrates[4] – find a common identity under the term 'evangelical' with like-minded Christians from Protestant churches. In other words, it is in the theological essentials of the gospel of Jesus Christ that their primary identity lies.[5]

This highlights how Evangelicalism should best be interpreted. On the one hand, to connect it intrinsically to Protestantism is to define it too narrowly. An 'evangelical spirit' can be identified outside the boundaries of classic evangelical Protestantism. Irish Evangelicals, for example, happily identify in Saint Patrick the hallmarks of authentic evangelical faith, namely in his deep awareness of the grace of God, a high view of Scripture, a living personal faith, humble repentance and passionate evangelistic zeal in making known the 'good news' of the gospel. The evangelical theologian Donald Bloesch can for example identify evangelical themes in such figures as Ambrose, Augustine of Hippo, Bernard of Clairvaux, Thomas Aquinas and Thérèse of Lisieux who spoke of a lift rather than a ladder to heaven – the lift of free grace.[6] On the other hand, to analyse evangelicalism in purely sociological terms – as a grouping within wider Protestantism who label themselves as 'evangelical' – is to define the term too broadly. Such an approach effectively detaches the term from its theological core. The result is that it becomes a virtually meaningless term, much like 'Christian' is (mis-)understood today.

An Agreed Belonging

The approach I prefer is to define Evangelicalism primarily in theological terms. Evangelicals are orthodox Christians who stress a dual commitment to the final and exclusive authority of the Bible and to the saving power of the gospel as achieved in the atoning death of Jesus Christ on the cross. This approach of focusing on the presence of such core essentials of evangelical belief helps to anchor Evangelicalism in the historic orthodox creeds of the Christian church. It is in this theological sense that Evangelicals primarily understand themselves. For example, EAI-2004 can thus begin stating 'Evangelicals are Christians who … confess the historic faith of the gospel' declared by the Scriptures. In this perspective, evangelical faith is firmly rooted in and connected to the church catholic, it is not merely an esoteric, marginal and novel sub-set of Christian identity. Rather, at its best, it is a movement of spiritual renewal within the wider church, calling the church back to its theological and biblical foundations. As Donald Bloesch puts it, 'It seeks to confess not a party line (a characteristic of sects) but the holy catholic faith.'[7]

This is why evangelical Christians of many different hues can feel a sense of shared identity – it flows out of a shared assent to and experience of core theological doctrines. Stanley Grenz puts it this way: 'What is central to evangelicalism is a common vision of the faith that arises out of a common religious experience couched within a common interpretative framework consisting of theological beliefs we gain from the Scriptures.' There is a sense of agreed belonging to what it means to be a Christian – at the heart of Evangelicalism is a 'shared experience cradled in a shared theology'.[8] Now of course this is a somewhat idealistic generalisation. Much depends on what is understood as theologically central. A universally agreed list of core beliefs does not exist among Evangelicals. But Grenz makes an important point. Without such a sense of a shared theology and experience it would be virtually impossible to talk of a movement called Evangelicalism at all. This is where it becomes helpful to introduce what John Stott calls evangelical essentials and *adiaphora* (matters of indifference).[9] It is general agreement on the 'primary' or core issues that acts to bind evangelicals together, however loosely, in a recognisable movement. Conversely, it is disagreement on the 'secondary' issues that helps to explain the confusing spectrum of evangelical opinion and practice.

Figure 1 illustrates the relationship between core and secondary beliefs. The inner circle represent the 'non-negotiables' that define historic Evangelicalism and demonstrate (Evangelicals will claim) how their faith stands in unbroken continuity with orthodox Christianity.[10] This is why John Stott can state boldly that evangelical Christianity, founded on the teaching of Jesus himself, is 'authentic Christianity, true, original and pure'.[11] Similarly Jim Packer can argue provocatively that 'Evangelicalism is not just one "ism" among many that our age has bred.' It is later diversions in his view, such as Catholicism and Liberal Protestantism, which are 'eccentricities and novelties'.[12] Any movement that denies one of these core truths (for example the claim that Scripture is God's inspired Word or that Jesus' work on the cross is the sole all sufficient means of salvation) in effect detaches itself from historic evangelical Christianity. However, disagreements over topics in the outer circle do not carry the same implication. These are the matters where evangelicals come to different conclusions on how Scripture is to be applied in practice. It is these 'secondary issues' that are my main concern in this chapter since they are the key to unlocking the question of evangelical diversity. It is not that these matters are unimportant. To the contrary, detailed and often passionate attention is paid to them. Rather they are 'secondary' in the sense of not impacting on 'gospel issues' such as the nature of

God, salvation or the truth of God's revelation in Scripture. In this respect, evangelicalism is a movement that is best determined by its centre (the inner circle), not its boundary (the outer circle).

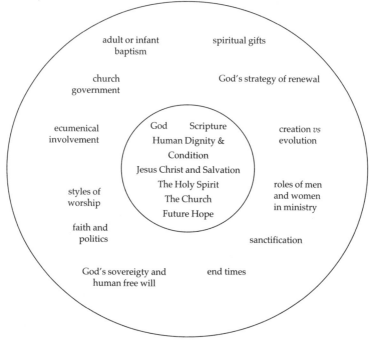

Figure 1: Unity and Diversity:
Primary and Secondary issues within Evangelicalism

If it is the variegated understanding of these secondary matters that shapes the complex landscape of contemporary evangelicalism, it is worth commenting on the areas of difference in practice. Whole books could be written on most of these issues. I will have to be ruthlessly brief and what follows is only meant to highlight the issues not describe accurately the various positions.

Spiritual gifts – have spiritual gifts (*charismata*) described in the New Testament ceased or are they for today?

Adult or infant baptism: should infants be baptised in the

prayerful expectation that they will later come to saving faith for themselves as they are nurtured by Christian parents within the covenant community of the church, or is baptism only for adult believers on profession of faith?

God's strategy of renewal: are Pentecostal and charismatic churches God's chosen tools in his strategy of renewal of his church in the twentieth and twenty-first centuries?

Church government: what form of church organisation is the most biblical? – for example, hierarchical denomination (Anglicans – archbishop, bishops etc); pastor and elders, local church autonomy (Baptists, some independent evangelicals, charismatics and Pentecostals); no formal leadership (Brethren, some independent evangelicals); equality of elders (*presbuteroi* – hence Presbyterian) responsible to a wider denominational authority.

Creationism *vs* evolution: is Genesis to be taken literally or not? Did God create the universe in a literal six days or over millions of years? Did God create man through the processes of evolution or not?

Ecumenical involvement: at what point does participation in dialogue and common activity with the Roman Catholic Church begin to conflict with evangelical truth? How should evangelicals relate to other faiths?

Styles of worship: what content, form and style of worship is most honouring to God and best reflects his character to an outside world?

Roles of men and women in ministry: are particular avenues of ministry (such as preaching and governing) only open to men or not?

Faith and politics: what level of socio-political involvement should Christians have in the world around them?

Sanctification: what level of holiness is attainable in this life to Christians empowered by the Holy Spirit? Is a 'second

level' experience of the Holy Spirit to be expected (Pentecostals and charismatics) or not?

God's sovereignty and man's responsibility: should all of the
Christian life be lived under the perspective of God's sovereign rule over all things (Calvinism) or should human free
choice be given similar weight (Arminianism)?

End times: what details are possible to discern from the Bible
on when will be the second coming of Christ and how will
God bring about the end of this world and all forces opposed
to him?

The conclusions evangelicals reach on these issues will play a
major role not only in what church they attend, but what 'type'
of evangelical they will be. This is why evangelicals have not
chosen to organise themselves within one church. Instead they
have divided into different 'tribes' or 'streams' according to
their preference, for example, on style of worship, structure of
church government, understanding of baptism or practice of
spiritual gifts and so on. It is not easy to categorise different
types of evangelical in Ireland today. Below is one possible re-
construction:[13]

(i) Reformed evangelicals

Reformed theology owes much to the Reformation and the
Puritans and emphasises themes such as the grace and sovereignty of God. Existing within major denominations such as the
Presbyterian Church in Ireland (PCI), which is strongly influenced by evangelicals. In recent years a series of evangelical
ministers have been appointed in the Republic with an emphasis
on biblical preaching, mission and church development. A long
established trend of Presbyterian decline post-Partition is beginning to reverse and some significant growth has occurred, particularly in Kilkenny and Dublin.

(ii) Charismatic evangelicals

The worldwide phenomenon of the charismatic movement
began to affect Ireland in the late 1960s. Five distinctive characteristics of the charismatic movement are: (i) a major post-con-

version enriching of personal Christian experience; (ii) speaking in tongues (for some); (iii) the use of all spiritual gifts described in the New Testament; (iv) the importance of worship 'in the Spirit'; (v) a particular understanding of God's strategy of renewal (of which more later). Charismatic Evangelicals represent a significant proportion of Evangelicals in Ireland, existing in a loose network of like-minded churches across the country. One of the largest charismatic communities in Ireland is Trinity Church Network (formerly Fellowship Bible Church) with congregations in central Dublin, Artane and Lucan. Arminian in theology, it has close links with ICTHUS in London.[14] Another is CORE, a charismatic Anglican church in Dublin.

(iii) Pentecostal Churches

Pentecostal theology emphasises the need for 'second blessing' in the Christian life through an experience of 'baptism in the Spirit' that empowers the believer. Stress is laid on particular spiritual gifts such as tongues, healing and prophecy. Various networks of differing types of Pentecostal churches exist in Ireland, including the denominations of Elim (which started in Monaghan town) and the Assemblies of God (AOG) and a small network of 'Plumbline' churches. St Mark's Family Worship Centre (AOG) on Pearse St, Dublin is one of the largest Pentecostal churches in the Republic. It is worth noting that Pentecostalism is the fastest growing sector of Christianity in the world today.[15] The vast majority of African ethnic churches developing in Ireland (see below) are Pentecostal.

(iv) Evangelical Minorities

Many Evangelicals are members of denominations where they form a minority. Examples include the Methodist Church (started of course by a famous figure with passionate evangelical convictions – John Wesley) and the Church of Ireland. The Church of Ireland has a significant number of Evangelicals within it, especially in Northern Ireland. Within the Republic Evangelicals have tended to be marginalised and for example have been largely excluded from representation within its predominantly liberal Theological College. However, the appointments of evangelical Bishops Harold Miller (Down & Dromore), Ken Good (Derry & Raphoe) and Kenneth Clarke (Kilmore, Elphin & Ardagh) around the turn of the millennium indicate the not insignificant influence of Evangelicalism within the denomination. If, as has occurred within the Episcopal Church of America, the Church of Ireland accepts the ordination of practising homosexuals, evangelicals will inevitably interpret such a step as a violation of biblical authority and a break with historic Christian orthodoxy.

(v) Evangelical Congregational groupings

These are independent churches that have formed themselves into loose coalitions, but resist a formal denominational structure or identity. They are without exception strongly evangelical. Included within this cluster are the Baptist churches, formerly united within the Baptist Union of Ireland and since 2003 gathered within an Association of Irish Baptist Churches (AIBC). Overwhelmingly evangelical and stressing the autonomy of the local church, the numbers of Baptist churches in the Republic has grown from approximately ten to more than twenty in the last twenty-five years. Some of these are new churches; others are former independent evangelical fellowships which have joined the Baptist Association. This in itself is an interesting development. Motives are difficult to isolate, but the need for belonging to a wider established grouping with all the benefits of a sense of identity, spiritual accountability and resources have probably played a major part in this trend. The largest Baptist church in the Republic of Ireland is Grosvenor Road in Dublin.[16] The Brethren Churches can also be located within this category. An Association of Irish Evangelical Churches (AIEC) was established in the early 1990s and has a membership of about forty churches partly belonging within this grouping.

(vi) Independent evangelicals

Many of the new churches and fellowships, which have emerged in Ireland in the last thirty years or so, retain an independent outlook. Some tend to be separatist in character, with a stress on theological purity or a pietistic spirituality. This in turn can lead to a withdrawal from the outside world and from other evangelicals who, for example, belong to 'mixed' denominations or who engage in ecumenical dialogue. Others have taken a more positive outward stance, engaging with contemporary culture and seeking to relate the good news of the gospel to contemporary Irish society using accessible forms of communication and styles of music.[17] Less structured and highly flexible, independent churches are less formal than denominational churches and tend to appeal to evangelical Christians from an Irish cultural background.

(vii) Ethnic evangelicals

A major and astonishingly rapid development on the Irish church scene has been the arrival of considerable numbers of ethnic Christians, a significant proportion of whom are evangelicals. Many 'black churches' of African origin now exist in Ireland, representing various shades of Pentecostal theology. A number of networks and denominations exist, one of the most influential being the Redeemed Christian Church of God. Informal research suggests that there are over forty churches belonging to this denomination meeting all over Ireland and at least another eight in Dublin (some of which have hundreds of people attending). It is estimated that there are approximately another thirty to forty other similar churches scattered across the state. Examples of other ethnic evangelical churches include those of Chinese and Romanian extraction. Without making a value judgement on this issue, for a mixture of theological, cultural and linguistic reasons, these churches tend to retain their ethnic identities rather than assimilate within existing Irish evangelical churches.

(viii) Evangelical Catholics

The Evangelical Catholic Initiative (ECI) emerged in 1992 out of the publication of the pamphlet *What is an Evangelical Catholic?*, first published in 1988 with ecclesiastical permission and endorsed by a group of lay and clergy signatories. The document claims to reflect the beliefs of 'millions' of Catholics worldwide who 'have received the basic gospel, accepted Jesus as personal Lord and saviour and are manifesting the fruit of the Holy Spirit in their daily lives.' Examples of individual Catholics' stories of faith have been published in *Adventures in Reconciliation* – with a foreword from Cardinal Cahal Daly.[18] Writing elsewhere Paddy Monaghan of ECI claims that between 1972 and 1978 some '10,000 Catholics came into a deeper, or first time, personal relationship with Jesus as Lord and Saviour and were baptised in the Holy Spirit.'[19] He goes to make the astonishing (and unsubstantiated) claim that by 1993 there were over 100,000 evangelical Catholics in Ireland.[20] Much of course depends on who is counted as being 'evangelical'. ECI's approach seems to include people who would describe themselves as either 'committed Christians, Charismatic Catholics, renewed Catholics, born again Catholics, or simply Catholics who love the Lord'.[21] Other Evangelicals in Ireland would not share this definition and think the figures are fantastically inflated. Initial figures from an EAI database of Evangelicals in Ireland currently being compiled suggests a figure for self-designated Evangelicals of c. 20,000 in the Republic of Ireland made up from 220-250 denominational and non-denominational churches across the country.[22]

The ECI leaflet states that evangelical Catholics affirm the following: salvation cannot be earned; there is only one mediator between God and man, the person of Jesus; and that the Mass is not a repetition of Calvary – Jesus died once for all and priest and people enter into that one, all-sufficient sacrifice by grace. This is not the place to debate the merits, or lack of them, of evangelical Catholic theology,[23] save to say that the status of evangelical Catholics is a highly contentious subject within Irish Evangelicalism and is an issue to which I will return below.

Fracture Points

If Irish evangelicals fall into numerous types, it is not surprising that there are a number of tensions and potential fracture points within what is a diverse Christian community. These 'fracture points' exist mainly within the 'outer circle' of secondary differences pictured in Figure 1. Many of them have been around a long time and are not unique to Ireland. Most (but not all) Evangelicals have had to learn to live with the reality that many of their secondary theological differences have been around for decades if not centuries and show no signs of imminent resolution. For example, not only different but mutually opposing conclusions on what the Bible teaches exist on the use of spiritual gifts within the church, adult and infant baptism, how and when God created the world and how and when the world will end. Space does not allow discussion of most of these tension points save to make two points.

First, it should not be surprising that such differences exist. Throughout church history there have been many issues on which Christians disagree. Second, since these are secondary and not gospel issues, the real challenge for Evangelicals is how they respond to the reality of diverse views. This is a question to which I will return in the conclusion. At this point I want to home in on just two areas that have a particular Irish dimension and in my view represent pressing threats to unity within the Irish evangelical community.

1. Church identity

Evangelicals have never been agreed on a single model of church life. The movement's theological stress on faith alone *(Sola Fide)* and the Scriptures alone *(Sola Scriptura)*, allied to the importance of personal conversion, has tended to relegate ecclesiology to a Cinderella doctrine whereby the church is too often viewed as an optional extra in the individual believer's personal relationship with God. Baptist, Presbyterian, Methodist, charismatic, Pentecostal and Brethren churches, all appealing to the authority of Scripture, come to quite divergent conclusions

about how to apply biblical principles concerning church organisation in practice. The reason for this is that Scripture itself does
not set out a 'blueprint' of church government. While evangelicals in general have learned to accept this *status quo* and work together across ecclesiological boundaries, it is an issue that causes
periodic bouts of real tension. The question of church identity
has the potential to divide Irish evangelicals on at least three levels. Let me try to explain and justify this claim.

(i) level one: 'purity *vs* reform'
In Britain in the late nineteenth century, a rising tide of theological liberalism acted as a catalyst for some Evangelicals to call
their brothers to separate from 'mixed' denominations. This
'purifying' impulse was seen for example in C. H. Spurgeon's
call for withdrawal from the Baptist Union.[24] In 1966 his 'call'
was famously echoed by Martyn Lloyd-Jones at the Assembly of
the National Association of Evangelicals. With John Stott in the
chair, he argued passionately for evangelical separation from
denominations influenced by liberalism. Stott publicly dissented, arguing that increasing evangelical influence should be the
basis for spiritual reform bringing the denominations back to
their theological and biblical roots. This significant event within
British evangelicalism was symptomatic of a recurring area of
disagreement between 'separatists' who view the 'reformers' as
naïve and divisive. This same tension is evident within Irish
evangelical churches. Those in the 'new churches' tend to be independent, wholly evangelical and highly flexible in their
church structures. They tend to view evangelicals within the denominations along a spectrum of opinion ranging from friendly
co-operation, to 'technical recognition' (where their legitimacy is
accepted but there is little, if any, relational interaction) to virtual irrelevance (where there is an assumption that genuine
Christians are only found in non-denominational evangelical
churches).[25] On the other side, evangelicals in the historic denominations often have an uneasy attitude to 'new churches'.
Some act to encourage and partner with such churches, seeing in

them a new and effective strategy for mission in an increasingly post-Catholic and post-institutional culture. Others are at times appalled at the new churches' 'entrepreneurial ecclesiology', spiritual competitiveness, lack of accountability structures, instability and potential for authoritarian leadership. Such evangelicals are Anglicans or Presbyterians (for example) first – their identity is intrinsically linked to their denominational heritage and ethos. While some take time to connect with fellow evangelicals on the 'outside', a denominational evangelical will feel more at home within their organisation's life and structures. Inevitably commitment to their church's life will leave little time and energy for building relationships with the wider Irish evangelical community.

(ii) Level two: 'national identity'

At a second level, the issue of church identity has been given an extra 'twist' in light of this island's frankly sectarian history. One consequence of the overwhelming success of Catholic nationalism in the nineteenth and twentieth centuries was that to be Irish was to be Catholic. The 'evangel' as embodied within evangelicalism was perceived as alien to Irish culture and identity. Viewed as intrinsically 'British', it was seen as potentially threatening and at times part of a wider political agenda of religio-political control.[26] One consequence of this is that many Irish evangelicals from a Catholic background find it culturally as well as theologically difficult to imagine becoming part of a 'Protestant' church – especially when they are usually staffed, funded and run by Northern Irish Christians! Issues of identity run deep – to the very essence of individual self-understanding. While evangelicals will agree that in Christ all other loyalties, whether cultural or political are relativised under his Lordship, many Irish evangelicals will resist any (perceived or real) requirement to leave their national identity by 'becoming' a Protestant. However, others have found spiritual homes in denominational churches, some of which have experienced significant growth embracing Christians from both Catholic and Protestant backgrounds. In my experience these churches have

been able to transcend the legacy of Irish history by majoring on
a common biblical and evangelical identity and relegating their
cultural Protestant ethos to the background of church identity.
In this sense, the questions facing evangelicals in Ireland are not
unlike the debates in the Acts of the Apostles on how to
incorporate Jewish and Gentile believers into a new common
Christian community.

(iii) Level three: God's strategy for renewal
A third level at which church identity poses a threat to unity is
in how particular churches interpret their role within God's sovereign purposes. While this is far from a new issue, it represents
a continuing and real area of tension between charismatic/
Pentecostal streams and other evangelical churches. In the early
twentieth century when Pentecostalism arrived in Britain, it was
passionately denounced by some conservative Evangelicals convinced that its 're-discovery' of spiritual gifts (such as speaking
in tongues, prophecy and healing) had nothing to do with the
Holy Spirit. Similar reactions faced the charismatic movement in
the late 1960s, coupled with distrust of its elevation of experience over doctrine, its trans-denominational appeal and tendency
to value the 'present word of God', as in prophecy or words of
knowledge, as opposed to the written word of God.[27] Some
charismatics in turn, reacting against a perceived lifeless orthodoxy in many evangelical churches, turned their backs on the
evangelical churches of their youth. In other words, there was a
sharp distinction between being a charismatic and being an
evangelical. Times have moved on. In 1977, reformed theologian
J. I. Packer's influential book, while disagreeing with much
charismatic theology, could recognise that each side could mutually enrich the other.[28] There is evidence that this has indeed
happened. The charismatic movement has profoundly influenced older 'classic' Evangelicalism and highlighted the need
for the Holy Spirit to be given his proper place at the core of
church teaching and experience. Evangelical churches have
been encouraged to seek new life in the form of a rediscovery of
the biblical emphasis on every member ministry (as against a

reliance on ordained clergy), refreshing worship styles, the necessity of incorporating emotion alongside a rational understanding of Christian faith. Many charismatics in turn are rediscovering the importance of doctrine, the final authority of the Bible and the value of connecting to the theological and historical heritage of the church. Increasingly in Ireland, as elsewhere, the older denominational barriers are breaking down. The 'founding members' of EAI include every shade of evangelical imaginable, including those on either side of the debate on spiritual gifts. There is an increasing sense of warmth and informality among an inter-connected network of individuals and churches that bodes well for the future.

However, having said all this, real differences remain, particularly over how to interpret the significance of particular churches within God's strategy for renewal. Charismatics have always been controversial as they push the boundaries of accepted orthodoxies. They have been called 'the pioneers of Evangelicalism' whose success suggests that 'the future of Evangelicalism looks increasingly charismatic'.[29] Yet success can engender some regrettable attitudes. Some Pentecostals and charismatics talk of different 'waves' of the Holy Spirit bringing renewal to the church in the twentieth century. The first wave was that of Pentecostalism in the early 1900s. The second the charismatic movement of the 1960s. The third wave is often associated with figures like the noted late American leader John Wimber of the Vineyard Fellowship. The assumption behind original Pentecostalism was that, because some of his people had sought him in a new way, God had restored to the church gifts that had been lost for centuries. Such thinking continues to shape attitudes towards those not 'baptised in the Spirit' or 'walking in the gifts' or 'open to the Spirit'. All too easily other churches can be seen, either explicitly or implicitly, as 'second class' and of less spiritual significance in God's strategy of renewal than those riding the latest wave of the Spirit. Charismatic attitudes can give the impression that they are the new dawn for the evangelical movement in Ireland and that they do not need to, nor desire to, work together with non-charismatic evangelicals.

This sense of spiritual self-sufficiency is seen in how charismatic churches tend to press ahead with their own agendas – whether for example in mission or setting up training schools of ministry – with little recognition of the activities of other evangelicals. In Ireland, despite a warming of some relationships at leadership level, there is still little relational unity between the charismatic/Pentecostal streams and other Evangelicals. There is evidence that charismatic churches are mirroring the Pentecostal denominations as they move into more structured networks around the country. As they do so, a key question for the future is where will their primary identity lie? Well informed observers have detected something of an identity crisis within charismatic circles.[30] Will their identity be first as charismatic Christians and then as evangelicals? In other words an attitude summed up by the statement, 'I am a charismatic and an evangelical' where the two identities are complementary yet remain quite distinct. Or perhaps as charismatics who see themselves as Christians who have transcended their evangelical roots, perhaps out of a negative experience, into a deeper experience of God's Spirit? This view is captured by the statement, 'I was once an evangelical but now I am a charismatic.' Or will they grow to see themselves as charismatic evangelicals who can say 'I am a charismatic evangelical; that is I am first an evangelical but with a charismatic outlook and experience'? The last option holds out most hope that evangelical difference in this area of church identity will not degenerate into evangelical fragmentation. A degree of humility, an ability to engage in searching self-criticism and a willingness to listen and learn from each other is needed on all sides if the diverse Irish evangelical movement is to move forward in unity.

2. Attitudes to Catholicism

If the first fracture point is an internal one, a second issue that causes sharp division within contemporary Irish Evangelicalism is an external one: 'What constitutes an appropriate biblical approach to Roman Catholicism?' Evangelicals exhibit a spectrum of responses to the Catholic Church. Here I will briefly sketch four outlooks on the spectrum and comment on why they exist.[31]

On the more theologically conservative end of the spectrum are the *theological separatists* – those who completely repudiate ecumenical activity as a betrayal of Reformation principles. The weight of opinion within the independent and newer churches (who usually have a majority of members from a Catholic background) is overwhelmingly negative against any form of ecumenism that seems to imply that the official dogma of the Roman Catholic Church is not seriously at odds with biblical teaching on a number of vital issues. It is the experience of many of these evangelicals despite the fact that the Catholic Church is christologically orthodox, that when members of that church they never heard the 'good news' of salvation through faith alone in Jesus Christ. The 'free gift' of the gospel through faith in Christ was obscured by extra-biblical doctrines such as the status and role of Mary, papal infallibility and sacramentalism – a stress on ritual rather than the necessity for personal faith. In this perspective, whilst the Irish church may be undergoing profound change from its authoritarian past, the fact that its official doctrine remains unchanged, means that any ecumenical relationships are premature, inappropriate and confusing. These evangelicals are quite willing to accept that individual Catholics (just like individuals Protestants who also need salvation!) can know Christ regardless of church affiliation, but they draw the line at attempting to reconcile evangelical theology with official Catholic doctrine. In this view, the term 'evangelical Catholic' is theologically incoherent (even an oxymoron) since it attempts to marry two incompatible positions. Theological separatists would have been unlikely to participate in the nationwide 2002 *Power to Change* campaign endorsed by all the main denominations. These evangelicals would be uncomfortable with engaging in mission with the Roman Catholic Church without an agreed understanding on the content of the message being communicated.

It should be noted that this attitude in Ireland is grounded not only in deeply held theological convictions, but also in personal experience. During the 1970s-1980s many Irish evangelicals encountered a considerable degree of hostility and exclusion from their communities if they left the all-embracing fold of the Catholic Church. This was still the era of what Tom Inglis calls 'monopoly Catholicism'.[32] Being Irish was a package deal and religion was the wrapping paper. Leaving the church was tantamount to betraying one's family, one's community, one's history and even one's identity. I know people who were disinherited and others whose family members did not speak to them in years. New groups trying to find a place to worship in their towns faced a blanket of exclusion, sometimes being forced to find a location some distance away. The response of some within the Catholic Church was at times close to scare-mongering and often misinformed. Some evangelicals were denounced from the pulpit. The work of Martin Tierney, then Director of the Catholic Communications Institute, while perceptive in many ways, managed to lump the Elim Pentecostal church in with cults such as the Moonies and the Hare Krishna Movement among others.[33] The Irish media, unused and unable to think in categories outside the simple duality of 'Catholic' and 'Church of Ireland', demonstrated how the wider society was ill equipped to deal with alternative religious identities. One of the most significant examples, among others,[34] of this was the 1982 'Ballaghaderreen affair', widely reported in the Irish media. When a charismatic group broke away from the Catholic Church and began baptising its members, the Western Bishops were prompted to publish a pastoral letter. In it they talked of how some 'non-denominational Christians' had established 'missions' through which people leaving the Catholic Church 'in many cases ... begin to seem like different people' to such a degree that 'they have been, not so much converted as taken over.'[35] The media perception of the new fellowship was overwhelmingly negative, mistakenly associating evangelicals as synonymous with non-Christian cults such as the Jehovah

Witnesses or Mormons, rather than as orthodox Christians.[36] Christians who were neither Catholic nor Protestant did not fit (and often still do not fit) in any known category. Such attitudes are waning (but far from gone). 'Old' Ireland was a place for insiders who belonged to the story of the (Catholic) nation. It was a cold place for those who found themselves on the outside of the all encompassing religio-political consensus.

On the other end of the spectrum are the *pragmatic ecumenists*. These are evangelicals, usually in the denominations which have official relations with the Catholic Church, who while acknowledging continuing significant differences between evangelical and Roman Catholic theology, gladly participate in the ecumenical process. They view it as a means to reflect Christian unity, not through all-embracing church structures, but as a means of bridge building with the wider Catholic community. This can include joint worship ('if the service contains nothing contrary to evangelical conviction') and witness ('provided there is agreement on the content of what is being proclaimed'). While Catholicism contains error, truth is also present. Rome can be understood as a Christian church in that all denominations are imperfect manifestations of the invisible church, which is not limited to any one denomination. Significant changes within Catholicism since Vatican II are taken as opportunities to establish 'new, positive relationships' with Roman Catholics.

Somewhere between these poles are two other groups. The *spiritual pragmatists* are those who stress a common experience of the Holy Spirit rather than concern for denominational allegiance. Structural questions related to ecumenical relationships then become virtually irrelevant and there is no impetus towards denominational unity. These Christians, mainly within charismatic and Pentecostal circles, emphasise the biblical truth that the Holy Spirit is a Spirit of unity. Where individuals together experience his empowering presence in worship, the theological niceties of official church dogma become a distraction and barrier to true unity in Christ. These evangelicals will be much more open to dialogue, common mission, worship and fellowship with evangelical Catholics than many other of their fellow evangelicals.

Fourthly are the *moral pragmatists* – those who are happy to adopt a policy of 'co-belligerence' with Roman Catholics on matters of common moral and social interest.[37] This policy seeks to advance Christian values through practical co-operation, whether for example in local community initiatives or anti-abortion campaigns. This position may allow for individual and informal meetings for prayer and fellowship with other believers and 'open and honest' dialogue, but it resists any formal, interchurch associations. These evangelicals remain cautious about actions that suggest theological differences are relatively unimportant in light of common experiences of the Spirit (contra spiritual pragmatists) or that they are close enough to allow common worship services (contra pragmatic ecumenists). The moral pragmatists are located at the more conservative end of the evangelical spectrum.

This summary of various evangelical attitudes to the Catholic Church helps to explain why the issue of 'evangelical Catholics' is such a sensitive one. Those associated with ECI, like Paddy Monaghan, argue for acceptance of evangelical Catholics by their fellow evangelicals saying 'Is it not time for the cold war among evangelical Christians to end?'[38] As we should expect given the discussion above, evangelicals exhibit a range of responses to Monaghan's plea. Trevor Morrow, for example, minister of Lucan Presbyterian Church, is willing to embrace evangelical Catholics arguing that to create extra requirements for believers – such as leaving the Catholic Church – is to add to the gospel itself and depart from the great Reformation doctrine of justification by faith.[39] While not wishing to deny the authenticity of any individual's faith, others dissent from this position, deeply uncomfortable with ECI's apparent attempts to conflate evangelical truth within official Roman Catholic teaching despite substantial and unresolved differences between Catholic and evangelical theology. Even evangelical organisations open to dialogue and building constructive relationships between

The former Methodist Church enjoys a central location at the Mall, Castlebar, Co Mayo. This historic building is still used for worship by Castlebar Christian Fellowship

A section of the congregation at a rural evangelistic
Outdoor Service

Evangelical enthusiast Alfred Styles
of the Dublin Central Mission of the Methodist Church

George and Gwen Pierce
Serving with the Pwo Karen
in Thailand

Forward movement – moving the church up the road! Ireland's unique Churchmobile was a familiar sight for twelve years mainly on the roads of Kildare, Wicklow, Wexford, Carlow and N. Tipperary. Built in Dublin in 1972 it seated 30-40 people, had its own folding spire, bell and collapsible pulpit.

Ballyfermot Community Church, opened in 2002, is part of the Elim Pentecostal church network.

Bishop Ken Clarke with his wife Helen

Irish Evangelical ministers at Cork conference, L to R: Ferran Glenfield (Rector, Kill o' the Grange, Dublin), John Faris (Presbyterian Church, Cork), Sean Mullan (Dublin West Church), Paul Kingston (Retired Methodist minister).

Deep in conversation after the Presidential inauguration at Dublin
Castle: Ms Mary Banotti, Dr John Alderdice, Rev Frank Sellar
(Adelaide Road Presbyterian Church).

Rev Warren Nelson
who led the work of
the Bible School at
Coalbrook, near
Thurles, Co
Tipperary, until it
merged to become
the Irish Bible
Institute.

The Dublin YMCA Male Voice Choir visited churches, halls and out-door services all over Ireland in the second half of the 20th century.

The Metropolitan Hall in Lower Abbey Street attracted large congregations to interdenominational evangelical meetings. The Sunday evening '8:30' was a popular meeting place for successive generations of young people and married couples.

Kilkenny farmer George Harper in traditional mode. He lived out his faith in a strongly rural setting.

Powerscourt, Co Wicklow. In the 1820s Theodosia, Lady Powerscourt hosted the great prophetic conferences from which developed the Christian Brethren movement. *Photo: Fergus Ryan*

The Evangelical Alliance's Theological Task Group in 2004. L to R: Ken Wilson (Methodist Church, Bray), Fergus Ryan (Trinity Church Network), Patrick Mitchel (Irish Bible Institute), Sandra Tutty (St Mark's Family Worship Centre), George Morrison (Grace Bible Fellowship), John Samuel (Grosvenor Baptist Church), Stephen Johnston (Carlow Presbyterian Church), Bob Mihuc (Christian Training Centre, Greystones), Suzanne Cousins (Grosvenor Baptist Church), Margaret Childs (Christian Brethren, Limerick).

Trinity Church, Gardiner Street, Dublin. It was opened in 1839 providing space for the crowds who attended the preaching services of Rev John Gregg. The building was closed as a place of worship in 1909 and became a Labour Exchange. Services will be held again in this large edifice when the Trinity Church Network occupies it in 2004.
Photo: Fergus Ryan

Catholics and evangelicals conclude their analysis of the theology of ECI by describing it as 'incoherent, eclectic and confused.'[40] The reasons given for this conclusion are that, even while the genuineness of their Christian faith is not in question and while ECI affirmations may be recognisably Evangelical in tone, they are held in tandem with other beliefs that 'are incompatible with evangelical conviction'. Furthermore, Thomson argues that Evangelicalism only has meaning within a fundamental theological and confessional core. If this core is abandoned, Evangelicalism is reduced to meaninglessness. If it is maintained then 'we have to say that "evangelical Catholics" are not evangelicals.'[41] This conclusion is tempered by a willingness to 'enter into a constructive debate' with evangelical Catholics on how to work together, 'not on the basis of a shared evangelical identity but on a shared Christian faith.'[42]

Neither the reality of the phenomenon of evangelical Catholics nor the sharply differing evangelical responses elicited by their presence are likely to disappear.[43] The very presence of evangelical Catholics – including it seems perhaps President Mary McAleese[44] – reflects something of the small but increasing influence of Evangelicalism in Ireland. It also highlights the movement's propensity for untidiness and loose ends. Some evangelicals can live with this reality; others are deeply troubled by it, interpreting it as a sign of theological drift and impending fragmentation. It would be tragically ironic if this aspect of Irish Evangelicalism's modest recent advance had the indirect consequence of provoking serious evangelical division.

In the end – a call to maturity
Faced with this spectrum of evangelical identity, an unprepared Irish observer, used to the ubiquitous presence of, until relatively recently, what was regarded as the 'one true church', may be tempted to conclude that the world of Irish Evangelicalism is hopelessly divided and too complex to understand. This would be a shame. Rather, its diversity is at once the movement's great strength and yet also its Achilles heel. It is a strength because

such a spectrum speaks of continual reformation, open discussion, flexibility, and innate wariness of institutional power structures such as those that have so disfigured Irish Catholicism. At their best, Evangelicals continue to search for spiritual authenticity and renewal, at both an individual and corporate level as they seek to live lives of faithful discipleship to Jesus Christ. In this light, evangelical diversity is a sign of vibrancy and life. Differing conclusions among Evangelicals of how best to understand the Bible hermeneutically (how its meaning can be applied today) reflect what is often a healthy debate. It represents the democratic impulse flowing from the doctrine of the 'priesthood of all believers' whereby each Christian has direct access to the Father through faith in Christ without the need of any institutional mediator. Hierarchical authoritarianism, while regrettably far from absent within Irish evangelical circles, is an outlook at odds with a faith that stresses the need for a personal faith in God and the need for believers to understand the Scriptures for themselves. Many Irish Evangelicals, having grown up within an Irish Catholic Church at the height of its power, find a liberating freedom in the informal openness of evangelical communities.

Yet the movement's diversity is simultaneously its greatest weakness. Evangelicals have a habit of disagreeing badly. After over sixty years of Christian service, John Stott continues 'to be profoundly grieved by our evangelical tendency to fragment.'[45] Developing an ability to live with difference, or disagree well, is one of the key challenges facing the fledgling Irish movement and one in which it does not have a good track record thus far. What I mean by this is that it is crucial to 'pick fights' on issues that really matter, and not, as is often the case, on secondary issues that only address issues internal to Evangelicalism but otherwise are relatively marginal. For Irish Evangelicals, in other words, what is needed is a *maturity* to discern what is a topic on which the truth of the gospel turns and what is an issue of secondary importance. Maintaining a united front by holding firmly on to the centrality of the gospel is, I would suggest, a crucial priority in an increasingly pluralistic and aggressively secular Irish culture.

Let me conclude with some thoughts on 'diversity in unity'. A challenge for Irish evangelicals is not only to learn to accept difference, but to be open to be enriched through potentially threatening debate. Emotions can run high. Different people will bring different experiences and attitudes to the questions at stake. However, the uncomfortable reality is that equally committed, godly, scholarly evangelical Christians will come to well supported but diametrically opposing perspectives on a whole range of subjects. The discussion can be healthy if participants can engage with alternative views while maintaining respect for those holding them. In other words, can Evangelicals who are passionate about truth, learn to disagree in love and not to attack their fellow Christian's integrity or question their salvation? At a community level, evangelical diversity also poses searching questions. How can churches that follow one practice on a secondary issue still co-operate with and support other churches following a different path? It is not constructive or accurate for one side to claim its view is the only truly biblical one if Scripture is obviously not monochrome. Secondary issues need to be kept in their proper place. Maintaining a right perspective will mean that words such as the following are kept constantly to the fore whatever happens to be the hot issue of the day: 'Equally loving, godly, and thoughtful Christians can work together in either model and testify that the centrality of Scripture has been upheld in the context of humble service carried out for our Lord.'[46] Or as the Puritan Richard Baxter wisely cited long ago:

Unity in essentials,
Liberty in non-essentials,
Charity in all things.

Appendix 1

Evangelical Alliance Basis of Faith 2004

Evangelicals are Christians who accept the revelation of the triune God given in the Scriptures and confess the historic faith of the gospel that they declare. They here assert beliefs that they regard as crucial to the understanding of the faith, and which should issue in mutual love, practical Christian service and evangelistic concern.

We believe in:

1) God
The only true God, holy, loving and glorious, who exists eternally in three persons, Father, Son and Holy Spirit. The sovereignty and grace of God in creation, providence, revelation, redemption and final judgement.

2) Scripture
The divine inspiration of the Scriptures of the Old and New Testaments and their consequent entire trustworthiness and supreme authority in all matters of belief and behaviour.

3) Human dignity
The dignity and equality of all people, created in God's image to live in love and holiness.

4) Human condition
The universal sinfulness, guilt and lostness of all people as a result of the Fall, making them subject to God's wrath and condemnation.

5) Jesus Christ: His person and work
Jesus Christ, fully God and fully man, born of the virgin Mary; his sinless life, his substitutionary atoning death on the cross, his bodily resurrection, his ascension into heaven, his victorious reign and future return. He is the only mediator, and his sacrificial death the sole and all-sufficient ground of redemption from the guilt and power of sin and from its eternal consequences. By the grace of God alone through faith in Christ sinners are justified and receive the gift of eternal life.

6) The Holy Spirit
The illuminating, regenerating, indwelling, empowering and sanctifying work of God the Holy Spirit.

7) The Church
The universal church of which Christ is the Head, expressed in local congregations of believers and committed to the proclamation and demonstration of the gospel throughout the world. The priesthood of all believers and the divine institution of Baptism and the Lord's Supper.

8) Future Hope
The personal, visible and victorious return of the Lord Jesus Christ in power and glory to establish fully his universal reign. His final judgement of all people with justice, bringing those who have rejected him to eternal punishment and believers to eternal life.

To God be praise for ever
Moladh go deo le Dia

Bibliography

Bloesch, Donald G., *Essentials of Evangelical Theology Volume One: God, Authority, and Salvation,* (Peabody, MA: Prince Press, 2001 2nd Edn.)

Bloesch, Donald G., *The Future of Evangelical Christianity: A Call for Unity Amid Diversity* (New York: Doubleday, 1983)

Blomberg, Craig and Beck, James (eds.), *Two Views on Women in Ministry* (Grand Rapids, MI: Zondervan, 2001)

Calver, Clive and Warner, Rob, *Together We Stand: Evangelical Convictions, Unity and Vision* (London, Hodder and Stoughton, 1996)

Evangelical Catholic Initiative, *What is an Evangelical Catholic?* (1988)

Evangelicals and Catholics Together in Ireland (n.p., n.p., n.d.)

Flanagan, Declan, *What is an Evangelical Catholic?: A Response by Declan Flanagan* (Salt & Light Publications: Dublin, 1991)

Grenz, Stanley J., *Revisioning Evangelical Theology: A Fresh Agenda for the 21st Century,* (Downers Grove IL: Inter Varsity Press, 2003)

Inglis, Tom, *Moral Monopoly: The Rise and Fall of the Catholic Church in Modern Ireland,* 2nd edn. (Dublin: University College Dublin Press, 1998)

Johnstone, Patrick, *Operation World* (Carlisle: OM Publishing, 1993)

Johnstone, Patrick and Mandryk, Jason, *Operation World: 21st Century Edition* (Carlisle: Paternoster, 2001)

Jordan, Glenn, *Not of This World?: Evangelical Protestants in Northern Ireland* (Belfast: Blackstaff and the Centre for Contemporary Christianity in Ireland, 2001)

Liechty, Joe, *Roots of Sectarianism: Chronology and Reflections* (Belfast: The Irish Inter-Church Meeting, 1993)

McGrath, Alister, *A Passion for Truth: The Intellectual Coherence of Evangelicalism* (Leicester: Apollos, 1996)

Mitchel, P, *Evangelicalism and National Identity in Ulster 1921-1998* (Oxford: Oxford University Press, 2003)

Monaghan, Paddy, 'What is an Evangelical Catholic?', *Lion & Lamb*, 14, Special Issue, Autumn 1997, 11-14

Monaghan, Paddy and Boyle, Eugene, 'Catholic evangelicals look for-ward with confidence: an open letter to Protestant Christians in Ulster', *Belfast Telegraph*, 20 September 1994.

Monaghan, Paddy and Boyle, Eugene (eds.), *Adventures in Reconciliation: Twenty-Nine Catholic Testimonies,* (Guildford: Eagle, 1998).

Morrow, Trevor W. J., 'Adventures in Reconciliation', *Christian Irishman* (July / August 1998)

Packer, J. I., *'Fundamentalism' and the Word of God* (London: Inter-Varsity Fellowship, 1958)

Packer, J. I., 'A Path Through the Jungle' in *Frontiers*, 3 / 3 (Spring 1999)

Ryan, Fergus, '"12c": A History of Abbey Street Chapel and its Congregation' in *Irish Bible School Journal* (1999)

Smith, David, *Mission After Christendom* (London: Darton, Longman and Todd, 2003)

Stott, John W. R., *Christ the Controversialist* (London: Tyndale, 1970)

Stott, John W. R., *Evangelical Truth* (Leicester: Inter-Varsity Press, 1999)

Thomson, Alwyn, *Beyond Fear, Suspicion and Hostility: Evangelical - Roman Catholic Relationships* (Belfast: ECONI, 1994)

Thomson, Alwyn, 'A World of Difference: The Evangelicals of ECONI', *Lion and Lamb*, Special Issue, No. 14, Autumn 1997

Tierney, Martin, *The New Elect: The Church and New Religious Groups,* (Dublin: Veritas, 1985)

Tidball, Derek, *Who Are the Evangelicals?,* (London: Marshall Pickering, 1994)

Western Bishops' Lenten Pastoral 1983, 'Renewing our faith in the Church'

Notes:
1. Derek Tidball, *Who Are the Evangelicals?,* (London: Marshall Pickering, 1994) p 12.
2. Out of the necessity to limit discussion, the focus of this chapter is evangelicals in the Republic of Ireland. For an excellent introduction to the world of Northern Irish evangelicalism see Glenn Jordan, *Not of This World?: Evangelical Protestants in Northern Ireland* (Belfast: Blackstaff and the Centre for Contemporary Christianity in Ireland, 2001). For a nar-rower political focus see my book, P. Mitchel, *Evangelicalism and National Identity in Ulster 1921-1998* (Oxford: Oxford University Press, 2003).

3. Alister McGrath, *A Passion for Truth: The Intellectual Coherence of Evangelicalism* (Leicester: Apollos, 1996) p. 22.

4. EAI was formally launched on 8 May 2004.

5. See Appendix 1 for the text of the EAI Basis of Faith (EAI-2004). Producing bases of faith is a longstanding evangelical tradition. In part 'identity markers' and in part defending against error, their primary function is to provide an agreed theological foundation by which to maximise evangelical unity.

6. Donald G. Bloesch, *Essentials of Evangelical Theology Volume One: God, Authority, and Salvation* (Peabody, MA: Prince Press, 2001 2nd Edn.) p 8.

7. Donald G. Bloesch, *The Future of Evangelical Christianity: A Call for Unity Amid Diversity* (New York: Doubleday, 1983) p 16.

8. Stanley J. Grenz, *Revisioning Evangelical Theology: A Fresh Agenda for the 21st Century* (Downers Grove IL: Inter Varsity Press, 2003) p 34.

9. John Stott, *Evangelical Truth* (Leicester: Inter-Varsity Press, 1999) p 141.

10. The list of issues listed within this circle is adapted from EAI-2004.

11. J. R. W. Stott, *Christ the Controversialist* (London: Tyndale, 1970) p 13.

12. J. I. Packer, *'Fundamentalism' and the Word of God* (London: Inter-Varsity Fellowship, 1958) p 38.

13. Adapted to an Irish context from Clive Calver and Rob Warner, *Together We Stand: Evangelical Convictions, Unity and Vision* (London, Hodder and Stoughton, 1996).

14. ICTHUS is a charismatic fellowship in London that emerged out of denominational evangelicalism. It later developed into a network of like-minded fellowships.

15. David Smith records how the extraordinary growth of South American Pentecostalism is confounding expectations of Western secularisation theorists. One writes that the conversion of 40 million Latin Americans to 'a genuinely indigenous version of Pentecostal and evangelical faith' is an event of epochal significance which exposes the inadequacy of the paradigms governing the study and teaching of the sociology of religion. David Smith, *Mission After Christendom* (London: Darton, Longman and Todd, 2003) p 120.

16. For further discussion of the history of the Baptists in Dublin see Fergus Ryan, '"12c": A History of Abbey Street Chapel and its Congregation' in *Irish Bible School Journal* (1999) pp 3-8.

17. See for example the appearance of Dublin West Community Church on RTÉ's *Morning Service*, 11 January 2004.

18. Paddy Monaghan and Eugene Boyle (eds.), *Adventures in Reconciliation: Twenty-Nine Catholic Testimonies*, (Guildford: Eagle, 1998).

19. Paddy Monaghan, 'What is an Evangelical Catholic?', *Lion & Lamb*, 14, Special Issue, Autumn 1997, 11-14, see p 11.

20. Monaghan cites figures listed in the 1993 edition of *Operation World*, a handbook of worldwide facts and figures produced by an evangelical

mission organisation called Operation Mobilisation. The 2001 edition of the handbook lists 125,000 evangelicals from all backgrounds as well as some 246,000 charismatic Christians. Yet rather confusingly it also states that evangelicals from Pentecostal, independent and Protestant churches number about 1.6% of the population, the lowest percentage of any country in the English-speaking world. See entry for 'Ireland' in Patrick Johnstone, *Operation World* (Carlisle: OM Publishing, 1993) and Patrick Johnstone and Jason Mandryk, *Operation World: 21st Century Edition* (Carlisle: Paternoster, 2001).

21. ECI, *What is an Evangelical Catholic?*, p. 2.

22. These admittedly approximate figures include both independent evangelical churches and individual denominational churches with an evangelical ethos.

23. For a careful evangelical response to the ECI document see *What is an Evangelical Catholic?: A Response by Declan Flanagan* (Salt & Light Publications: Dublin, 1991). Flanagan was then Pastor of Grosvenor Road Baptist Church, Dublin.

24. Warner and Calver, *Together We Stand*, p 64.

25. For example, in 2004 a number of independent churches, meeting in a denominational church to promote 'church unity' in an area of Dublin, managed to omit to invite any denominational churches – including the one in which the service was being held!

26. See Joe Liechty, *Roots of Sectarianism: Chronology and Reflections* (Belfast: The Irish Inter-Church Meeting, 1993).

27. Tidball, *Who are the Evangelicals?*, p 73.

28. J. I. Packer, *Keep in Step with the Spirit* (Leicester: Inter-Varsity Press, 1977).

29. Calver and Warner, *Together We Stand*, p 67.

30. Ibid., p 68.

31. What follows is adapted from A. Thomson, *Beyond Fear, Suspicion and Hostility: Evangelical-Roman Catholic Relationships* (Belfast: ECONI, 1994).

32. Tom Inglis, *Moral Monopoly: The Rise and Fall of the Catholic Church in Modern Ireland*, 2nd edn. (Dublin: University College Dublin Press, 1998).

33. See chapter 5 'A Catalogue of Cults' in Martin Tierney, *The New Elect: The Church and New Religious Groups*, (Dublin: Veritas, 1985).

34. Another case to hit the media was in 1983 when a bookshop in Athlone run by Elim Pentecostals was picketed by people from Charlestown after the parents of a local girl called Emer Kennedy had claimed that she had been 'abducted' by the church.

35. Western Bishops' Lenten Pastoral 1983, 'Renewing our faith in the Church.'

36. For an excellent exploration of Irish media attitudes to evangelicals in this period see Alison Cook, 'News Coverage of Irish Evangelism, 1978-1991: A Case Study of Ideology in the Media', unpublished thesis.

37. The term 'co-belligerence' was first adopted by evangelical writer and thinker Francis Schaeffer.

38. Monaghan, 'What is an Evangelical Catholic?', p 14.

39. T. W. J. Morrow, 'Adventures in Reconciliation', *Christian Irishman* (July/August 1998) pp 6-7.

40. A. Thomson, 'A World of Difference: The Evangelicals of ECONI', *Lion and Lamb*, Special Issue, No. 14, Autumn 1997, p 9. ECONI stands for Evangelical Contribution on Northern Ireland, an organisation committed to peacemaking and reconciliation.

41. Thomson, 'A World of Difference', p 10.

42. Ibid., p 10.

43. Indeed the whole question was re-ignited with the publication of *Evangelicals and Catholics Together in Ireland* (ECTI) and J. I. Packer's visit to Dublin on 31 July 1998 to coincide with the launch of the booklet. Packer had been involved in the highly contentious American evangelicals and Catholics Together (ECT) initiative which he describes as a venture bringing together Protestant evangelicals and Roman Catholic evangelicals committed to a dual mission of evangelism and social witness. For further reference see J. I. Packer, 'A Path Through the Jungle' in Frontiers, 3/3 (Spring 1999) pp 3-5 and other related articles in the same issue. See also *Evangelicals and Catholics Together in Ireland*.

44. See for example 'Catholic evangelicals look forward with confidence: an open letter to Protestant Christians in Ulster', written by Paddy Monaghan and Eugene Boyle and signed by (among others) Mary McAleese, *Belfast Telegraph*, 20 September, 1994.

45. Stott, *Evangelical Truth*, p 9.

46. A conclusion on dealing with differing evangelical views of women in ministry. See Craig Blomberg and James Beck (eds.), *Two Views on Women in Ministry* (Grand Rapids, MI: Zondervan, 2001).

CHAPTER 9

Evangelical Experience
and the Potential for Human Growth

Tony Walsh

The Christian message is concerned with the promotion and nurturing of human potential in its widest sense. This is increasingly acknowledged within Irish evangelical Christianity and is evidenced in a new engagement with life, with culture and indeed with how it is beginning to view itself. Perhaps this is a reflection of the increasingly multi-cultural and post modern nature of Irish society, whose new found confidence values the expression of a wider range of views and realities than ever before. Such a change has allowed the emergence of many alternative discourses from their previous states of embattled defensiveness. Perhaps the evolving nature of Evangelicalism is something that has been waiting to happen; something that needed time for an evolved confidence to emerge.

In tandem with these developments it has been fascinating and enriching to watch the wide range of people from all sorts of backgrounds who now identify themselves as 'evangelical'. This was not always so in the past; in fact as a child I remember playing a game that consisted of identifying the Evangelicals on Sundays at Dublin suburban bus stops; it seemed at the time that this was easily done; there was a common sense of rather tight lipped and well-scrubbed sobriety, a determined sense of other-worldness and non-engagement with their fellow travellers. This has changed radically. In more recent years, as a practising psychotherapist I've been fascinated with what appears to be a growing number of Evangelicals who choose to participate in therapeutic conversations. To me this doesn't mean that a disproportionate percentage of the grouping are needy or unbalanced, rather it indicates a commitment to self understanding and a recognition of areas or aspects of life that need attention. The juxtaposition of these reflections has led me to wonder increasingly about the relationship between evangelical spirituality and emotional health, and more particularly to reflect on what in the evangelical experience may be promoting human growth and development.

Traditionally evangelical Christianity and psychotherapy have tended to see each other as poles apart; in fact there has been only very limited converse between the two. The core message of the Christian gospel is about the development of human growth and potential. So is the core message of psychotherapy. The musings in this chapter, while far from comprehensive, are reflections on the common task of both and a challenge to evangelical believers to respond to what is core both to their motivation and often their practice. These thoughts are drawn from a number of sources – personal reflection, dialogue with colleagues and from my own relationship with evangelical spirituality. However, by far the most significant influences are conversations with clients who have shared their insights on many areas of life including spirituality. Such conversations seem deeply privileged spaces, as fellow humans wrestle with the business of making sense of life. Or as they try to find ways of coping with crisis, loss, pain and issues of meaning and identity. I have included some brief vignettes, suitably altered to preserve anonymity. These conversations frequently resonate with one's own processes and dilemmas; they are after all part of the inescapable reality of life.

At the outset it must be said that evangelical Christianity does not generally receive a good press in orthodox psychological circles. The stereotype of closed-minded, inward looking groups, investing in a black and white range of limited realities is common. Evangelicals are perceived as reacting negatively towards, among others, scientific enquiry, women clergy, gay relationships and liberal theology. They are hence and quite understandably dismissed, being seen as having little, if anything, to say that is of significance in the area of psychological health.

In fact the movement in all its forms has frequently been seen as psychologically unhealthy, tending to nurture neurosis, denial and escapism. Sadly, such characterisations are not always invalid. However I would like to suggest that such understandings of evangelicalism at the beginning of the twenty-first century are limited, accruing from an incomplete or at times a fundamentally flawed analysis. Perhaps they always have been so. On the contrary a healthy evangelical Christianity has the potential to offer both a framework of meaning and a range of structures that constitute life-enhancing and useful frameworks for human growth and development.

Evangelicalism not Fundamentalism

Part of the main traditional difficulty in exploring evangelicalism and one which has led to a range of misunderstandings has been a tendency to confuse it with fundamentalism; evangelicals have sometimes compounded this difficulty by themselves equating definitive belief structure with fundamentalism. Desiring to adhere to the 'fundamentals' of Scripture, they have sometimes accepted the title 'fundamentalist' uncritically. At other times the fear of not identifying a truly biblical faith has led some to flirt with, if not to embrace, a full orbed fundamentalism. But Evangelicalism and fundamentalism are not indistinguishable. Some Evangelicals are fundamentalists, others are not; likewise some Catholics, Hindus, Muslims and even Buddhists are also fundamentalists, others are not. There is little in any variety of fundamentalism that is nurturing of emotional maturity, of tolerance or of richness and variety. Many evangelicals, while having a clear belief structure, are not fundamentalists. Such distinguished thinkers as John Stott and Miroslav Volf differentiate clearly between Evangelicalism and fundamentalism, seeing the latter as militantly exclusivist. Martin E. Marty further defines this when he suggests that the difference is primarily one where fundamentalism is essentially oppositional by nature. Glen Jordan in his recent work on Evangelicalism in Northern Ireland also makes a clear distinction between the two, defining evangelical Christianity as the attempt ' to live in the world in the light of the Bible, recognising that one is not in possession of the whole truth.' In this definition there is real conviction and commitment coupled with a sense of provisionality and openness to change, growth and possibility that is missing in traditional fundamentalism. To seek a truly biblical model of belief and lifestyle it is not necessary to be fundamentalist. As much of the movement within Ireland increasingly grapples with this challenge, the ability to critically asses its own way of being, its own structures and its own 'sacred cows' is creating new possibilities. Frequently in the past discussion with Evangelicals or any exploration of their particular emphases has become bogged down in a contentious review of belief and dogma; this is regrettable in that it has disallowed the recognition of the richness of spiritual experience and practice which is at its centre. Evangelicalism embodies far more richness than its doctrinal positionings. However, a preoccupation with dogma has tended to both dominate the scene and simultaneously discourage an exploration of the lived experience which lies behind it. The manner in which these discussions have been carried out has tended to communicate a very frosty and contentious image. Its reluctance, or at times outright refusal to enter dialogue, its preoccupation with doctrinal pedigree, has conveyed a sense of tightness and exclusivity which is far from the warmth of the spiritual experience that it avows and which is so often central to the life of its members.

In this reflection I want to distinguish between the dogma and that experiential core and to focus on what may be called evangelical spirituality and experience. It seems it is at this 'heart' place that Evangelicalism has so much to offer which is nurturing of growth and development; it is also this emphasis which distinguishes Evangelicalism from other religious movements.

Encountering the Heart

John Wesley spoke of his 'heart being strangely warmed' as the initiation of his spiritual journey. Personal testimony has always been central to Evangelicalism: the story of the changed heart gives both meaning and structure to life. At the very core of evangelical belief and practice is that moment of personal conversion, where the individual first enters into relationship with the divine, where the heart knows itself to be touched, enfolded by the love of that Great Heart. This experience is radical, transformative and profound, where the 'I' enters into a personal encounter with 'the eternal Thou'. As Martin Buber puts it, '...all superstitions about God, all talk about him, all theology is sacrificed to the voice that speaks...' The power of this moment is between God and the individual. There is a yielding of self, of will, to the greater reality. This experience is not foreign to the mystical traditions within Christianity; it is just understood somewhat differently there and is more rareified and less common, but available to all.

Within evangelical thought the emphasis on the personal nature of Christian initiation identifies agency as resting with the individual and this has a number of implications. In emphasising heart encounter it relocates emphasis and agency from the externals of church structure, meditative technique, rite or human agent, it centres it instead in the individual's heart engagement that gives meaning to life. The theme of heart health and heart focus as central to human wellbeing has become a pre-occupation of psychotherapy in recent years. James Welwood speaks of 'the healing relationship as an intimate encounter that can awaken the heart'. The heart is traditionally seen as being at our centre; its health a measure of our overall health. Themes such as heart, spirit and soul are now common currency in on-going training workshops for therapists as well as in workshop presentations geared for a wide range of client groupings. Of course they mean something different here than in traditional evangelicalism; or perhaps they don't. Re-kindling the heart energy and focus has become a central core of much of what is central to both spiritual and therapeutic endeavour.

The related development of a meaning-making framework through which to make sense of the vagaries and vicissitudes of life has been a constant theme in many schools of therapy, most particularly among the existentialists. This preoccupation can be seen as related to the need for a centre or value system by which to live, and by which to organise and give a structure to the complexities of life. In the Western world the dramatic decline in the influence of the historic denominations and the continued growth of a nakedly consumerist philosophy has left a vacuum in society. This has created a sense of existential meaninglessness and ideological emptiness in the experience of many. In responding to this vacuum psychotherapy has become increasingly aware of the importance of finding ways of acknowledging the transcendental or mystical in human experience. Evangelical belief honours the experience of heart as central to this. The moment of divine connection with the human heart is core; here we find meaning, confirmation and identity. In this endeavour perhaps both Evangelicalism and therapy are not so far apart; perhaps both are struggling to name a need that is central to the human condition.

The Search for Identity

Both modern and postmodern analyses of society point to the confusion that lies at the core of human processes of self identification. In traditional societies the defining of individual identity is based on relationship with others. There are a finite and clear number of relational possibilities available within the tribe, family or community. A modern analysis suggests that today's societies offer a vastly expanded and deeply confusing array of possible roles; and a modernist sociological analysis questions whether the idea of a real self is useful or valid at all. Postmodernism celebrates disintegration, seeing the experience of self as without substances and exchanging this for an array of lifestyle possibilities and choices with an overriding emphasis on appearance and style. These theoretical frameworks in many ways echo the symptomatic confusion that many of us experience as part of the clamour of today's life; nothing is simple; who, what and indeed if we are, is open to questioning. Hence identity becomes an 'issue', a site of confusion and contention. The message that is at the core of Evangelicalism does not negate the theoretical analyses that are part of our society, and are perhaps a reflection of its dilemmas. However, a spirituality which confirms the centrality of an experience of self acts as a sheet anchor from which to explore and negotiate swiftly flowing and complex waters.

Derek, at thirty-five had been twice married, had had countless relationships and an exciting and insecure career in the world of computer technology. The level of his depression was alarmingly profound as he questioned everything: his life, his values, his ability to relate, his sexuality. He felt lost and frightened, 'a form of self without a core,' as he described himself. It would be trite and disrespectful to suggest that a moment of spiritual encounter completely changed all this; it did not. However what it did provide were moments of secure personal identity and restfulness that constituted stepping stones from which to explore the dilemmas of his life. The beginnings of a healing process. This emphasis on individual encounter with God, of God consciousness, is all the more significant within evangelical reality as it is an experience that believers are encouraged to attend to and nurture throughout their lives. It is a relationship based on an experience of the deep and profound and unqualified love of the divine for the individual and a growing openness and responsiveness to being unconditionally accepted. For generations psychotherapists of many schools have re-iterated the conviction that the core experience of unqualified love is the deeply significant *sine qua non* for any human to achieve their potential.

This emphasis on the individual recognises the inherent difference of each individual, a difference that will be expressed in the need for varying contexts of spiritual expression. Diversity is also central to evangelical Christianity, its inbuilt tendency towards limited formality and its relative lack of formal structure allows it to provide such diversity. This variety is expressed in different forms of church organisation and structure and in varying shades or emphases of belief and practice. There are evangelical denominations, or denominations where the majority view is evangelical and many where there is an evangelical minority; there are also many independent or loosely linked groupings of congregations, fellowships and house churches. This range, while acknowledging a basic central core of evangelical belief, also in reality celebrates a breadth of emotional and spiritual expression that implicitly acknowledges human difference. People vary in so many ways and this requires a variety of spiritual expression and practice. Personality also changes and evolves over the human development life cycle; what fits for me as a teenager, a young adult, will not necessarily meet my need in mid-life or in old age. In a recent book of devotions Sam Portaro challenges the Anglican Communion to forget its preoccupation with unity and uniformity and to celebrate instead the challenge of diversity. In that diversity Christ ministers to a diverse range of human need and experience. This unity and diversity, while at times confusing to outsiders, is one of the prime strengths of the evangelical movement. Such diversity is particularly evidenced within worship. This is in marked historic contrast to the majority denominations in Ireland who have tended to emphasise ritual, set liturgy and uniformity of pattern. While this is meaningful for some, many find the accessibility and variety of evangelical worship with its choice and alternative forms deeply appealing. 'I love the quiet simplicity of the morning meeting; we sit in silence around that very ordinary table with its loaf of bread and its glass of wine. Often few people speak or prayer audibly, but everyone is free to do so if they feel led; there's a great sense of equality, of spontaneity. God's presence is so real and there are no frills or complexities to distract you. But I sometimes like to go to one of the newer churches where there's the dramatic life and energy of worship bands and praise groups with lots of noise and enthusiasm. Both experiences nurture and ground me at different times. Meeting with God is what's important in either place.'

Francine, a young woman working through the experience of sexual abuse, gives a vivid picture of the contrast between the communion service at the small Brethren Assembly where she has found spiritual meaning and her periodic attendance at worship in a lively Pentecostal church in Dublin. Mark, whose early childhood and adolescence were chaotic finds on the other hand the more formal structure of a Presbyterian service, with its emphasis on doctrinal teaching, more emotionally appealing: 'The structure and predictability give me a sense of safety and orderedness; I know that this says more about me than anything else.' Both Francine and Mark illustrate how the diversity of evangelical worship facilitates the meeting of very different personality needs while acknowledging a core experience of spiritual unity.

The challenge of connection
While the nurturing of a sense of individuality is central to human wellbeing, identity is forged in the experience of connection with significant others. Counselling and psychotherapy are primarily concerned with the holistic development of individuals and indeed with the emergence of societal substructures which nurture such possibilities. While varying theoretical schools will tend to emphasise slightly differing priorities, common themes do emerge. Traditionally psychotherapy and counselling activities have been preoccupied with identity formation, and with the integration of life's experience in a healthful way within the boundary of that identity. This implies the development of a sense of individuality that is secure and distinct enough to maintain its coherence and independence while simultaneously permeable and elastic enough to cope with change, trauma, ambivalence and dependence. Certain conditions are seen as helpful in order to achieve this. Paramount among these are a range of trusting relationships in which an individual can feel supported, validated and cared for; the person centred approaches to counselling are particularly concerned to emphasise this need. It is also important that such relationships provide a

context in which the individual can challenge and be challenged and learn to cope successfully with a range of divergent personalities and roles. The knowledge of support and acceptance from others and the availability of a range of safe places in which to explore and process the difficulties and traumas of life and in which to experience challenge and validation are central for growth and stability.

Connection with others has also been a central component of evangelical emphasis; it is expressed historically in the class meeting of early Methodism, the cell groups of today's 'new churches', and the various meetings for fellowship, Bible study and prayer which are part of the life of any evangelical church. At best in these there is an emphasis on nurturing growth, in the development of deep relationship and in expressing care and support. The evangelical understanding of church values the idea of the local church or assembly of believers rather than that of denomination or organisational network. While this is not universally unproblematic it avoids both the distancing and anonymity of traditional denominational structures. It promotes notions of communal responsibility and militates against institutional power abuse and the dangers of bureaucratisation. It is in the local body of believers that the individual and the group work out the implications of their spiritual commitment. It is assumed that people need each other and a healthy interdependence is nurtured. Spiritual or psychological growth is perceived to be dependent on the existence of warm and accepting human relationships which both nurture, but also challenge and stretch. In evangelical theory and practice this local group is charged with the recognition, development and nurture of the unique talents and gifts of each member. Thus the Apostle Paul's powerful metaphor of the local group of believers as a physical body, where no one part can work without the other, and where the whole is dependent on the working of the subparts for its functioning. Each member is hence accountable to the wider group as well as the group being accountable to the individual members. In the tension between individual and communal life that evangelical Christians are increasingly allowing themselves to stretch and be stretched, to challenge and be challenged. In their local church cell group where a deeply trusting bond has been formed between members, Martina and David are being supported in a process that gently but firmly confronts certain behaviours and ways of thinking that have previously marred their relationships with significant others. While all sorts of dangers can exist in such practices, when such a context is carefully and respectfully managed the warm and yet challenging atmosphere of such a group emulates the positives of a group therapeutic experience.

Conclusion

Evangelical Christianity is the fastest growing sector of the Christian church both internationally and in an Irish context. It is primarily and essentially a movement which emphasises three realities: the individual, the transcendental and the community. It invites a recursive relationship between the three. The centrality of the transcendental, indeed the necessity of experiencing the transcendental not at a remove but as part of everyday living is seen as an essential part of the full human experience. This emphasises the uniqueness of each individual; their personal responsibility in responding to God and life is expressed through the sense of variety central to evangelical structure, practice and worship. The highlighting of the individual in community invites a process of growth and challenge within the warm and trusting relationship of the local church and its subgroupings. While the transcendent is not controlled or even mediated by the body of believers, this body is the primary context in which the individual is called upon to explore, express and test their faith.

While many practices and emphases exist within Evangelicalism which are particularly attuned to the nurture of human growth and development, some are more strongly embedded within local practice; others tend to be more embryonic or emergent, needing increased emphasis and development. In order to maximise its potential for nurturing human development and human growth Evangelicalism needs to attend to certain issues.

Firstly, it needs to recognise the potential towards promoting human growth and development that exists within many of its core practices. In the past it has tended to focus on sharing particular theological or dogmatic insights. There is also, however, much of profound value in its practices and traditions; these should become the focus of both further development and of its sharing with the wider world

Secondly, evangelical Christianity needs to acknowledge the area of human growth and development as one that is central to its mission; it already does so sporadically and in certain contexts; it needs to do so explicitly and universally. The relative informality of its structures, its inbuilt tradition of being able to hold variety and divergence of practice in creative tension mean that it is particularly well placed to do so. The availability of a comprehensive range of training programmes focusing on the development of wider ranges of worship and worship-leading skills, as well as small group leadership, would be of help to the wider world; it is well placed to facilitate such programmes. To do this it needs to clearly and explicitly acknowledge the unity of purpose that binds Evangelicals together as well as the great gift of variety that is part of their heritage.

Thirdly, the confrontational and often abrasive attitudes that have marked its relationships with other groupings do not serve it well. Neither do they serve the Lord nor the people his church exits to serve. While the movements' preoccupation with doctrinal purity and with the maintenance of biblical standards is important, its way of communicating these has frequently appeared to be informed more by practices redolent of siege mentality and extreme defensiveness rather than care and a willingness to communicate meaningfully and effectively. This mindset and the attitudes that accompany it do not tend to the promotion of growth or health in either the holders of these positions or those among whom they exist. A movement that is locked within an identity pattern formed by threat, insecurity and defensiveness will be unable to reach out to a society that needs its message of spirituality and wholeness; in fact the very nature of its message becomes deeply compromised by such mindsets.

Evangelical Christianity has much to offer that is related to the promotion of health and wholeness; it exists in an Ireland and in a network of communicational relationships that are increasingly willing to listen to its wisdoms. It is part of a society which is increasingly hungry for spiritual experience; it would be tragic if Evangelicalism failed both its Master, itself and that society, by a reluctance to communicate its richness.

CHAPTER 10

All in the Family

This selection of pen portraits identifies and describes the spiritual anchorage of a wide variety of people who, through the centuries have embraced the Christian faith within the fellowship of evangelical experience. They differ widely, socially, politically, intellectually and geographically but find commonality in the way they confessed Christ and served his cause. Some are household names in Irish history, others lived their lives quietly and expected little recognition.

Their stories help to illustrate the broad sweep of evangelical experience and demonstrate its appeal to a wide spectrum of people of all ages and backgrounds.

Robert W. Abbott (1926-2003)

Bob was born in Moate, Co Westmeath in the early years of the Irish State's existence. In his own words it was not a good time to be an economically challenged Protestant. The family had to move when he was a small child as there were few jobs for Protestants and little trade for minority businesses. They eventually settled in Athlone, shortly before his father's untimely death, finding work and accommodation as caretakers of the old garrison church. Unable for financial reasons to attend secondary school, he continued his education at the local technical school; in this tough but fair atmosphere Bob received an introduction to Latin, English literature and critical inquiry which was to remain with him all his life. At seventeen he moved to the Harding Boys' Home, an apprenticeship and a career in engineering, centred in Dublin. While the family were Church of Ireland, they were also regular attenders at meetings in the small Methodist and Baptist churches in the town. It was in the latter contexts that Bob first met Johnny Cochrane, and it was through a conversation with the evangelist that he committed his life to Christ.

These formative experiences of environment, education and spirituality were important elements in forming his personality, his value system and his faith. While never bitter he refused to concur with the comfortable view that everything was rosy for the minority in the early years of the State, and he said so. In his own words: 'Wherever you turned the world seemed to be against us. We simply knew we had to keep our heads down and say nothing.' Over time he came to an absolute conviction regarding the equal right of Protestants to be honoured as completely, if differently Irish, as the majority and in their duty both to commit to the State and to voice their opinions as Irish men and women: 'to tell it like it was'. Early experiences of 'being different' and suffering for that difference, as well as in other ways, gave Bob a commitment to justice and to speaking out, as well as a deep empathy for any who were marginalised or displaced; and his experience of Christ refined and honed this reality. In later life he became deeply committed to working with and for refugee and asylum seeking immigrants to Ireland. For him the Christian message was never to be confined to the sanctuary or divorced from issues of social and political justice. In fact his faith, while motivating him, was never a place of escape; a living relationship with a living Saviour meant allowing oneself to be challenged at every level – intellectually, behaviourally, politically and theologically. This view was nurtured by a year at Cliff College and a short period spent as an evangelist in rural Ireland. He did not believe in easy answers. As an experienced Methodist local preacher his ministry was always practical, challenging and down to earth. To him preaching was about real communication with real people and whether on the street corner, at a fair or at little meetings up country laneways where half a dozen met to pray, was as much a privilege as when speaking to hundreds. He never skipped the difficult or 'awkward' bits of the Bible, believing that God's Word was there to be wrestled with and to challenge us. His prayer life was equally earthed in reality. Bob loved the hymn book, particularly those hymns characterised by clear theology and good poetry: Watts, Wesley and more recently Pratt Green were constant favourites; he loathed shallow sentiment in hymns as everywhere else and often dug out little known hymns with strange metres because they fitted his theme!

He believed above all in seeing the holy in the common; he sometimes said that to him a cup of tea taken with another human was as much a sacramental meal as the Lord's Supper. Bob had a remarkably wide range of interests and was never happier than when sharing these with others. He loved nature, was an erudite conversationalist, a knowledgeable and deeply skilled plantsman, and experimented happily for hours with engines, natural remedies, church account books and latterly with art. His particular *bête noirs* were meaningless shibboleths, croneyism, platitudes and spiritual sentimentalism and he would speak out heatedly against these in the church or outside it. Despite all this or perhaps because of it, Bob had deep friendships with people of all backgrounds throughout the length and breadth of Ireland. His extensive toolbox went everywhere with him and many a stranger stuck on the side of a country road was thankful for his company, skill and ingenuity. In all this Bob was supported by Vera. Together they rejoiced in their four children and later in their grandchildren; together they mourned for Ivan, a preacher like Bob, who died at the age of 32.

Bob Abbott was called home in Raheny Hospice, on 29 April, 2003. He leaves a legacy of faith in action. Like the men of An Blascaod Mór, we may not see the like of him again.

Cecil Frances 'Fanny' Alexander (1818-1895)

Millions know, love and sing words penned by Mrs Alexander (nee Humphreys) but are unaware of her place in the life of the Irish church. Born in Dublin, a teenager in Co Wicklow, a Rector's wife in Tyrone and Donegal and, when her husband became Bishop of Derry, keeper of a large inviting household in the centre of Derry. She was an unlikely evangelical, related to and socialising with 'the rich man in his castle' – her phrase – and she admired aspects of High Church life and the Oxford Movement. But she was a simple believer in the Redeemer and had been deeply influenced by the Powerscourt circle of keen evangelicals and by a Reverend James Smith when she was in Strabane. Her memorial will always be her hymns, of which she wrote dozens; indeed she made hymn singing popular though she neither was a singer nor played any musical instrument. Many of her hymns were written for children and were based on the Apostles' Creed. She managed to package depths of good theology in simple words: 'He died that we might be forgiven' from *There is a green hill* and 'And our eyes at last shall see him / Through his own redeeming love' from *Once in Royal David's city*. From another less well known of her hymns we have 'It was my pride and hardness / That hung Him on the Tree.'

Throughout her life she gave herself to others less fortunate than herself: she started a School for deaf girls in Strabane, she was a tireless visitor among the poor and sick in her husband's parishes and also when he was bishop; her faith worked.

Thomas Barnardo (1845-1905)
'I hope to die as I have lived, in the humble but assured faith of Jesus Christ as my Saviour, my Master and my King.' These words, inscribed on his memorial, sum up the Christian faith of the famous child philantrophist.

He was born in Dame Street, Dublin the fourth of six children born to John and Abigail Barnardo. His mother came from English Quaker stock and his father was a Hamburg-born immigrant of Jewish ancestry.

As a two-year-old child Tom was critically ill. A doctor confirmed that he was dead and a coffin was prepared but he was snatched back from the gates of death and survived. He grew into a precocious child and as a teenager he was influenced by the rationalistic ideas of Voltaire and Tom Paine, declaring himself an agnostic.

During the 1859 Revival period vast crowds attended the

preaching of Henry Grattan Guinness in Dublin's Metropolitan Hall. A number of his brothers and friends were converted and reluctantly Tom agreed to attend evangelistic meetings in the city. His spiritual awakening shook him deeply and in the Pauline tradition he quickly began to spread the faith he had long laboured to destroy. He attached himself to the Brethren meeting in Merrion Hall and after hearing Hudson Taylor in 1866 volunteered for missionary service in China.

He went to London to study medicine in preparation for service in China but was so moved by the destitution and poverty in the East end of the city that he rented a dilapidated donkey shed and opened his first ragged school for the homeless urchins on the streets. In 1870 he founded his first home for boys in Stepney Causeway and put a sign over the door: 'No destitute Child ever refused Admission.' Following his marriage to Syrie Elmslie, seven children were born. Three died in infancy and one daughter, Marjorie, had Down's Syndrome. This influenced him to set up homes for children with physical and learning disabilities.

He maintained a strong connection with leading Evangelicals including Lord Shaftesbury and the noted banker Robert Barclay. With generous donations from wealthy Christians he founded a temperance society, bought a well-known gin shop and converted it into the People's Mission Church and opened the country's first Coffee Palace.

By 1878 fifty orphanages were opened in London; this was followed by a Village Home for girls in Ilford. By the time Barnardo died in 1905 there were nearly 8,000 children in his 96 residential homes, more than 4,000 were boarded out.

This remarkable man, described in his youth as 'hot tempered, self willed and highly imperious' was mellowed by God's grace and carried in his heart a passion for the spiritual and material well-being of needy children. His funeral was attended by thousands and through his visionary labours Barnardos became a household name and still carries on a work of care and compassion for children in Ireland and Britain.

Thomas Berry (1805-1877)

One of the leading evangelists in Victorian Ireland grew up in the quiet Connacht village of Easkey, Co Sligo. He was the son of a school inspector, Denis Berry, who had been appointed by the London Hibernian Society to superintend their schools in Sligo, Mayo and Roscommon. Joining the small congregation in his home village he quickly threw himself into evangelistic activity. He was one of the first agents of the Baptist Irish Society which had been founded in 1814 with the twin purposes of providing schools in rural Ireland and evangelising through Scripture Readers and itinerating preachers.

Berry started his ministry with some trepidation: 'I found myself relieved of all embarrassment whilst I was preaching Christ and him crucified and although I commenced with timidity, I was surprised to find myself filled with greater courage than I expected.'

Setting out into the surrounding countryside he quickly built up an extensive circuit and recorded in his diary: 'On Lord's day prayer meeting at eight, preaching at twelve and at half-past six in this town. I preach alternately on Tuesday, Thursday and Friday at Kiloran, Dinoad, Durish, Clooncurra, Beltra and Drumnagoole.'

Berry trained at the Ballina Baptist Seminary which had as one of its objectives the training of young men to preach in Irish and also to procure some knowledge of the classical languages. His ministry fell into three distinct parts: in north Connacht in Sligo and Mayo, at Abbeyleix in the south Midlands and astride the Shannon at Athlone.

His early ministry brought him to Abbeyleix where he opened eleven preaching stations and personally visited 1,200 families in the area with famine relief. One of his daughters recorded how she remembered her mother 'three days in the week standing for hours at the open window dispensing food to starving crowds that came from every quarter'. He built up a healthy little congregation in spite of opposition from a strong Orange Lodge in the town. But the wholesale emigration after the worst years of the Famine led to the decimation of the church and before moving to Athlone only the pastor and his family were left.

Berry spent his last 25 years in the Midland town, established a circuit of eight preaching stations and built up a substantial evangelistic enterprise. He was also instrumental in fostering the churches in Moate and at Rahue, near Kilbeggan.

Throughout his ministry Berry was something of an innovator, preaching at wakes, keening houses and rural gatherings of every kind. There was a close relationship in many places with the clergy of the Established Church, other Dissenting ministers and where possible, courteous attitudes to Roman Catholic priests.

When he died the shops in the town closed as a mark of respect. His funeral to Cornamagh cemetery was attended by 'a great company of the townsfolk, leading tradesmen and ministers of all denominations'.

Robert Andrew Boggs (1908-1989)

Robert Boggs spent most of his working life as minister of the historic Carson Memorial Baptist Church in Tobermore in Co Londonderry. Named after the renowned Ulster theologian and preacher, Alexander Carson, the church held a prominent place in the small village.

His mother was a city girl, daughter of a textile worker; his father came from a hill farm between Plumbridge and Strabane, Co Tyrone. His parents met at a 'service of song' in Cliftonpark Avenue Baptist Church.

The family lived initially just off the Shankill Road, Belfast, where his father had a grocer's shop. While still young, the family moved to Stranmillis, where he grew up. He played in the Boys' Brigade pipe band, remaining a strong BB supporter all his life. He attended Belfast Model school, situated in the Lower Falls, until it was burnt down during the Home Rule controversy. On leaving school he worked with an advertising agency for four years. He left this to do a matriculation course in preparation for the Irish Baptist College in Dublin, where he went in 1928 and studied under the Principalship of Thomas Harold Spurgeon and the tutelage of the veteran teacher of homiletics Pastor L. E. Deens.

He came to Christ on 22 November 1922, during a Nicholson campaign in St Enoch's Presbyterian church at Carlisle Circus, Belfast and, after baptism joined his home church in Gt Victoria St.

Active Christian service began in the Christian Endeavour society, in young people's gospel services and in open air work. He also sang in East Belfast Gospel Testimony choir, and at this time he met his future wife, Gwen Williamson. They had a family of three daughters and one son.

After his first pastorate at Grange, Co Antrim he settled in Tobermore in 1938 caring for a rural church at Carndaisy Glen and a Mission hall at Upperlands. He was very involved in the life of the village and fostered an excellent working relationship with the Presbyterian and Church of Ireland churches in the village. This co-operation included the setting up of a united Boy's Brigade Company which still continues. He was affectionately known as the 'bishop' of South Derry because of his warm friendship and concern for ministers and pastors of all denominations. A noted raconteur, his infectious wit and art of story telling added greatly to his influence far beyond his own communion.

As well as preaching up to five times each Sunday, and up to three times each week, he took an active part in the work of the Baptist Union of Ireland, serving on its Council from 1946 to 1982 and as President 1955-56.

Robert Boggs was a gifted preacher noted for clarity and brevity. He was an ardent persuader of men, women and young people. He believed passionately in the dignity of the Christian ministry and was a strong advocate of adequate training and preparation. He encouraged and participated in all kinds of evangelistic outreach and was well received south of the border, especially at evangelistic Field and Farmyard Services in the Midlands and South East.

At heart he was a solid Ulsterman and loved nothing more than sharing the good news and building up the church through open air preaching (including the Lammas Fair at Ballycastle), Bible Conventions and Evangelistic Missions.

But he was also a fervent supporter of all initatives designed to apply the truths and values of the gospel to society at large and believed that to be effective, evangelical Christians needed to be both salt and light in the wider world.

Joseph Boyse (1660-1728)

Dublin's Wood Street congregation became an important centre of Presbyterian witness in the seventeenth century. A man of Yorkshire descent, with roots in New England and pastoral experience in Amsterdam, became its minister in 1687.

Joseph Boyse stayed in Dublin for the rest of his life and is remembered as a warm pastor and evangelist who ministered with great acceptance in the leading dissenting congregation in the city. An admirer of Richard Baxter, he was an expository preacher in the Puritan tradition.

At the time Arian views were finding acceptance among some ministers and Boyse strongly defended Trinitarian orthodoxy in his book *A Vindication of the True Deity of our Blessed Saviour* (1703). When a major controversy broke out in the Synod of Ulster on the question of subscription to the Westminster Confession of Faith, Boyse upheld and promoted orthodox doctrine but opposed mandatory subscription.

He also engaged in pamphlet warfare over the question of episcopal *v* presbyterian forms of church polity and worship. His arguments, while forcefully expressed, showed an eirenical spirit and pleaded for co-operation and mutual respect between the two traditions.

A prolific writer, he became a champion of biblical Christianity and managed to combine strong convictions with generosity of spirit. He suggested that all churches own each other as true churches and maintain occasional communion in order to witness to charity, and that pastors accept each other as true ministers of the gospel and rejoice in one another's work, help one another in their ministries, speak well of each other and band together to defend the reformed religion.

'I am persuaded that if ever the native Irish be brought to the knowledge of God's word it must be by having it read to them publicly in a language they understand and not by thrusting Bibles privately into their hand, of the ineffectiveness of such we have had an experiment of 150 years.'

The writings, thought forms, theological insight and gracious disposition of this distant Dublin leader offer an interesting template for furthering evangelical co-operation in the twenty-first century. Believing passionately in the catholicity of Christ's church, he tried to find an accommodation with the ascendant Church of Ireland but Archbishop King gave him little room to manoeuvre. Insistence on re-ordination of dissenting ministers he judged as 'a rejecting of us altogether and a manifest injury to the church of God'.

This Englishman with a thoughtful theology, impressive credentials and a reasonable attitude speaks far beyond his own time and might well contribute to consolidating the efforts of those who are working towards a workable Evangelical Alliance in contemporary Ireland.

Amy Carmichael (1867-1951)

The renowned Irish missionary and writer was born into a well-off family of Scottish descent. Her father was a flour miller. She grew up near Millisle, Co Down, the eldest of seven children and was a regular worshipper at Ballycopeland Presbyterian Church.

The family later moved to Belfast, after Amy had spent three years at the Wesleyan Methodist Boarding School in Harrogate. Early stirrings of God's Spirit came through a CSSM mission in the town. In her own words she recalled: 'Mr Arrowsmith told us to sing 'Jesus loves me, this I know' and then to be quiet. During those quiet few moments, in his great mercy the Good Shepherd answered the prayers of my mother and father and many other loving ones, and drew me, even me, into his fold'.

In Belfast she was attracted to the work of the Belfast City Mission and the YWCA in Donegall Square. With the support of Dr Park, the minister of Rosemary St Presbyterian Church, she was able to start a get-together for the mill girls who wore shawls instead of hats and were known as 'shawlies'. Collecting money from sympathetic friends she obtained a piece of ground from a large mill owner and erected 'The Welcome', a Gospel Hall in Cambrai Street in West Belfast which is still used as an evangelical church.

During a visit to Keswick Convention she felt the affirming and renewing work of the Holy Spirit. This led her to offer herself for missionary service. In 1865 she was commissioned by the Church of England Zenana Missionary Society to go to Dohnavur, India where she served for fifty-six years without a furlough. A major part of her work was devoted to rescuing children from temple prostitution. She founded the Dohnavur Fellowship which became a place of safety and refuge for more than a thousand children during her lifetime. To them she was known as Amma, which is the Tamil word for mother.

After a tragic accident in 1931 much of her time was spent confined to the mission compound. She was a prolific writer with thirty five published books to her name. Works like 'Edges of His Ways' and 'Gold at Moonlight' reveal the depth of her spirituality. She carried a mystical streak in her Christian character, and explored the Scriptures in various translations to draw out the meaning.

Her commitment and selflessness set her apart as a greatly revered disciple who was sold out to Jesus Christ. She reflected an intensity of devotion mingled with Christian idealism in some of her best known lines :

Give me the love that leads the way,
The faith that nothing can dismay,
The hope no disappointment tire,
The passion that will burn like fire,
Let me not sink to be a clod:
Make me Thy fuel, Flame of God.

Amy Carmichael is probably the best known Irish evangelical missionary of all time and through her prose and poetic writings she has helped thousands towards a closer walk with God.

Johnny Cochrane (1900-1971)

Johnny Cochrane represented the type of evangelist who stands in the tradition of Billy Bray and Billy Sunday. Labelled as the 'Hallelujah milkman' he was known throughout Ireland and preached in every county. The main thrust of his work in the Evangelisation Scheme of the Dublin YMCA, accompanied by his companions in service, Victor Evans of Greystones and Dubliner Arthur Reyner, was a series of evangelistic meetings held in church halls, parochial schools or Nonconformist chapels and meeting houses. He sought, and often obtained, the goodwill and support of clergy of all denominations.

He grew up in Lower Dorset St, Dublin in a modest home. Early spiritual influences came through his membership of the Boy's Brigade and attachment to Dublin YMCA. After a spell in the navy he went to work on the Great Northern Railway. The tragic death of a companion before his very eyes stirred him deeply. When the renowned evangelist W. P. Nicholson came to the Metropolitan Hall Johnny was persuaded by his sister to attend and was captured by Christ in a dramatic conversion on 6 December, 1925. He had only a basic education and set about gaining a knowledge of the Bible, reading up to fifteen chapters daily. Large portions of Scripture were committed to memory which he could recite freely. He became a member of the YMCA and commenced work as an evangelist in January, 1933.

The remit was to hold missions in Protestant churches but he quickly developed a collateral ministry in fairs and markets. This activity was launched in Mountmellick, Co Laois on Tuesday 21 February 1933, and his final foray was at the Fair of Charlestown, Co Mayo on his 71st birthday, 1 April 1971, nearly forty years after its inception.

Johnny Cochrane was at his best as a communicater in the open air, whether evening preaching sessions in the heart of

Dublin or in fairs and markets, mainly in the south and west of Ireland. While often attracting hostility, his sense of humour and skilful usage of an apt phrase, often deflated his antagonists and got him out of a tight corner while preaching on the street. There were times when this was dangerous work. At Ballinrobe, Co Mayo he recorded:

> 'They nearly ate one another for the tracts and then nearly ate me! Just before train time we were attacked and beaten up by 30 or 40 men, our Bibles thrown into the river. We were then kicked to the railway station, packed like cattle into the train and warned never to come back.'

As a young evangelist he met Kitty Baker and told the YMCA Committee of his desire to get married. A stalwart member cautioned him by reminding him that the Apostle Paul was an itinerating evangelist and never married. The intrepid evangelist reputedly responded, 'The Apostle Paul never met my Kitty'!

Whether in draughty church halls, poorly lit parochial schools, neat Nonconformist chapels, simple Gospel Halls or bustling street corners, Johnny Cochrane had only one message: 'Christ is All' and with distinctive eloquence, great passion and spiritual anointing he pleaded with his hearers to believe the gospel and receive eternal life.

He was unconventional, courteous, direct and persuasive. A man for his own times raised and used by God, he is remembered with affection all over the island.

John Nelson Darby (1800-1882)

John Nelson Darby became so important in the history of the Brethren Movement that in many parts of the world the Plymouth Brethren are still referred to as 'Darbyites'. A member of a highly-placed family, he took his middle name from his godfather, Admiral Lord Nelson; his uncle was Admiral Darby, famous for his exploits on the Nile, and his father John Darby lived at Leap Castle, Co Offaly. A precocious student, young Darby entered university at the age of 15 and graduated from Trinity College Dublin in 1819. After a long and difficult conver-

sion, he was ordained a deacon in 1825 and a priest in 1826 by
Archbishop William Magee of Dublin and became curate of
Delgany in charge of Calary Parish in Co Wicklow. There he described the local Catholics as being almost as wild as the mountains in which they lived. He fasted regularly, was known for his
austerity, was diligent in his pastoral visits, upheld Anglican
teachings on apostolic succession, and looked with tolerant pity
on those who claimed to be Christians but were not members of
the Established Church.

At the time, he claimed between 600 and 800 Catholics were
joining the Church of Ireland each week. But he soon grew unhappy at the links between church and state. While convalescing
in Dublin after an injury, he came in contact with some of the
early Brethren, and as he studied the Bible under their guidance
his disillusionment with the Established Church grew. He con-
cluded that Saint Paul himself would not be permitted to preach
in the church if he were not ordained, whereas a 'worker of
Satan' could if he were in holy orders! Darby resigned his curacy
in 1829, although he did not formally resign his Anglican connections for several years. He published his views in 1829 in
Considerations of the Nature and Unity of the Church of Christ, the
first of an avalanche of Brethren pamphlets.

By now, Darby was holding millenarian meetings in the
drawing room of Powerscourt House in Enniskerry. Despite the
best efforts of the evangelical rector, Robert Daly (later Bishop of
Cashel) to keep Lady Powerscourt within the Church of Ireland,
Darby and his followers succeeded in persuading their hostess
to join the new movement. Other early figures in the new movement included Charles Stewart Parnell's uncle, John Parnell,
who travelled to Baghdad on an evangelical mission with
Francis Newman, brother of Cardinal John Henry Newman.

Darby spent the rest of his life writing, speaking and travelling on behalf of the Brethren. However, he was ruthless in controversy, accusing his opponents – including those who allowed
the use of music in worship – of contradicting God, not Darby.
The movement split in 1835, with Darby leading the 'Exclusive

Brethren' and his opponents remaining with the 'Open' Brethren. His followers were soon known as the Plymouth Brethren, taking their name from the town where he helped establish the large Brethren assembly of the day. The spread of the movement owed much to his extensive travels throughout Europe from the 1830s and in America in the 1870s, when he directly influenced the revivalist Dwight Moody and the 'rapturist' C. I. Scofield. In a French Catholic newspaper in 1878, Darby claimed the Brethren rejected both Catholicism, because of the sacrifice of the mass and the separate priesthood, and Protestantism, because of its sectarian divisions and worldliness. By the time he died in Bournemouth in 1882, he had broken with nearly all his early friends among the Brethren. His writings were published in 34 large volumes.

William Edmondson (1627-1712)

God calls his servants from most unlikely places. William Edmondson, the pioneer of the Quaker movement in Ireland, served as a soldier in Cromwell's army. He must have witnessed awful atrocities but set those things behind him and, leaving the army, came to settle in Ireland as a shopkeeper. On a visit back to England for further supplies he was convinced of Christ's call through the preaching of a Quaker minister. On his return to Ireland he lived at Lurgan and in Co Cavan. He used every opportunity to tell all he met of how Jesus Christ could meet every condition without the intermediary of priest or formal religious duties. He preached tirelessly in open air markets or in churches, if he were granted access. Sometimes his zeal caused offence and often he suffered imprisonment for his fearless witness.

He settled finally near Mountmellick and from this central location he travelled throughout the country, encouraging the small meetings which were being established.

As an Englishman who renounced violence and privilege he was at risk from all sides, but put his trust in the Lord whom he served. Once his house was set on fire while his family was in bed and he and his sons were marched off to be shot by a party of raparees. At the last moment they were reprieved because he was recognised as one who had used his influence to get cattle seized by the Williamite forces returned to his Irish neighbours.

When John Wesley came to Edenderry, Co Offaly in July, 1765 he had an altercation with the Society of Friends. Someone gave him Edmonson's *Journal* which impressed him deeply when he wrote:

'What faith, love, gentleness, long-suffering! Could mistake send such a man as this to hell? Not so. I am so far from believing this that I scruple not to say Let my soul be with the soul of William Edmonson.'

As the pioneer of the Society of Friends in Ireland, Edmonson represents both the zeal and courage associated with evangelical Quakerism.

Alan Flavelle (1924-1986)

Alan Flavelle grew up in Lurgan in the congregation of Hill Street Presbyterian Church. While in his late teens he committed his life to Christ during a Mission conducted by Tom Rees.

Several years later, he felt the call of God to enter the Christian ministry. He studied at Queen's University and later undertook theological and pastoral studies at the Presbyterian College. He became student Assistant in Fitzroy Avenue Church, Belfast and remained as full time assistant after ordination.

In 1956 he was called to be minister of Mourne Church in Kilkeel, the largest rural congregation in the General Assembly. In his early years there he married Anne McConaghy, continued studies at London University and gained an enviable reputation as a gifted preacher, diligent pastor and an outstanding evangelist. He was recognised for his wide reading and ability to think his way through the big issues of theology. Through his ministry in Mourne many young people heard God's call to serve Christ in many parts of the world.

In 1972 he moved to Lowe memorial congregation at Finaghy in South Belfast. Here his ministry took on new directions as he

sought to grapple with the challenges of a suburban congregation in an age of rapid change, and in the setting of the Troubles.
Not only was he to prove again his preaching and pastoral abilities, but increasingly he was in demand as a seminal thinker, a
gifted teacher and a powerful motivator of others. He took particular delight in encouraging and influencing students through
the work of UCCF, and in a more personal way he acted as a
mentor to many students for the ministry. He was involved in
conducting a number of telling evangelistic missions. His gifts
as a Bible teacher were recognised also in an invitation to speak
at Keswick Convention. He served as Chairman of the Portstewart Convention Committee and of the N. Ireland Committee of the Overseas Missionary Fellowship.

Within the Presbyterian Church he was a recognised leader
of evangelical thought, acted as extern examiner to the College
in Systematic Theology and was also a contributor to the IVF
New Bible Dictionary. He resisted attempts to have him nominated
as Moderator of the General Assembly but was given an Honorary
Doctorate from the Presbyterian Theological Faculty.

His early death on 17 May 1986 was an enormous loss to the
church and to the evangelical cause in Ireland and beyond. He
contributed to the witness of the gospel in the south and promoted the idea of an Association of Evangelicals. When the Irish
Bible School was being launched in Co Tipperary he was an enthusiastic supporter.

Alan Flavelle was outstanding in his generation, a modest
man who was naturally gifted as a leader and inspirer of others.
He was above all someone who walked with God and whose life
bore the marks of total commitment to Christ.

Reginald H. Fry (1917-2003)

Among many dedicated servants of God in the middle to late
twentieth century, the name of Reggie Fry stands out. Known,
respected and loved by thousands of people, young and old, he
had a unique gift of relating to, and interesting himself in, the
lives of all those who came within his circle of friendship.

Born in Dublin into a well-known family associated with the legal profession, he came to Christ at an early age, and as a member of the Merrion Hall Assembly, he was involved in Sunday School and young people's activities from his youth. He was educated at Avoca School in Blackrock and then qualified as a Chartered Accountant. After a short time in practice he moved into commercial life, and was a director of a group of companies for many years.

A lifelong bachelor, he frequently commended this way of life to his associates. This gave him freedom to be involved in Christian activities and missionary enterprise on a broad scale. His greatest interest lay in ministering to the spiritual needs of young people. Early experience with Crusaders led on to the founding of Boys' Evangelical Camps, where during nearly 50 years, many were led to faith in Christ, and went on to serve the Lord in their own churches and interdenominational organisations, like Dublin YMCA. He was an energetic participant in camps for many years, and right up to the age of 80 was a regular and welcome visitor to these activities. He gave generously of his time and resources to help and counsel young people, both in person and by extensive correspondence. Cheerful and fun loving by nature, his sound advice, always based on Scripture, was greatly valued. Copies of his 'letters' on matters relevant to the Christian life were often enclosed with his correspondence.

Business changes in mid-life afforded the opportunity for early 'retirement' during which he devoted his energies to revitalising a number of Christian ministries in Dublin. He assisted his family legal firm for a time and never lost his keen interest in Irish business life. In his later years he was deeply involved in developing the establishment of Christian fellowships in many parts of Ireland, and provided ministry and encouragement to a wide circle of Christians from all backgrounds.

He was someone who aimed to faithfully 'serve his generation by the will of God'. During his long and active life he pointed many young people to Christ and is remembered all over Ireland as a zealous evangelist.

John Gregg, (1798-1878)

He described himself as being from one of the obscurest parishes in the most neglected county in Ireland – Clare. But this did not deter him. Of great mental and physical vigour, he became an outstanding preacher of the gospel in English and Irish, and preached in every county of Ireland. Though highly educated he worked hard to have a plain style, direct and forceful that all could understand. He knew little of God while growing up but was converted on coming to Dublin under the ministry of the Reverend Benjamin Mathias at Bethseda Chapel in Dorset Street. He studied at TCD becoming MA, BD and DD. After a short ministry in Portarlington he became Rector of Kilsallaghan, Co Dublin but was famed far and wide and established evangelical teaching in the heart of Dublin. In 1835 Trinity Church, capable of seating 2,000, was built in Lower Gardiner Street specifically as a preaching place for him, and people from every walk of life thronged to hear him, though he was not approved of in some church circles. He was fearless in denouncing sin, he told one very proper lady that she was drunk, and when she protested that she did not drink, he said 'drunk with self-importance, self-conceit, self-reliance, self-delusion and self-satisfaction'. Referring to latest ecclesiastical trends coming over from England, he described them as 'frippery in doctrine and trumpery in dress'.

He went on to become Bishop of Cork in 1862, often going for weeks at a time by coach to visit West Cork parishes. He lived just long enough to see the completion of the present St Finbarre's Cathedral, and indeed laid in place the top stones of the spires six weeks before he died. He was the grandfather of Archbishop Gregg (Dublin 1920-39, Armagh 1939-1959).

T. C. Hammond (1877-1961)

Thomas Chatterton Hammond grew up in Victorian Cork and was converted while connected with the YMCA there when he was in his teens. He soon became involved in evangelism and in time was ordained (1903) for the ministry of the Church of

Ireland. Theological controversy was strong in the early decades of the twentieth century in Ireland and Hammond was a robust and well informed defender of evangelical truth. At times he found himself preaching in the open air with police protection. For nearly twenty years he was Superintendent of the Irish Church Missions with a staff of up to fifty engaged in evangelism and relief work. He wrote a large number of pamphlets and some books, the most significant of which was a basic compendium of Christian doctrine called *In Understanding be Men* (1936). With the proliferation of evangelical books we have today it is hard to appreciate the impact of this book – a whole generation of evangelicals were nurtured on it. When he was almost sixty Hammond began a second phase of ministry when he moved to Sydney. He was Principal of Moore College there, wrote more books and was, at the same time, Rector of a city church. He never retired and died 'in harness'.

He combined profound scholarship with a warm simple faith and never lost his impish Irish sense of humour. His reputation in Ireland was coloured by the rough and tumble of the days he lived in but he laid safe foundations on which sound progress has been made. He was a safe pair of hands as a theologian and of world stature; he did not get the same following as those who launched out in new directions but with clear, reasoned, warm consolidation and presentation of the truths of the eternal gospel he was a craftsman who has built well.

George Harper (1911-1999)
The senior member of one of the largest and best known families within Irish Evangelicalism lived for most of his married life on the southern end of the Harper homeland at Annamult, near Bennetsbridge, Co Kilkenny. George was born at Cramer's Grove outside Kilkenny city but the family origins were in the townland of Coon, near Castlecomer. All his life he was the archetypical countryman – close to the land, connected to his neighbours, delighting in the abundance of nature.

As a colourful story teller, he relished relaying how his grandfather Edward had eloped with Margaret Bolton because her family did not consider him a suitable match for their daughter! With tongue in cheek and typical generosity George added 'in the end it turned out all right'.

As the elder statesman of a family of nine boys and one girl, George continued the Harper tradition of working the land. As he grew up he maintained the practice of attending his local Parish Church, but through the ministry of the Faith Mission pilgrims and the teaching of Isaiah 53 he came to a living personal faith in Christ. His search for a partner in life 'who shared the same spiritual experience and the same experience of farm life' came to an end when he fell in love with Tillie Shirley of Coolcullen, Co Carlow during a tent mission led by YMCA evangelists Johnny Cochrane and Victor Evans.

Eventually they settled in what became their family home at Annamult and set about rearing their eight children. Their home became a welcoming place for all sorts of Christian workers, missionaries and friends who needed rest and refreshment. Tillie Harper was always cheerful and unflappable, sharing whatever she had with whoever turned up. When food was low on one occasion, she went into the fields, shot several rabbits and served up a stew for her unexpected guests.

George and Tillie were delighted that so many of their children not only shared their faith but five of them ended up in full-time Christian service with evangelical agencies – Helen with Dublin Christian Mission, June with the Wordlwide Evangelistic Crusade, Ruth as a missionary with the Methodist Church in Africa, Herbert in Scripture Union at Avoca Manor and Edna with the European Missionary Fellowship.

George Harper with his warm heart and rougish sense of humour won the respect of the community. He became an elder in Kilkenny Presbyterian Church, maintained a keen interest in the work of the Faith Mission and supported all kinds of interdenominational evangelism at home and abroad.

He felt deeply the loss of his wife Tillie, the sudden death of his daughter June and of his son-in-law Albert Shaw. But he bore his grief bravely with faith and fortitude.

He was the kind of Christian who, more than most, learned to disagree without being disagreeable. When the charismatic movement was getting going George acted very much as a bridge-builder between evangelical Protestants and Roman Catholics who were experiencing the renewal of the Holy Spirit. His approach was tactful, prayerful and saturated in faithfulness to Christ and the Scriptures.

His desire to see the third millennium was not granted but he was grateful for a long life, well lived and poised to achieve the chief end of man, to glorify God and enjoy him for ever.

Barbara Heck (1734-1804)

Two candlesticks flank the pulpit chair in John St Methodist Church, New York city. They are lit every Sunday to commemorate the work of their original owner.

Barabara von Ruckle (Ruttle) was born at Ballingrane, Co Limerick as part of the Palatine community who had fled religious persecution by the forces of Louis XIV in Southern Germany in 1709 and settled in West Limerick.

When John Wesley arrived in Munster he visited the German colony around Rathkeale and was appalled at how they were penalised, partly because of their industrious ways. Partly through pastoral neglect he found a people who had become 'eminent for drunkenness, cursing, swearing and utter neglect of religion'. Wesley, who was fluent in German, brought them the message of the gospel and many responded. Barbara publicly professed her faith in Jesus Christ as a teenager and resonated spiritually with Mr Wesley.

Due to difficult social conditions a number of the refugees decided to emigrate, including Barbara and her new husband Paul Hescht (Heck). In 1760 New York had 14,000 people and the young Palatine was stunned by the spiritual carelessness evident all round her. Finding some of her relatives playing cards she flung them into the fireplace crying out, 'Now look at your idols; there are your gods.' At the same time she pleaded with her cousin, Philip Embury, to begin a preaching ministry but he responded by telling her that he had neither a church or a congregation. Undaunted, she challenged him, 'Preach in your own home and I will gather a congregation.' From a small beginning of four people, consisting of Barbara and Paul Heck, a labourer and a female servant, the first Methodist Church in the new world was planted.

Eventually a meeting house was erected and when the American War of Independence loomed the Hecks with their five children moved upstate, but they were burned out and fled to Montreal. Here Barbara commenced her mustard seed sowing again; she gathered the first Methodist class on Canadian soil and eventually a saddlebag preacher arrived to lead the fledgling church.

From tiny beginnings in West Limerick and a series of trials and challenges, she became the spark that ignited a great flame. On 17 August 1804 , when she was seventy years old, one of her sons found her sitting on a chair with her German Bible open on her lap. Her courageous soul had gone home to God.

A high white granite monument stands over her grave with this inscription:

Barabara Heck put her brave soul
against the rugged possibilities of
the future and under God brought
into existence American and
Canadian Methodism and between
these her memory will always form
a most hallowed link.

Thomas Houston (1804-1882)

In the early seventeenth century, Scots Presbyterians who were fleeing persecution in their own land settled in the province of Ulster. Those of their descendants who wished to maintain a strong attachment to the Scottish Covenants began to hold separate meetings for fellowship towards the close of that century, and these congregations formed the root from which the Reformed Presbyterian Church of Ireland, or 'Covenanters', grew.

A leading Covenanting minister of the nineteenth century was Dr Thomas Houston, whose early life was spent in the Cullybackey congregation under the ministry of the church-planter, William Stavely. Ordained to the ministry at Knock-bracken, County Down, on 8 April 1828, he served there for fifty-four years, until his death on 27 March 1882.

Houston's intellectual and literary abilities were recognised early when the Synod invited him to publish a magazine for the denomination, and the first edition of *The Covenanter* appeared in December 1830. When the church established a Theological Hall in 1854, he was appointed first professor of Exegetical & Pastoral Theology & Ecclesiastical History and continued in this post all his life.

Dr Houston was a prolific author, publishing such works as: *A Treatise on the Lord's Supper; The Intercession of Christ; The Dominion and Glory of The Redeemer; The Faithful Minister's Walk with God; Divine Psalms against Human Paraphrases & Hymns,* together with a four-volume set of shorter writings. Under his ministry the Knockbracken congregation reached its numerical peak, with 260 members listed in 1860. This church was the mother of the Belfast Covenanting congregations, as its members settled in the city and began centres of witness there.

Thomas Houston matured into a profound theologian and great-souled pastor, with a concern for evangelism and revival. His unpublished diary, a transcript of his dealings with his Saviour, movingly reveals a Christian with a passion for holiness and greater closeness to God.

Thomas Kelly (1769-1854)

Although born in Dublin on 13 July 1769, Thomas Kelly will always be associated with the village of Ballintubbert on the Kildare/Laois border. He is buried in the parish churchyard not far from the family seat at Kellyville.

He is best known for his prolific output in hymnology and is credited with over 700 compositions and is often thought of as being the author of some of the finest hymns in the English language. Among the best known are 'Look ye saints the sight is glorious', 'We sing the praise of Him who died', 'Praise the Saviour ye who know Him' and 'The head that once was crowned with thorns'. Over a period of fifty years he produced several editions of his hymnal entitled *Hymns on various passages of Holy Scripture*.

His father was a judge and Thomas, who was educated in Portarlington, Kilkenny and Trinity College, set out to follow a career in law. While studying for the Bar at the Temple in London he came under the influence of the Puritan William Romaine and came to accept the doctrine of justification by faith. Ordination into the ministry of the Church of Ireland followed in 1792. He served in two Dublin parishes, St Luke's and Irishtown. The following year the renowned Dissenting preacher Rowland Hill came to Dublin and influenced several young clergy in the Established Church. Kelly had scruples about remaining in the national church and eventually withdrew and set up independent congregations. These were run on Congregational lines. He had no shortage of funds and was able to erect buildings for worship, especially in Athy and Dublin.

It is recorded that the Dublin headquarters of his sect were, ironically, in Mass House Lane, off Inn's Quay, near the city centre. Nicknamed 'Kellyites' his congegations were never large, between thirty and forty people gathering in their Duke St Meeting House at Athy each Sunday. They were to remain an active group outside the national church for about half a century and eventually died out.

While in Athy Kelly established a weaving workshop for the young men of the town. An uneasy relationship existed between him and his Catholic neighbours and he was inevitably accused of proselytism. In one piece he writes to tell of James Byrne, a weaver from Kilberry who joined Kelly's people and was ostracised by his family and neighbours. He laments that when he died there were not enough people present to carry his body to the grave. Byrne had been accused of becoming a 'Swaddler' – a nickname for the early Methodists – and was disowned, in

Kelly's words because he 'read the Word of God and dared to
think for himself'.

In 1799 Kelly married Elizabeth Tighe of Rosanna, Co
Wicklow, whose mother had been of close friend of John Wesley.

In spite of some controversial theological writings he was a
generous Christian whose liberality found ample scope during
the years of the Great Famine. He remained an occasional
preacher in old age, retiring to Dún Laoghaire to live with his
son-in-law Rev William Wingfield. One admirer described him
as 'a man with a catholic spirit and a love of all good men'.

Rose La Touche (1849-1875)

A member of the well known Huguenot banking family which
settled in Ireland after the Revocation of the Edict of Nantes,
Rose La Touche's place in history is mainly connected to her
stormy relationship with the noted Victorian author and critic,
John Ruskin. Although physically fragile, she became a person
of great spiritual stamina during her short, sad life.

As an evangelical Christian she shared the lively faith of her
father, John who, while holidaying in Mentone, France met C. H.
Spurgeon and was savingly united to Christ. Following baptism
by the 'Prince of Preachers' in the Metropolitan Tabernacle in
London, 'the Master' returned to his estate at Harristown in Co
Kildare where he started evangelistic meetings which later became the nucleus of Brannockstown Baptist Church.

His talented wife, Maria, while welcoming her husband's
change of direction, wasn't enthusiastic about his move into the
Baptist Church. She wrote: 'I do really twenty times a day bless
Mr Spurgeon (though of course I had far rather it had been the
Archbishop of Canterbury or even Cardinal Manning) for rescuing the 'Master' out of the blighting narrowness of a life entirely
given to sport, and enabling him to see the beauty of things he
never gave a thought to when he was young.'

Rose, the younger daughter of John and Maria, was deeply
influenced by her father's Christian life and witness. When she
was nineteen she wrote:

'As I grew older I listened and took in all my father's doctrines. He taught me that there was but the one thing needful,
one subject worthy of thought, one aim worth living for, one
rule for conduct, namely, God's Holy Word. He used to say
that the things that concerned God were the only real and important things'.

While sharing her father's evangelicalism, Rose worshipped
with her mother at St Patrick's Church, Carnalway which stands
on the edge of Harristown demesne. She had a deep respect for
Scripture – 'I used to take the Testament and read it like a book,
because I suppose its beauty struck me so, and I thought of
Christ as a friend one could really love – as a father loved.'

Like her father, and many of her La Touche relatives, she had
a philantrophic spirit and went round the villagers with gifts
and religious tracts. While she imbibed Ruskin's social con-
science – 'I think it was Mr Ruskin's teaching when I was about
twelve years old that made me first take to looking after the
poor' – she was shattered by his questioning of the reliability of
Scripture.

Their whole relationship is filled with pathos and tragedy.
Brought up in a strict evangelical home in London, he publicly
rejected evangelicalism at a Waldensian church in Turin and his
loss of faith shattered Rose. Her parents refused to allow them to
marry, mainly because of her suitor's religious scepticism.

In her *Diaries* Rose unveils her inner spiritual strength in the
face of deep distress and disappointment. Three years before her
death at twenty six years, she wrote these lines, which evince
much disappointment and calm resignation:

I in those hours have learnt that life is sad,
Sad to heart-breaking did we walk alone,
I who lost much which I never had,
Yet which in ignorance I held mine own,
Would leave that clouded past, its good and bad,
Within His hands to whom all things are known.

As one of the most renowned young women in Victorian Ireland
because of Ruskin's place in her affections, she is also remem-

bered as a devout Christian whose faith was refined and strengthened in the furnace of affliction.

Adam Loughridge (1915-2001)

North Antrim was the home country of the Loughridge family for generations. Of Scottish stock they worshipped in Kilraughts Reformed Presbyterian Church. It was here that Adam Loughridge grew up. Here too his early spiritual formation took place. When he sensed God's call in 1930 to enter the ministry, he sought the guidance and support of his minister and the congregation of which he was part.

As a student he excelled from his days at Ballymena Academy through Trinity College and eventually doctoral studies at Geneva College at Beaver Falls, USA. He managed to combine clear theological thinking with warm pastoral care and diligent expository preaching. Ministering in four Covenanting congregations at Newtownards, Portrush, Ballymacashon, Co Down and Cregagh Road, Belfast, Professor Loughridge's work was characterised by faithful exposition, winsome evangelism and clear application of God's Word to every part of life.

He became Principal of the Reformed Theological College in Belfast and taught in the Reformed Presbyterian College in Pittsburg and at Belfast Bible College. In the lecture room he gave his students a love for church history, a love for the Scriptures, a love for preaching and a love for people. These were all kindled by the warmth of his own heart.

Adam Loughridge was exemplary in his wide reading and generous attitude to those who were scattered across the denominational spectrum. In the harsh climate of church life in Northern Ireland he managed to hold to a conservative theology while extending courtesy to his many friends in the academic, political and ecclesiastical world. Young people found him an understanding and gracious pastor and mentor.

He was a keen supporter of interdenominational co-operation and served for many years as Chairman of the Scripture Gift Mission Advisory Board. Events for Bible teaching and spiritual challenge such as Portstewart Convention attracted his enthusiastic endorsement.

He loved to garner knowledge of God's doings and dealings in past generations and his account of the origin and development of his own denomination, *The Covenanters in Ireland*, opens a clear window into the story of a small but significant body of Christian people.

The evangelical cause in many places has been enhanced by the quiet influence of this careful scholar and gifted teacher who in his life and witness has spread around 'the sweet fragrance of Christ' (2 Cor 2:15).

H. D. McDonald (1911-2003)

One of the leading evangelical theologians in Britain, Dermot McDonald was born in Dublin on 29 October 1911. Like many young people of his era he was converted at Merrion Hall and threw himself into Christian witness in the city. He cut his teeth in outdoor preaching and not infrequently had rotten eggs and tomatoes thrown at him, the Garda occasionally coming to the rescue! He had a Dubliner's native wit and fondness for debate. During an open air meeting some students from the Baptist College in Harcourt St debated with him about believers' baptism. After careful thought young Derry Mac, as he was affectionately known, was baptised and joined Harcourt St Church, where Louis Edward Deens was pastor.

In 1931 he entered the college and despite a long and crippling illness completed his course and became Mr Deens' assistant. Moving to England he fulfilled two pastorates going first to Stockton-on-Tees and then to Woolwich Tabernacle.

Pursuing philosophical and theological studies and gaining several degrees, he joined the staff of London Bible College and was awarded a Doctorate from London University. From 1964 to his retirement he served as Vice-Principal of LBC, and among other things became visiting professor at several seminaries and universities in the USA. One of his academic tasks was to supervise the doctoral thesis of George Carey, who later became Archbishop of Canterbury.

He was a prolific writer and was the author of nineteen works. His many books cover a wide range of biblical, theological and philosophical topics, among them *Jesus Human and Divine* and *The New Testament concept of Atonement: the Gospel of the Calvary Event*. Three lucid commentaries came from his pen – on Galatians, Ephesians and Colossians. He contributed to several important encyclopaedias including the *New Bible Dictionary*, and the *New International Dictionary of the Christian Church* and has written innumerable articles for evangelical journals.

While maintaining a high standard of scholarship, Dr McDonald never moved away from the profound simplicities of the gospel of Christ. He strongly defended the historical Christian faith. Stated succinctly in his own words, 'The gospel would not have survived if it were not anchored in secure historical facts. We are not saved by accepting a churchly Christ-idea but by encounter with the reality of God in the historical actuality of Jesus Christ the Lord.'

He had a deep love for and interest in the progress of the kingdom of God in his homeland. Several staff members and scores of students at London Bible College were Irish and they benefitted not only from the theological expertise of a notable scholar but also from his warm personality and infectious wit. When presented with an illegible script from a student he wrote, 'I marked this more by faith than sight as I cannot read it!'

Dermot McDonald was an engaging preacher, biblical, precise, clear, orderly and convincing. Some see him as one of Ireland's gifts to the wider church and through his written works his influence lives on and throws clear light on many of the great questions which continue to confront pastors, evangelists, missionaries and all believers in God's revelation in Christ.

Francis Makemie (1658-1708)

The father of American Presbyterianism was an Ulster Scot, the son of immigrants who settled in the Laggan district of East Donegal. The Makemies were part of the Plantation of Ulster, and Francis was born at the time when the Laggan presbytery was formed. His spiritual preparation for the ministry began with 'a work of grace and conversion wrought on my heart at fifteen years of age by and from the pains of a godly schoolmaster who used no small diligence in gaining tender souls to God's service and fear.'

In 1680 an appeal came to the Laggan presbytery from Colonel William Stevens, a member of the governing council of the American colony of Maryland, for a minister to serve the people of the colony. Makemie answered the call and as an evangelist itinerated along the coasts of Maryland, Virginia, North Carolina and the island of Barbados.

Because of financial limitations in the infant colonial congregations, he pursued a 'tent-making' ministry engaging in trade, and married the daughter of a successful merchant who had helped support him. He travelled twice to London to raise funds and recruit ministers and his great achievement was to join with other ministers in forming the first presbytery on American soil in 1706.

He has also been honoured as a champion of civil and religious liberty in America and was arrested in New York for preaching illegally. He fought his case, as someone who had experienced the injustices suffered by Nonconformists in Ireland, and was acquitted by a jury.

Makemie's theology emerges from his writings. In a published sermon he emphasised the need for Christians to give evidence of 'the mature fruit and consequence of regeneration ... without a suitable and agreeable Conversation (lifestyle), men cannot lay claim to the New Birth.'

In a work entitled *Truth in a True Light,* he appealed for Protestant co-operation 'in the great work of the gospel for the manifestation of God's glory and the conviction, conversion and salvation of souls'.

His evangelicalism was not narrowly pietistic – he urged the inhabitants of Virginia and Maryland to give attention to economic, social and urban development alongside the organisation of the church. A statue raised in his honour in 1908 in

Philadelphia describes him as:
> A devoted and able preacher of the
> Gospel, a Christian gentleman, an
> Enterprising man of affairs, a public
> spirited citizen, a distinguished
> advocate of Religious Liberty.

This talented and adventurous Ulsterman died when he was fifty, but from humble beginnings in Ramelton went on to spread the gospel and organise church order in the train of Calvin's people in North America.

T. S. Mooney (1907-1986)

There is little doubt that T. S. Mooney was one of the most prominent and influential laymen of his generation. Born outside Coleraine in 1907 he was converted to Christ in his early teens at a mission led by two Faith Mission pilgrims in Cullyvenny Primary School. On leaving Coleraine Academical Institution he wanted to become a minister or a lawyer but God had other plans for his life. In 1925, he began his working life in the Londonderry branch of the Belfast Banking Company, retiring from the same office 45 years later as Assistant Manager.

The Divine Providence which prevented him entering the ministry, strategically placed his home in the shadow of Magee College, then a college for training Presbyterian ministers. God used him to encourage successive generations of young men entering the ministry. There is certainly no chance relationship between T. S. Mooney's influence and the rise and usefulness of the Evangelical Union in Magee. Apart from his natural gifts of warmth, wit, and wisdom this archetypical bachelor, who needed remarkably little sleep to sustain a punishing schedule, was a voracious reader with a photographic memory and the ability to argue his position lucidly and simply. He had one of the finest libraries of Christian books in Ireland – James Philip said of him that he knew few laymen who were better or more deeply read – and was, therefore, a tremendous source of strength to many budding, but theologically unsure, students.

In Londonderry his Christian work was in 7 main areas – Great James Street Presbyterian Church, later Kilfennan, where, amongst other things, he was Clerk of Session and Bible Class Leader; his beloved Crusader Class; the Christian Workers Union; the Young People's Convention which he founded in 1936; the Londonderry City Mission, the Londonderry Temperance Council and the Londonderry auxiliary of the Bible Society. His service in all these organisations spanned more than half a century.

On a wider front he was a council member of the Qua Iboe Mission, treasurer of the Portstewart Convention and a member of 26 Committees or Boards of the Presbyterian Church in Ireland. A measure of his energy and commitment to Christian work is the fact that in the 12 months before he died he clocked 19,000 miles in his car!

TS was an engaging Bible teacher and expositor with a great gift for the use of alliteration, and the appropriate illustration. Meticulous in preparation, he had the ability to communicate biblical truth in a relevant, attractive way either in the informal setting of the Castlerock Crusader Camp surrounded by 50 sweaty boys, in the more formal setting of the Inter Varsity Fellowship annual conference at Swanick where, in the early sixties, he became the first layman to give the Bible Readings, or in some small mission hall with only a handful of folk present.

It will come as no surprise that the power for TS's service came from his disciplined prayer life. He did not talk about it but those who shared a room with him at conferences testify to the fact that he rose each morning at 6.00 a.m. and was shortly on his knees at his beside, his Bible open and his prayer list laid out in front of him. How appropriate that those who entered his home on Friday, 24 January 1986 should discover that the Lord called him home while engaged in this daily activity.

Edward Nangle (1799-1883)

Canon Edward Nangle is the man most closely identified with the controversies surrounding the evangelical response to the famine on Achill Island. Although earlier biographers tried to play down his family background, Edward Nangle was born into a strongly Roman Catholic 'Anglo-Norman' or 'Old English' family in Co Meath who had been intermarried for generations with families of similar background. His father, Captain Walter Nangle, was brought up a Catholic, and two of his three wives were Catholics too. However, Edward was the son of Walter's second wife, Catherine Sall, the daughter of a Dublin Protestant merchant. Although there is no record of his birth or baptism, he was probably raised as a Catholic until Walter decided he should have a Protestant education, sending Edward to Cavan Royal School, where his contemporaries included Thomas Fowell Buxton, the nineteenth century Liberal abolitionist, and Robert Daly, the celebrated evangelical Bishop of Cashel.

A wild and reckless young student, he opted instead for ordination 'as a means of securing an eligible social position,' but failed miserably in his first two curacies in Athboy, Co Meath, and Monkstown, Co Dublin. In Arva, on the borders of Cavan and Longford, he was deeply influenced by the local Primitive Methodists and by the Rev William Krause, later preacher at the Bethesda Chapel in Dublin. Once again, however, he had difficulty in holding down his curacy, and appears to have suffered a nervous breakdown.

After a classical conversion experience, he emerged committed to working among the Irish-speaking people of the West. With the outbreak of famine in 1831, he helped bring a cargo of Indian meal to Westport, where he made friends with the rector, William Baker Stoney, and on whose first prompting he visited Achill Island. Moved by the destitution of the people, he drew up his first initial plans for the Achill Mission. Land was provided at Dugort on a long lease and a low rent, and a new committee included Daly and many of the leading evangelicals of the day. Nangle settled with his family on Achill in 1834, and they were soon joined by an assistant clergyman, scripture readers, a teacher and Dr Neason Adams. Within weeks, four schools were catering for over 400 children and a printing press was established to publish the *Achill Missionary Herald* and to print prayer books, Bibles and tracts in Irish.

His work was extended to neighbouring Inishbiggle and Clare Island; Saint Thomas's Church was built in Dugort; 2,000 acres of land were purchased for redistribution among the tenant farmers; more land was enclosed, wild moor was reclaimed and crop rotation was introduced; schools, orphanages and a dispensary provided education and health care; the Slievemore Hotel, built in 1839, introduced modern tourism; piers, roads were built, transforming transport and fisheries.

Nangle became Rector of Achill and a canon of Tuam Cathedral in 1850. However, he found it easier to work as a missionary than as a parish clergyman, and after 18 years there left Achill in 1852, and despite regular return visits, his relationship with the mission committee became increasingly acrimonious. He remained Rector of Skreen in Co Sligo for 21 years and retired to Dublin, where he died in 1883 at the age of 84, forgotten by many of his colleagues and with only his second wife by his side. He was buried in Dean's Grange in a grave that remained unmarked for many years.

A cultured man, Nangle could play the violin with virtuosity, knew his Haydn and Mozart, painted in watercolours, and was familiar with Byron's poetry, a very different character from the man left with a lasting reputation as a headstrong firebrand and unfair allegations of 'souperism'. Nangle was a practical missionary, deeply concerned for the spiritual and material wellbeing of the Irish-speaking people of Achill. An ironic consequence of his mission was the unintended benefits for the island's Catholics: the Vincentian missionaries Villas and Rinolfi were sent there by his fiery opponent, Archbishop John McHale; the Franciscans opened a monastery in Bunacurry; and schools were opened after years of pitiful neglect.

W. P. Nicholson (1876-1959)

Within Northern Ireland, and to a lesser extent further south, the name of William Patteson Nicholson was widely known in the first half of the twentieth century. Sometimes called 'Willie Nick' he earned a reputation as a hard hitting, straight speaking, sharp tongued preacher.

After a wild youth spent at sea, he was converted in 1898 and his spiritual awakening was almost as dramatic as that of John Newton. His early ministry was in Glasgow where he trained at the Bible Training Institute and served as an evangelist with the Lanarkshire Christian Union. After emigration to America he was ordained an evangelist with the Presbyterian Church, USA, and joined the staff of the Bible Institute of Los Angeles.

In the 1920s Nicholson came back to his native Ulster at a time of political and social unrest. He held Crusades in towns all over the north and people flocked in their thousands to his meetings. His style had a particular appeal to the shipyard workers in Belfast. On one memorable occasion the spacious Assembly Hall was so full that the workers from Harland and Wolff are said to have torn down the railings to gain admission.

By any standards he had the ear of the common people and preached with great power and conviction. Conversions were numerous and the spiritual awakening was of such proportions that anecdotal evidence has been handed down that a special shed was set aside at Belfast shipyard to house the stolen property returned by those who turned to Christ at the Nicholson mission. In large provincial towns he preached forthrightly in plain Ulster language and while some were offended by his coarseness, multitudes were turned Godwards.

He used the Bible effectively and ranged over the foundational truths of the gospel as he understood them, clothing his words with homespun stories, vivid illustrations, catchy sayings and at times, personal insults.

To the surprise of many he was invited to participate in a Student Mission at Cambridge University, with William Temple (the Bishop of Manchester, later to become Archbishop of Canterbury) as the other missioner.

Nicholson's preaching created something of a sensation and left a deep impression on the lives of many students.

In his latter years he returned to Ireland and is buried at Clandeboye Cemetery, near Bangor, Co Down.

The Nicholson meetings did more than anything else to spread evangelical Christianity in Ulster in the twentieth century and propelled scores of young people into pastoral ministry, evangelistic activity and missionary service.

Gideon Ouseley (1762-1839)

One of Ireland's most renowned evangelists was born at Dunmore, County Galway, the son of an anti-clerical member of the gentry and a devout mother. He was privately educated for a career in the Anglican Church but failed to win a place at Trinity College, Dublin. He married into a wealthy family but squandered his fortune through indulgent living and litigation.

Ouseley lost his eye in a shooting accident and, while recovering, his heart turned to spiritual things. He was converted in 1791 when a Methodist quartermaster came to his native town and conducted evangelistic meetings for his soldiers in the local inn. His conversion was decisive, dramatic and transformative and set him on the road for half a century of intinerant preaching with irrepressible zeal.

He laboured for a time as an independent evangelist, but in the aftermath of the Irish Rebellion of 1798 was invited by the Irish Methodist Conference to join a team of Irish-speaking preachers, Charles Graham and James McQuigg. Their remit was to reach the Irish peasantry and, in the words of David Hempton, they were devoted to 'reclaiming Irish Catholics, lukewarm Protestants and the irreligious in a period of social tumult and political upheavel' After visting Enniskillen on Christmas Day 1800 they reported that 'superstition and formal religion are flying like chaff off the summer threshing floor'. These early revivalists witnessed significant growth, reflected in the fact that Methodist societies grew from 16,000 in 1799 to 36,527 in 1820.

Ouseley was an evangelist of tremendous ability although some wealthy Dublin Methodists dismissed his popular style as all 'nonsense and noise'! His ambition was to preach in every settlement in Ireland and it was not unusual for him to travel several thousand miles a year, preaching between twelve and fifteen sermons a week. An eccentric figure, he had a gift for communicating with the poorest members of rural society, with whom he felt an intense sympathy. His methodology worked well – he rang a bell when entering a town, stood in front of chemist shops to ward off missiles and used homespun rural illustrations to get his message across. Above all, he had an intense passion for evangelism and falls within the category of a zealous soulwinner. The key to much of his effectiveness was the use of the Irish language and his willingness to mix with the ordinary people at patterns, wakes, fairs and even cock fights.

Ouseley inherited his father's anti-clericalism and carried on a long pamphlet controversy with the Roman Catholic Church. This reflected the outlook of many evangelicals of the time and naturally drew the opposition of the Catholic clergy.

A large monument marks his burial place at Mount Jerome Cemetery, Dublin opposite the restored Mortuary Chapel.

In Mountmellick, Co Leix the local congregation still worships in the Gideon Ouseley Memorial Methodist Church.

George Lawrence Pilkington (1865-1897)

In a now closed church near Tyrrellspass, Co Westmeath a memorial tablet gives a glimpse of the short but fruitful life of a nineteenth century Irish missionary. It says, 'The congregation of Newtown and some friends have placed this tablet here in memory of George Lawrence Pilkington, missionary of the Church Missionary Society. He finished the work begun by others and left to the people of Uganda the Bible in their own tongue. He was laid to rest in their country having fallen in battle on behalf of those he loved and taught. One of whom, Aloni, spoke in his dying ear the words of hope 'nze kuzukira nobulamu ...' 'I am the Resurrection and the Life, he that believeth in me shall never die, John 11:25, 26 '

What led this young man, son of a prominent barrister and

landowner, to Africa? He had a profound conversion while studying Classics in Cambridge and his first thought was to hold a mission with Cambridge speakers in Tyrrellspass with the Rector's approval. There was great fervour for mission in his College and Pilkington saw foreign service as a prime consideration. He set off for Uganda with three others in 1890. During the foot safari from the coast through German East Africa, now Tanzania, he learned much of the language of the Baganda tribe, and studied the grammar because his assignment was linguistics and Bible translation. A beautiful window in Naminembe Cathedral, Kampala, depicts him at a table doing translation.

After five years Pilkington came home and, with his sister who knew Hindustani, worked on sections of the Bible not yet translated. He could then return to Uganda with the Bibles ready for the eager and avid readers there. Pilkington's insights into mission are still of value. Primarily Africans for Africa was his message; he begged for workers capable of teaching the Ugandans, who could then do the job of twenty foreign staff. He saw Uganda with its eagerness, faith and ability as a fulcrum for evangelising the whole of Africa. He emphasised the value of knowing vernacular proverbs and similes to communicate the gospel. And he knew from personal experience that the whole must be in the power of the Holy Spirit. Out of his work a revival took place, some say a beginning to the well known East African Revival of later years.

Peter Roe (1778-1841)

The son of a medical doctor, Roe was one of the ice-breaking evangelicals who lived just as the formalism and deism of the eighteenth century was giving way to the warm faith that transformed the nineteenth century Church of Ireland, leading to a time in mid-century when it is estimated that half the members of that church were evangelicals. He was greatly influenced by the early Methodists but was a model Pastor as a church clergyman when many were careless or non-resident. When it came to due Church order he was beyond criticism and restored many aspects of pastoral work that had fallen into disuse. He was a tireless evangelist and eirenic apologist known throughout Ireland, though most of his work was based in the South East and especially in Kilkenny, where he was curate and later Rector (1805) of St Mary's. But his fame spread to England and he was invited to preach for John Newton of 'Amazing Grace' fame. While in London Roe noted that there were more preaching the gospel there than 'in all Ireland' and his prayer was that the Lord would raise up preachers in Ireland. With others of like mind he supported the newly formed agencies of good such as the Sunday School Society, the Bible Society and the Hibernian Church Missionary Society. He was ordained in 1779 and encouraged other clergy to meet in societies for study and fellowship. When one bishop frowned on such gatherings Roe pointed out that eight of the bishop's clergy met often as members of the local Hunt Club and no one reproved them. By his evangelistic zeal on the one hand and his loyalty to the church on the other he made it easy for many to follow in his steps, and that eight or ten bishops were evangelicals by the end of the century was in no small way because of Roe's example and influence.

William Russell (d. 1879)

Russell came from a remote farm near Littleton, Co Tipperary. When a student in Dublin he went often to hear the preaching of John Gregg and was greatly influenced by it and converted to a living faith. He shared in the awakening of missionary interest at the time and offered himself to the Hibernian Church Missionary Society for service in the Far East. He sailed for China in 1847. Some of his colleagues quickly succumbed to disease and he was alone for a while. But in Ningpo he met the daughter of other missionaries and in due course they married. She had already been many years in China with her parents and knew the language and customs. Building on this he went on to translate the New Testament and the Prayer Book into Chinese. He was an able and devoted evangelist, pastor and organiser. He was ahead of his time, visionary in his efforts to train

Chinese clergy. He also came into conflict with the powerful political influence of British traders, clashing with them over the nefarious opium trade.

By sheer stickability and loving faith he won an opening for the gospel in previously unevangelised areas and was made the first Bishop of North China seven years before his death.

Elise Sandes (1851-1934)

'I can never remember a time when thoughts of the littleness of life and the greatness of eternity did not stir my heart,' Elise Sandes wrote as she reflected on her early life.

She grew up at Oakvilla near Tralee, Co Kerry in a family of nine children and spent much of her childhood living with an aunt in a remote country home.

At the time of the 1859 Revival a young man was awakened under the preaching of Rev Denham Smith in Dublin and went to Kerry to conduct evangelistic meetings. Elise and her father attended a service in Tralee Presbyterian Church. Following the singing of 'Rock of Ages' and discussion with the preacher both Elise and her father came to faith: 'He a man of fifty and I a child of ten, tremblingly ventured to trust Jesus.'

As a teenager she went to Madame de Mailly's French School in Bray and obtained permission to attend revival meetings near the town. The sudden death of her father devastated her but through the support of the Crosbies of Ardfert Abbey and the Mahonys of Dromore Castle she caught a vision of spending her life in Christian service. Susan Crosbie and Marie Fry were instrumental in influencing her to commence a philantrophic and evangelistic ministry for soldiers and their families. It all started simply when she met a young drummer boy and invited him to her home and later held her first gathering for soldiers at Oakvilla in 1868.

Through co-operation with evangelical compatriots like Theodora Schofield, Mary Stokes, Miss Magee and Eva Maguire, Elise Sandes embarked on the passion of her life.

In the summer of 1877 the first Sandes Soldiers' Home was

opened in Cork. With the support of leading evangelicals, including titled people and influential leaders, Miss Sandes was instrumental in setting up Homes in Ireland, Britain and overseas. The list is impressive – Queenstown (Cobh), 1890; Belfast, 1894; Dublin, 1894; The Curragh, 1899; India – Rawalpindi, 1896, Murree and Quetta , 1898.

In the twentieth century expansion continued mainly in Ulster: Ballykinlar, 1901; Londonderry and Holywood, 1901; Magilligan, 1904; Dunree Fort, Co Donegal, 1927.

Homes started in Knockanarrigan, Co Wicklow (1904) and Coolmoney (1913), Catterick Camp in Yorkshire (1928) and in Jamaica in 1932. Wherever armies were stationed Sandes was there to offer warmth and hospitality in places as diverse as Ballincollig, Athlone, Dundalk, Waterford, Limerick, Kildare, Cahir, Mullingar, Glen of Imaal and Kilbride.

Her homes became a haven of hospitality and practical Christian care. Some had sleeping accommodation for service men on leave or in transition. Canteens, games rooms, reading rooms and in some cases a cinema offered facilities for military personnel and their families. There were regular meetings for prayer, hymn singing, Bible study and evangelistic preaching. In Elise Sandes words: 'A home full of light and gladness and music, where men would find warm human hearts, always ready to welcome, help and befriend them. A home where they would hear of the Only One who could free them from sin and make their lives glad and useful and victorious.'

Elise Sandes was raised by God to serve the needs of her own time. She won the affection of thousands of serving men and women, the co-operation of Military chaplains and the appreciation of the Army and Air Force in Britain and Ireland. Eight soldiers carried her coffin to her last resting place at Tyrella Churchyard, the whole battalion stationed at nearby Ballykinlar camp stood around her grave, joined by Lord Craigavon, Prime Minister of Northern Ireland.

Her lasting memorial is with those she dedicated her life to serving and the few Sandes Homes still left continue the min-

istry she pioneered for the sake of Christ and the well-being of
military personnel.

Joseph Medlicott Scriven (1819-1886)

The author of one of the world's best loved hymns, 'What a
friend we have in Jesus', was an Ulsterman named Joseph
Scriven. He was born near Banbridge in Co Down on 10
September 1819. A memorial window in Seapatrick Parish
Church features his hymn and a monument in the town centre
commemorates his work.

He was the son of Captain John Scriven, Churchwarden of
Seapatrick Parish Church and his mother Jane was the sister of a
Wiltshire vicar, Rev Joseph Medlicott.

After graduation from Trinity College, Dublin he fell in love
with a local girl and planned to marry in the summer of 1844.

On the day before their wedding when his fiancé was crossing
the River Bann on horseback, she was thrown into the river and
drowned in full view of Joseph who was waiting for her on the
far bank.

Early spiritual influences came from his association with the
emerging Brethren movement in Dublin. After emigrating to
Canada he lodged with the Courtney and Sackville families and
joined the local Brethren Assembly.

On a lonely night in 1857, weighed down with loneliness and
overcome with despondency, he poured out his heart to God
and his burden was lifted. At that time he penned the hymn
which spoke of being 'weak and heavy laden, cumbered with a
load of care'. It was not released or published but kept in his private papers.

Scriven was a regular preacher at street corners in Port Hope
where he was frequently ridiculed and mocked. He married
evangelistic zeal with social concern and became known as 'the
man who saws wood for poor widows and sick people unable to
pay'. He gave away all his private income for the benefit of others, including a coat his mother gave him for the cold Canadian
winters.

On return to Europe he fell in love with a girl in Plymouth, who forsook him for another suitor and left him heartbroken. Back in Canada he became deeply attached to Catherine Roche who was baptised by immersion in Lake Rico in the spring of 1860. She caught pneumonia and died in August. Scriven was devastated. Three times he had lost the woman he loved.

When he reached his late sixties he was worn out with disappointment. His old friend, James Sackville brought him to his home to spend his last days. One evening he came across the original copy of Scriven's hymn and asked him how he had managed to write it. He replied 'the Lord and I did it between us' and disclosed that he had written it to comfort his mother in Ireland during her illness.

Joseph Scriven is buried beside his beloved Catherine in the cemetery at Balieboro, Cavan County, Canada, on the shore of Rice Lake. A white obelisk marks his grave and a memorial monument stands in Port Hope, Ontario.

What a Friend we have in Jesus was published anonymously in 1865 and eventually found its way into Sankey's *Sacred Songs and Solos* and gained worldwide acceptance.

Dorothy M. Sinton (1895-1991)

Dorothy McClatchie was born in Portadown and grew up a member of the Church of Ireland. She was a lively girl, popular and outgoing, who made friends easily. She married a local farmer, John Henry Sinton, and they looked forward to a life of comfort and enjoyment. Some time after their marriage special meetings were held in Portadown by the sharp-shooting evangelist W. P. Nicholson. These meetings attracted much popular interest because of the unconventional approach of the preacher and the Sintons went along largely out of curiosity. Although unable to sit together because of the crowd, both were gripped by the message of salvation and at the end of the meeting both met at the front of the church where they each committed their lives to God.

They determined at once to express their new faith to those

among whom they worked and worshipped. They arranged special meetings in the Friends Meeting House at Tamnamore which continued each evening for several weeks at which some 35 neighbours experienced conversion.

Realising the need for biblical instruction for both themselves and the other young converts they established a Christian Endeavour society. This movement was to be a powerful influence in Dorothy's life and she became all-Ireland president of C.E.

John Henry and Dorothy Sinton were united in their service for their Lord and shared ministry in mission halls and churches in all parts of Ireland. They also made several extended visits to the USA.

John Henry was gifted with down-to-earth common sense and an outrageous sense of humour which commanded the interest and attention of his audience. Dorothy had great insight into the needs, aspirations and temptations of ordinary people. These qualities were used by the Holy Spirit to convey biblical truths and to challenge their hearers to a full commitment to Christ. Both had long and active lives, John Henry reaching the age of 91 and Dorothy her 97th year.

Frances Walker (1893-1966)

No one would be more surprised to find her name in a list of evangelical worthies than Frances Walker. 'Fan', as she was known, grew up Frances Godkin in the Ballyforan-Athleague area of Co Roscommon. She was the sort of person of ample build and warm personality who could be described as 'a mother in Israel'.

Her main contribution to evangelical life and witness was through her generous hospitality. Her husband, Ralph was a well known farmer at Cloncannon, Ballygar in East Galway who was highly regarded by his neighbours and associates. With his sister Hester, he ran an evangelical Mission Hall on the main street of Ballygar. Such an unusual venture was regarded with some caution by the small scattering of Protestants who lived in the area. In the first half of the twentieth century, Roman Catholics would have kept themselves at a safe distance from such activity, partly through fear of the unknown.

In the family home at Cloncannon colporteurs, travelling evangelists and street preachers were always welcomed and treated with respect. After a weary and discouraging day trudging up long lanes, with little interest and few sales, many a travelling Bible salesman was re-assured by the welcoming smile and the generous hospitality of Frances Walker. She kept a spare room, sometimes called the 'prophet's chamber', so that any evangelical enthusiast who turned up would be housed and fed. In those days the doors of many Irish farmhouses remained unlatched and it was said that at times colporteurs turned up for breakfast in the Walker kitchen, their host unaware that they had let themselves in the previous night and gone quietly to bed!

The witness borne by the Walker family was quiet and discreet. The neighbours knew about the 'strangers' who frequented their home.

In local fairs and markets when the street preachers turned up, sympathetic farmers like Ralph Walker kept a discreet distance. If they identified too closely with the travelling preachers, whether they were Methodist ministers, Irish Mission workers or YMCA evangelists, there was the distinct possibility that their livestock would remain unsold.

Frances Walker with her family of two sons and two daughters gained the respect of the local community in times of social, political and religious tension. With her winsome ways and prayerful disposition she managed to encourage all who came over her doorstep in the cause of the gospel and at the same time leave behind the sweet aroma of Christ in the neighbourhood where she lived all her life.

Eva Stuart Watt (1891-1959)

There are places in the world where heaven and earth seem to have touched together. But the late night revellers in the Dublin of the 1940s 'Emergency' might not have known that this was one of those places, nor noticed two of heaven's loveliest citizens bringing many wanderers to its gates.

Eva Stuart Watt and her sister Clara had abandoned their comfortable house in the Wicklow Mountains for the dark inhospitable streets of the city. Earlier, sheltering from the drizzle under the portico of the Custom House, Eva had made a vow to God: she would give away all of her already small income as deputation secretary of the Sudan United Mission and live solely by faith. Clara agreed.

Their parents had been pioneering missionaries in eastern Africa and Mrs Watt was the first white woman to reach the interior of Kenya colony. In the summer of 1939 Eva had travelled extensively in Eastern Europe with the Scottish evangelist James Stewart and was in Prague on the night of the Nazi invasion. Now, desiring no personal gain, nothing deterred her from following God's call to care for Dublin's young street girls. Eva and Clara lived on scraps that fell from the stalls in Mary Street. In 1940 they founded the interdenominational Young Ireland for Christ mission at Eden Quay, from which they carried on a widespread literature distribution. In one of her most effective leaflets, *Blood in the History of Ireland*, Eva quoted Thomas McDonagh's speech from the dock appealing to the example of Savonarola 'whose weapon was not the sword, but prayer and preaching'. Only righteous men could make our land a 'nation once again'.

After a long, colourful and caring life, Eva was buried at Glasnevin near an Irish soldier who had found righteousness through her ministry. The gravestone tells her simple story: 'Auntie Eva of Eden Quay Dublin, called home Easter 1959.'

CHAPTER 11

The Way Ahead

Sean Mullan

In the summer of 2002 a young girl was found dead in a field, killed by a lethal mix of alcohol and tablets. In an *Irish Times* column Fintan O'Toole reflected on the death of Geraldine Chambers and compared it to the death of Ann Lovett eighteen years previously. Ann Lovett was a pregnant teenager who had died giving birth at a grotto in her home town of Granard, Co Longford. O'Toole wrote of these two girls representing the old Ireland and the new Ireland. The old was defined by traditional religion, conservative morality and 'a culture of extreme repression'. By contrast the new Ireland is defined by declining religion, relative morality and 'a culture of extreme tolerance'.

The challenge that faces evangelical Christians in Ireland is how to relate to these two competing visions of what Ireland should be like. Many will want to slot evangelicals into 'old Ireland'. While Evangelicals may not have sat very comfortably with the Catholic Church on doctrinal matters, there is a lot of common ground in moral and ethical issues. Evangelicals and Catholics share much common ground on abortion, euthanasia, human sexuality, family life and many other issues. Indeed Evangelicals in the United States have tended to play a similar role to that of the Catholic Church in Ireland, using numerical strength to exert political pressure for traditional, conservative moral decisions from government.

But Irish Evangelicals have another option. The evangelical movement in Ireland is so small and unknown that it effectively has a blank sheet of paper to work on. The challenge facing the movement is how it will define itself and what mission it will adopt. The way forward is not to go back to the past. The days of institutionalised religion exercising religious and moral authority in the lives of large numbers of people are over. Many predict that the fall of institutionalised religion will be followed by the end of Christianity in Ireland. That is not beyond the bounds of possibility. It has happened and continues to happen in other European countries. Church attendance figures for most of Europe are in single percentage figures and, in most cases, still in decline.

How then will Evangelicalism make an impact on a modern European society as it journeys into secularism, pluralism and multiculturalism? Does it have a future? The contention of this writer is that it does. But much depends on how it responds to the changes taking place both within its ranks and within Irish society. It must see itself as a movement with a message for contemporary Irish society. It is not enough to critique the messages of others. It must present its own message and show that what it is offering is a genuine third way that is radically different from both traditional religion and from liberal, post-modern and largely secular thinking. If it is willing to face this challenge then who knows what lies ahead for it? Evangelicalism as a movement may be numerically tiny and not well organised or focused but there there are strengths within the movement that suggest its time may be coming. What are these strengths?

It will be personal

The Christian faith will only continue to have a significant impact in Ireland if it is lived out from a basis of personal conviction which produces a lifestyle that is attractive to others. Evangelicals have always emphasised a personal relationship with God as the centre of faith. It is not the religious label a person wears but what they believe that matters. It is not so much whether someone puts in an appearance at church as how his faith affects his life the rest of the week.

Evangelicals have often emphasised the personal dimension to the extent that faith had barely any social dimension. Faith was lived out in the community at large but in the more shel-

tered confines of personal prayer, Bible reading and small gatherings of like-minded people. But in recent decades Evangelicals
in many parts of the world have begun to take seriously the
challenge to develop a strong social dimension to their faith.
Leaders such as John Stott in England have pointed the way forward.

But Evangelicalism's greatest strength may now be its focus
on the personal aspect of faith. It means that faith exists apart
from institutions and structures. When the institution fails in
some way, the faith remains. It also means that large resources
and finances are not necessary for effectiveness. Sharing personal
faith with a neighbour or friend costs nothing except the time. It
means that the power for movement comes from within, not
from an external authority. In an era when people are moving
from the institutional towards the personal, Evangelicalism has
an opportunity to present a vision for a life that is constructed
around a personal relationship with God and then reaches out
into the community in acts of service.

It will be communal
Twentieth century Irish life was famous for its communal dimension. From the local pub to the parish hall to the GAA club
people met and related and engaged with each other to weave a
strong community life. But profound changes have taken place.
Much of this communal life was based on conformity. It was
easy to combine community and church life in the parish system
when 97% of the people in a locality were of the same religion.

Enter the new Ireland with enormous new housing estates
that have no communal centre, not a hall, a church, a pub or
often not even a football field. Tens of thousands spend hours
each day alone in their cars. Fewer people head out to cheer the
local team for they can watch world class football on digital
wide-screen cable television. Many chat on the net with people
in Japan or Fiji but do not know their next-door neighbours'
names.

Evangelicalism is a communal movement. It has developed a

strong emphasis on small groups of ten or twelve people who meet in homes where relationships are built. It can prove a catalyst for building lifelong friendships. Moreover because the foundation for those relationships is not what each can do for the other but what God has already done for all through Jesus, then those relationships prove tough and durable. It thus has the chance to provide a counter-cultural alternative to the increasing privatisation of Irish society.

But if it is to be effective this communal life must be attractive. The danger is that this community life quickly becomes exclusive rather than inclusive. Particular mores and standards are adhered to – often unspoken. A peculiar form of political correctness may grow regarding habits such as smoking, drinking or the use of colourful language. Groups often develop a particular way of speaking or turn of phrase which sounds strange to the outsider. In short, the danger is going back to a community based on conformity. The uninitiated soon feel isolated.

Evangelicalism at its essence is about non-conformity. Its message is that God accepts everyone, religious and irreligious, moralists and hedonists, saints and sinners. But the focus of communal life needs to be on welcoming outsiders in without requiring conformity as a condition of acceptance. That approach offers a real alternative to both the old conforming community and the newer individualism. It engenders an uncomfortable but liberating type of communal life.

It will be non-judgemental

The great crime in Ireland today is to judge another or be seen to do so. Most people will no longer accept anyone telling them how they should live their lives or what their personal moral standards should be. By focusing on moral failure, churches have alienated many people. The more recent exposés of wrongdoing by those whom many viewed as the moral police served to increase that alienation.

But what replaced the traditional moral religious approach to matters of right and wrong? In reality, nothing. The prevailing view is that everyone is free to set their own moral standards. The one non-negotiable is that no one may impose their views on anyone else. So everyone makes choices that no one else is free to question. We are almost unable to engage in any moral discussion because the bottom line is, 'You are entitled to your opinion.'

Evangelical moral standards are generally not that different from the mainline churches. On matters of personal integrity, relational, sexual and business ethics there is nothing particularly revolutionary about evangelical views. They would be seen by most to be traditional conservative moralists. But there is a significant difference. The evangelical understanding of the gospel should lead to a critical difference of approach. A central tenet of the gospel is that in essence no human being is different from any other. Every single person is the same. The heterosexual is no better than the homosexual. The celibate is no better than the adulterer. As the Apostle Paul put it in his letter to the Romans: 'There is no difference for all have sinned' (Rom 3:22). The evangelical thus has a basis for not judging someone.

The essence of the traditional religious/moral approach is that the solution lies in people doing better. This will lead those who think they are doing better to look down on those they think are doing worse. The liberal approach might appear to be different but it is not. It passes judgement on those who do not accept that approach. Try telling a liberal that you believe in absolute truth and absolute moral standards to see how far tolerance stretches. The greatest weakness of tolerance is that it will not tolerate intolerance. Evangelicalism has the opportunity to present a way of living that is both ethical and non-judgemental.

It will offer hope
In this era of great material prosperity there is a rising tide of hopelessness affecting many. Frightening rates of suicide and depression plague Irish society. Many are simply giving up. And hopelessness is not confined to those who have missed out on the benefits of the economic boom. Many of those taking their

own lives or being treated for depression have got good jobs and enough money to live comfortably. There is a growing sense that the boom has failed to deliver. People may have more but they have less to hope for. In recession years hope survives on the belief that things can only get better. But when things cannot really get better than they are, where does one go to find hope?

A traditional religious approach faces difficulties in a prosperous society. The power of pleasure overcomes the demands of duty and people flock to new shrines of worship like shopping centres, leisure complexes and sunshine holidays. Living dutifully in the present finds insufficient motivation in the promise of a somewhat nebulous future reward. And no hope is offered to those who have failed to fulfil their religious duty.

The evangelical understanding is that hope is based on who God is and what he has achieved through Jesus Christ. A core evangelical belief is that Jesus will return and establish a new and unending rule of peace, justice and joy. All of life is essentially about preparing for that return. But hope is not limited to something that will happen someday. It provides a paradigm for action in the present. It motivates believers to fight injustice in the belief that one day justice will be fully established. It enables people to face suffering in the belief that one day all suffering will be ended. It fuels campaigns against corruption and abuse with the conviction that all such work will one day triumph. This hope-based perspective challenges both the traditional religious approach, that makes hope contingent on fulfilment of duty, and the liberal secular approach that blandly assures us that things will get better.

It will be life affirming
Modern Irish society has moved into hitherto unfamiliar areas of behaviour in its thirsty search for pleasure. Sex, alcohol, drugs, health-fads, cosmetic surgery, spending sprees have all become well-tried prospective thirst-quenchers.

The religious perspective has traditionally seen repression as the best means of dealing with human passions. 'Don't sleep with your neighbour's spouse because it's wrong.' In the old Ireland this perspective worked in terms of producing the results. The potential social consequences of being caught proved a powerful deterrent. Now those consequences have virtually disappeared. And the act of sleeping with your neighbour's spouse is no longer unthinkable. It comes down to whether or not both parties want to do it.

The modern liberal approach says that this is fine. Each must do what he or she wants. But many travel the hedonistic road pursuing pleasure to find at the end of it that they are no happier than at the beginning. Except that now there is one less road to try. Meanwhile lives are ruined, homes wrecked and another crack appears in society's unravelling structure.

An evangelical approach to this issue begins by seeing life and pleasure as products of the God who created everything. Thus they are to be celebrated, enjoyed and lived out. It also recognises the existence of strong desires in every human being. These natural desires are not to be repressed but channelled into ways of living according to God's guidelines where they might find fulfilment. The moral guidelines of the scriptures are not seen as rules to be joylessly obeyed but a prescription for life that can be lived fully and enjoyed fully.

It will present a realistic approach to human nature

Evangelicals have almost always lived in societies where they were not the predominant religion and so have had to learn to live with those who think and act differently from themselves. Their understanding of how human nature works should help them to be able to do this successfully.

A good example of the kind of struggle this may cause is that of Everett Koop, an evangelical Christian doctor who in 1980 was appointed Surgeon General of the USA. His appointment was vehemently opposed by liberals who abhorred his strong anti-abortion, anti-homosexuality stance. In 1981 the first signs of AIDS began to emerge among homosexuals and drug abusers. Many conservatives saw it as divine judgement. There was little or no response from a conservative government to the disease. Koop was forbidden to address the issue of Aids. In 1986 with 10,000 cases Koop was finally asked to produce a report on it. He came out with a report that recommended heterosexual monogamy as the sure way of avoiding the disease but advocated early sex education and condoms as a means of prevention. His report contained this explicit rebuke to his own conservative evangelical community:

> 'At the beginning of the AIDS epidemic many Americans had little sympathy for people with AIDS. The feeling was that somehow people from certain groups "deserved" their illness. Let us put those feelings behind us … We are fighting a disease, not people.' (*The Surgeon General's Report on Acquired Immune Deficiency*, 1988)

Koop went on to say:

> 'Total abstinence for everyone is not realistic and I'm not ready to give up on the human race yet … I am the Surgeon General of the heterosexuals and the homosexuals, of the young and the old, of the moral and the immoral.'

Koop's approach is a good example of how evangelical Christians can present their perspective truthfully with fidelity to their own beliefs while at the same time reaching out to serve those who do not share their beliefs.

Towards a Third Way

The above strengths are just some of the reasons that Evangelicals need to speak loudly and clearly to contemporary Irish society. The need for another perspective is urgent. The demise of the traditional conservative religious society is not yet complete yet the liberal secular society that was to replace it is already showing serious structural flaws. There is little to celebrate in this modern liberal society. A 2001 report on human rights in Ireland stated:

> Ireland has one of the most unequal societies in Europe, a political system notorious for corruption and cronyism, standards of human rights far below international norms

and serious abuses of the human rights of mentally ill prisoners. There is an on-going need to challenge injustice, the infringements of human rights and the lack of accountability of government to the people. (Brian Harvey, *Rights and justice work in Ireland 2001: A new base line,* Joseph Rowntree Charitable Trust, York)
There is little to suggest that things have improved since then.

A history of Evangelicalism shows that when it was committed to serving society at large it prospered and grew. When it focussed on itself only it shrivelled and died. In the early church the Roman historians recognised that the Christians not only cared for their own poor but also for the pagan poor. In nineteenth century Britain Evangelicals engaged effectively in the two biggest challenges facing society, slavery and poverty. Their work led to the Emancipation of Slaves Act. In sixty years they formed 223 national, religious, moral, educational and philanthropic societies to help needy children. They had many women's aid groups with great names such as 'The Forlorn Females Fund of Mercy' and 'The Friendly Female Society for the Relief of Poor, Infirm, Aged Widows and Single Women of Good Character who have seen better days'. It may be that in the opening decades of the twenty-first century Evangelicals will have the opportunity to make a similar impact in Ireland.

There are few in Ireland who desire a return to the days of Ann Lovett and what her death represented. But there are also very few who want to see more youngsters like Geraldine Chambers perishing for lack of purpose, guidance and a clear sense of what life is all about. The question of whether a better way than either of these alternatives can be found remains open.

Could Evangelicalism provide the third alternative? The changes required within the movement for this to happen are enormous. But there are encouraging signs that there is a willingness among many to face the challenge, embrace change and move ahead. The message is adequate. The times are appropriate. The movement seems eager. The outcome remains to be seen.

The Contributors

MOYA BRENNAN is the lead singer with Clannad and in recent years has pursued a burgeoning solo career. She has recorded with U2's Bono, Paul Young, Bruce Hornsby and many others. She has over twenty Clannad albums, five solo albums, Grammy, Bafta and Ivor Novello awards to her credit. Her autobiography, *The Other Side of the Rainbow*, frankly charts her upbringing in rural Donegal, through hurtful and hedonistic years and into a search that led to her rediscovery of faith and solid footing in her life and work. Moya is a member of St Mark's Family Worship Centre, Pearse St, Dublin.

KEN CLARKE is Church of Ireland Bishop of Kilmore, Elphin and Ardagh. A native of Holywood, Co Down he served as a curate in Magheralin and Dundonald. After church planting in Chile with the South American Mission Society he was Incumbent of St James' Church, Crinken, Bray, Co Wicklow and then Rector of St Patrick's, Coleraine, Co Derry. He is married to Helen from Cork and they have 4 daughters, 2 sons-in-law and one grandson.

ROBERT DUNLOP grew up near Emyvale, Co Monaghan and crossed the border daily to attend school in Aughnacloy. He has been a Baptist minister since 1960 and following three years in Athlone settled in the rural village of Brannockstown, Kilcullen, Co Kildare where he has completed forty years pastoral ministry in the congregation.
He is a regular columnist with the *Leinster Leader* and also writes for Kilcullen's Community magazine *The Bridge* and *The Ballymore Bugle*. He teaches Irish church history in the Irish Bible Institute and in the Irish Studies Programme of Taylor University, Indiana, USA, based at Greystones. His wife Olive is a social worker and they have a son and daughter, Julie and Jeremy.

DEBORAH FORD is a graduate in Classics and Theology. She has spent three years in Kenya and is currently involved in a strategic review of the work of the Overseas Board of the Presbyterian Church in Ireland.

DREW GIBSON is a Presbyterian minister in Bloomfield, East Belfast. He lectured at Belfast Bible College for ten years and, before that, was a missionary in East Africa.

CRAWFORD GRIBBEN is Research Fellow in the Centre for Irish-Scottish Studies, Trinity College, Dublin. He is the author and editor of a number of books, including *The Puritan Millennium: Literature and Theology, 1550-1682* (2000), *The Irish Puritans: James Ussher and the Reformation of the Church* (2003), and *Prisoners of Hope? Aspects of Evangelical Millennialism in Britain and Ireland, 1800-1880* (2004). He is married to Pauline, is a member of Ballyclare Evangelical Presbyterian Church, and enjoys reading, visiting the theatre, and playing football with his dog, Rusty.

PATRICK MITCHEL is married to Ines and they have two children, Ciara and Catriona. He lectures in theology at the Irish Bible Institute in Dublin and is an elder in Maynooth Community Church (Presbyterian). He is author of *Evangelicalism and National Identity in Ulster 1921-1998* (Oxford University Press, 2003). His passions include golfing, writing and travelling.

SEAN MULLAN is from Cork but now lives in Dublin where he is a church leader with Dublin West Community Church in Blanchardstown and is also Director of the fledgling Evangelical Alliance Ireland. He is married to Ana from Argentina and they have three teenage children.

WARREN NELSON is a minister of the Church of Ireland, now living in retirement near Tullamore, Co Offaly. Although born in Belfast, he grew up in Drogheda and worked in the textile industry. He served in several parishes in Tipperary and Cavan and was the founder of the Irish Bible School at Coalbrook, Thurles. He continues to teach in the Irish Bible Institute in Dublin.

MALACHI O'DOHERTY is a journalist who lives and works in Belfast. He is the current Editor of *Fortnight,* a publication of social and political comment, and author of *The Trouble with Guns* (Blackstaff, 1988) and *I was a Teenage Catholic* (Marino, 2003).

FERGUS RYAN is senior leader of Trinity Church Network, Dublin, one of what have come to be known as the New Churches. Fergus's father was originally a Catholic from a Republican family actively involved with de Valera in the War of Independence, but later he became a theosophist. His mother was a member of the Church of Ireland, and he was brought up in that tradition. He is the author of the *Headway Discipleship Series.* For twenty-seven years Fergus was an Aer Lingus pilot, primarily on long-haul routes. He and his wife Sarah, who was formerly an Aer Lingus hostess, live in north County Dublin. Fergus is also an artist.

LYNN STANFIELD took a degree in geography and worked in the travel industry for some years before studying, and later teaching, theology at

Belfast Bible College. She is currently working with Finaghy and Strandtown Baptist Churches in Belfast.

TONY WALSH is a lecturer in the department of Adult and Community Education at the National University of Ireland and has been a psychotherapist for some twenty years. A founder of the Dublin Bereavement Counselling Service and the Institute of Psychosocial Medicine at Dún Laoghaire, he is co-editor of a recent book on Christian responses to suicide and a forthcoming one on sustainable community development. A member of the Methodist Council on Social Responsibility, and its focus group on Refugee Issues, he belongs to Clontarf Methodist Church in Dublin, and is married with a teenage daughter.

General Bibliography

Houghton, Elsie, *Christian Hymn-writers*, Evangelical Press of Wales, Bridgend, Glamorgan, 1982

Sandes, Elise, *Enlisted or My Story*, Office of Sandes Soldiers' Home, Curragh, 1915

Craig, Bartholomew, Parry, Robin, West, Andrew (eds), *The Futures of Evangelicalism*, Inter Varsity Press, Leicester, 2003

Loane, Marcus, *Makers of our Heritage*, Hodder and Stoughton, London, 1967

Hempton, David and Hill, Myrtle, *Evangelical Protestantism in Ulster Society 1740-1890*, Routledge, London, 1992

Dunlop, Robert, *Plantation of Renown*, the story of the La Touches of Harristown and the Baptist Church at Brannockstown, Naas, 1982

Burd, Van Akin, *John Ruskin and Rose La Touche, her unpublished Diaries of 1861 and 1867*, Clarendon Press, Oxford, 1967

Kilroy, Phil, *Protestant Dissent and Controversy in Ireland 1660-1714*, Cork University Press, Cork, 1994

Larsen, Timothy (ed), *Biographical Dictionary of Evangelicals*, Inter Varsity Press, Leicester, 2003

Jordan, Glenn, *Not of this World – Evangelical Protestants in Northern Ireland*, Blackstaff Press, Belfast, 2001

Ford, A., McGuire, J., and Milne, K., *As by Law Established – The Church of Ireland since the Reformation*, The Lilliput Press, Dublin, 1995

McGrath, Alister E., *Historical Theology – An Introduction to the History of Christian Thought*, Blackwell Publishers, Oxford, 1998

Ward, W. R., *The Protestant Evangelical Awakening*, CUP, Cambridge, 1992

Coad, F. Roy, *A History of the Brethren Movement*, Paternoster Press, Exeter, 1968

Holmes, Finlay, *Our Presbyterian Heritage*, Belfast, 1985

Bowen, Desmond, *The Protestant Crusade in Ireland*, Dublin, 1985

Ford, Alan, *Protestant Reformation in Ireland 1590-1641*, Frankfurt, 1985

Bowen, Desmond, *History and the Shaping of Irish Protestantism*, Peter Lang Publishing, New York, 1995

Noll, Mark A., *The Scandal of the Evangelical Mind*, Inter Varsity Press, Leicester, 1994

Herlihy, Kevin (ed), *The Religion of Irish Dissent 1650-1800*, Four Courts Press, Dublin, 1996

Comerford, R. V., Cullen, Mary, Hill, Jacqueline, Lennon, Colm (eds) *Religion, Conflict and Co-Existence in Ireland*, Gill & Macmillan, Dublin, 1990

Knox, R. Buick, *James Ussher, Archbishop of Armagh*, University of Wales Press, Cardiff, 1967

Noll, Mark A., Bebbington, David W., Rawlyk, George K. (eds) *Evangelicalism – Comparative Studies of Popular Protestantism in North America, the British Isles and Beyond 1700-1990*, OUP, New York, 1994

Douglas, J. D. (ed), *The New International Dictionary of the Christian Church*, Paternoster Press, Exeter, 1974

Noll, Mark A., *The Rise of Evangelicalism*, Apollos Press, Leicester, 2004